Straight, No Chaser

Straight, No Chaser

The Life and Genius of

THELONIOUS MONK

Leslie Gourse

SCHIRMER
BOOKS
An Imprint of
SIMON & SCHUSTER MACMILLAN
New York

PRENTICE HALL INTERNATIONAL
New York • Mexico City • New Delhi • Singapore • Sydney • Toronto

Schirmer Books
An Imprint of Simon & Schuster Macmillan
1633 Broadway
New York, NY 10019

Library of Congress Catalog Number: 97–10509

Printed in the United States of America

Printing number:

1 2 3 4 5 6 7 8 9 10

Library of Congress Cataloging-in-Publication Data
Gourse, Leslie.
    Straight, no chaser : the life and genius of Thelonious Monk / Leslie
Gourse.
       p. cm.
    Include's list of Monk's compositions.
    Sessionography: p.
    Videography: p.
    Includes bibliographical references (p.) and index.
    ISBN 0-02-864656-8
    1. Monk, Thelonious. 2. Jazz musicians—United States—Biography.
I. Title.
M>417.M846G68 1997
786.2'165'092—dc21 97–10509
  [B]   CIP
               MN

Contents

Percy Heath, who would become famous as the bassist in the Modern Jazz Quartet, had been in New York for only about six years in 1954 when he recorded with Miles Davis and Thelonious Monk for the Prestige label. It thrilled Heath to be "with all those great cats," he recalled. "My mother used to call Monk 'the onliest.' She got mixed up with his name Thelonious. I told her he sure was the onliest."

There is a race of strangers, of wayfarers, that persists upon the earth. They dwell with us awhile, calling us brothers, but we come to be aware that they are of an immortal stuff, somewhat more deific than ourselves, and only insofar as we receive and comprehend their utterance, only insomuch as we join our wavering, uncertain voices, may we partake in brief and finite measure of their communion.

From the preface to
This Man from Lebanon—A Study of Kahlil Gibran,
by Barbara Young

Dedication and Acknowledgments

This book is dedicated to
Dr. Edward Holtzn, *psychiatrist,*
whose uncanny understanding of Monk's musical genius and mental
condition guided me all the while I was researching and writing this book. Dr.
Holtzman provided me with insight, information, and encouragement.

I'd also like to thank Harry Colomby, Monk's brilliant and kindly manager from the early 1950s to the late 1960s, without whose generosity and information this book could not have been written.

I'm also enormously indebted to saxophonist Paul Jeffrey for his invaluable aid with information and insights.

These three good people gave me their valuable time without asking for anything in return. Without them, I would not have been able to complete this work.

A number of other people have made contributions, among them my editor, Richard Carlin, whose ideas were invaluable; and Marion Monk White, Dr. Billy Taylor, Idrees Sulieman, Lorraine Gordon, Teo Macero, Bob Jones, George and Joyce Wein, Johnny Griffin, Steve Lacy, Randy Weston, Ron McClure, Joel Forrester, Nat Hentoff, Percy Heath, Rudy Van Gelder, Eddie Bert, Johnnie Garry, Ray Bryant, Marian McPartland, Clark Terry, Dr. Everett Dulit, Maynard Ferguson, Larry Ridley, Brooks Kerr, Ben Riley, Stanley Dance, Putter Smith, Clarence Becton, Bobby Colomby, Grover Sales, Sonny Buxton, Ray Mosca, Leroy Williams, Samir Safwat, Pete Malinverni, and Nellie

Smith Monk, Thelonious S. Monk Jr., Monk Sr.'s nephews Thelonious Theo and Thomas Monk Jr., and Alonzo White Jr., Dan Morgenstern, and others—people whose stories and insights—some great and lengthy, others pithy—all shedding light—have been incorporated into this book.

AUTHOR'S NOTE

My primary intention in this book is to tell the story of Monk's life and shed light on his genius and the creation of his unique sound. Much of the analysis of his individual pieces comes from historical critical appraisals and explanations by musicians who play the music. Those analyses await augmentation by a musicologist or musician devoted to writing a note-by-note dissertation on Monk's music.

Preface

In 1993, eleven years after he died, Thelonious Sphere Monk Jr. received a Lifetime Achievement Award from the National Academy of Recording Arts and Sciences "for his demanding jazz compositions, unorthodox piano technique, and legacy of standards like *'Round Midnight* and *Straight, No Chaser*; the genius of his jazz recordings and performances attests to his stature as one of America's greatest artists."

In one of the less likely testimonies to his achievements, his name graces the side of a commuter train car on the Metro North line running from Manhattan to upstate New York and Connecticut. On West 63rd Street, where he lived for most of his life in a tiny apartment—virtually an urban shack crammed full of his family's possessions—a sign has been erected: "Thelonious Sphere Monk Circle." In the 1990s, the Thelonious Monk Institute became one of the most prestigious jazz organizations in the country, increasingly well endowed, the Institute has educated young students and awarded treasured prizes to rising young jazz musicians.

These are only a few of the honors that gradually accrued to Monk, a jazz pianist often vilified for his unorthodox playing style, odd harmonies, and spikey rhythms when he first came to public attention in

Thelonious Monk at the Five Spot, c. mid-1960s. Photo: Raymond Ross.

the early 1940s. He would *not* have been surprised at the posthumous honors, for even as a starving young artist, he had confided in those nearest to him that he would become famous one day. It was not conceit but impassioned commitment to his composing that inspired him to have such a glorious vision of his music. But for nearly two-thirds of his life, until he was forty, he remained little more than a lonesome, cult figure on the fringe of the jazz world. Many critics and musicians regarded him as an off-kilter composer, a mannered, inept pianist, and an eccentric man, and he suffered from chronic discouragement.

His personal life was at least as nightmarish. Once, in the early fifties, he disappeared into his apartment for weeks to compose, then emerged to find himself wrongfully arrested near his front door on narcotics charges. As a result, he lost his New York City cabaret card—a work permit—and, essentially, his ability to earn even a meager living. (One wonders if he had this experience in mind when he recorded "Everything Happens to Me.")

Monk's depression and erratic behavior may have had their root cause in his frustrations and were surely enhanced by his dalliances with all types of drugs. His mental difficulties became more pronounced when he started to use amphetamines masquerading as vitamins in the mid-1950s; his midlife, mental lapses were never properly or uniformly diagnosed or treated. Casual observers decided he might be manic depressive, schizophrenic, or simply profoundly depressed. But a psychiatrist, who treated him in 1971, rejected all those diagnoses; his diagnosis, revealed finally by a friend and associate, sheds new light on Monk's final descent into silence. Those who knew Monk best over a long period of time understood that he was, from the beginning, a very quiet, shy, sometimes withdrawn man who was completely preoccupied, even transfixed, with music. They also knew another side of Monk—the man who loved games, hijinks, jokes, and mischief and who had a clear understanding of the world he lived in.

There were just enough people with vision, good will, and excellent taste to help Monk lift himself out of the maze of failures that marked his early public career. His family believed in him, nurtured, and sustained him. Monk's career was boosted by an inexperienced, passionately devoted manager, Harry Colomby, who discovered an East Village saloon, the Five Spot, that provided Monk with a forum. There, he played his own compositions and crossed the line from the offbeat to the mainstream, as progressive jazz itself gained prestige. He never changed his direction or sacrificed an iota of his artistry. He had simply been ahead of his time.

Above all, Monk, the composer, strove to create a universe of sound with his compositions. Each piece he wrote gave him a sense of fulfillment; each blocked out the cacaphony of criticism that greeted his arrival and persistence on the jazz scene. He had suffered through the indignities of having his compositions labelled difficult and obscure and his personal behavior bizarre. But he was a master of the keyboard, playing in exactly the right way to interpret his own music and to modernize every composition he touched. He made dissonance beautiful, warm, and exciting.

Once he established himself as a star at the Five Spot, where his foibles revealed themselves as magical stagecraft, all of the opposition fell dead or at least into disarray at his feet. Critics rushed to try to explain why his music was so marvelous and alluring. Most of all, jazz fans had learned to make sense of his sound, and they loved it. They carried him, as it were, on their shoulders, to his commercial successes on recordings, in concert halls, and in nightclubs.

Through the years of hardships, Monk had learned to understand the vagaries of public disdain and acclaim. Most of all, his genius was for composing. That was his first love. He performed in public to bring his sound to audiences, and sometimes he found his public career a grueling ordeal. Definitely success came too late in life to such a shy, sensitive man, and the glory years could never erase his memories of the heckling he had endured. All along the way, he had sampled every kind of drink and drug—legal and illegal—to amuse and maintain himself through the bleak and trying times, and to find a way to tranquilize and socialize himself and triumph in a cold, mercurial, and sometimes dangerous world.

As a star who finally found acceptance for his genius, he had to endure a new criticism leveled by some listeners who decided they were tired of hearing him play his by-then familiar repertoire—although they still clamored for him to play the songs they knew best. They showed up primarily to hear him play such haunting songs as "Blue Monk," "'Round Midnight," and "Straight, No Chaser," but not to hear him play "Locomotive," "Skippy," the complex "Brilliant Corners," the poignant, romantic ballads "Ruby, My Dear," "Ask Me Now," and "Pannonica," the stately art song "Crepuscule with Nellie," or the muscular, swinging "Rhythm-a-ning," based on the chords of "I Got Rhythm,"[1] which could stand as the archetypal composition of the midcentury jazz revolution.

Even at the height of his career, Monk was an acquired taste, and praise seemed fleeting. About ten years after he had achieved a measure of fame at the Five Spot Cafe, the major record label, Columbia, that had promoted his work through the 60s, dumped him. His record sales, like those of so many jazz artists, failed to earn profits; rock reigned in the pop-music world.

Exhausted and depleted by his efforts and excesses, Monk walked away from his career and became a recluse. A friend offered him refuge in her house, and he went to live there, becoming less and less communicative. Nothing could coax him out of retirement. Eventually, almost nothing ever brought him out of the little room he inhabited in the big house to which he retreated. Friends and family clucked in the other rooms about what to do to help Thelonious feel well again, but they never discovered a method.

A group of younger musicians, including tenor saxophonist Charlie Rouse, who had played for about twelve years in Monk's quartet, formed a group called Sphere. Its members hoped that their first recording, *Sphere*, a tribute to Monk, would entice him to participate in the music world again. Even if he had been able to, it was too late. On the day they began recording, Monk died of an aneurysm.

Nobody has ever been able to imitate Monk's sound or inspire a group to play his music—or any music—exactly the way he did. But the momentum of his legacy has kept growing, and his admirers and interpreters abound.

This book introduces the story of Thelonious Monk, probably the quietest man who ever lived in the jazz world and who, quixotically, had one of the most dramatic, suspenseful, even action-packed existences of any creative genius. Eventually jazz-world insiders would say it did Thelonious Monk no good to be dubbed "the high priest of bebop" early in his career. The sobriquet made him seem like a Tibetan Buddhist monk, a Sufi mystic—an ascetic who was apart and above it all. The image—which emphasized the intensely introspective, often moody sound of a portion of Monk's repertoire in those post-World War II years—may have done little to reap commercial benefits for him or for the Blue Note record company that invented the phrase in 1947. But that is exactly what Monk was, stated in an amusing, poetic way. Although he was a very well-liked man, even beloved by his friends, he lived alone in his mind, a devout believer in his own creativity. And he could tolerate that degree of isolation, so that he could create new ideas for jazz, probably the most abstract and unpredictable of all the arts.

Because of his shy, retiring nature, his mental difficulties, and his trail-blazing techniques, Monk never achieved the success that he deserved. It took other energetic, young musicians in his generation—and beyond—to develop his revolutionary ideas for harmony, rhythm, and melody, and their inseparable handmaidens in his style—phrasing, accents, spacing, and pacing—to create a special sound. They became virtuosos, embellishers, organizers, and promoters. But Monk was the original different musician, and a paramount source and sorcerer for modern jazz.

NOTE

1. Like many of the other bop artists, Monk based six of his compositions on preexisting jazz standards; the rest were entirely original to him. The pianist and historian Brooks Kerr helped me identify Monk's source material for these compositions.

Straight, No Chaser

Growing Up in Manhattan

Barbara Batts Monk was tired of crossing the railroad tracks every day from her little house on Red Row, the "colored" side of town, to the houses where she worked as a maid for white people in Rocky Mount, North Carolina. By 1922, she already had three children, all delivered by a midwife. Marion, the eldest, was six years old; Thelonious Jr., four, came next, with his bright, big, round, staring eyes just like Barbara's in photos; two-year old Thomas was a bright-eyed child, too, whom everyone in the family would always call Baby. Barbara wanted to give the children broader horizons than they could see from the porch of their little house in a small, segregated, southern, country town. She set her mind on moving north.

Her husband, Thelonious Sr., worked as a day laborer. Thelonious Jr.'s birth certificate, dated October 10, 1917, gives his father's occupation as "ice carrier," but that was only one of the many tough jobs the tall, strong-looking man did to earn a living. Actually he was not as physically fit as he looked, because he suffered from asthma. Although that didn't prevent him from sharing responsibility for his family with his wife, the Monks' prospects for improving their lot in Rocky Mount were nil. Both parents could read and write, but they had very little

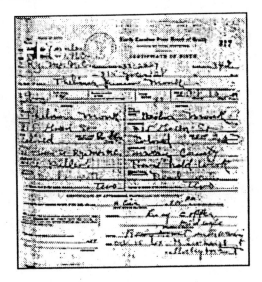

Birth certificate of Thelonious Monk

formal education or job training. The best they could do was to struggle along from day to day on the meager wages of laborers in a place that figured, at best, as a geographical speck on the map not far from Durham and Raleigh.

When Barbara told her husband that she wanted the family to move to New York City, he didn't want to go. Years later, Marion would recall her parents as quiet people. She never saw or heard them fight, but she believed their marriage could have been happier. Barbara Monk made up her mind to go to New York without her husband.

In 1922, Barbara said goodbye to the country world of her parents—Sphere Batts and his wife, Georgiana Knight Batts—packed her belongings, and took her children in a segregated railroad car to New York City. Thelonious Sr., who may have been sick at the time, stayed behind. Marion would recall nothing of her hometown, except for the little house with the porch where she had sat with the family and the backyard where she had played with Thelonious. But she would clearly

Marion Monk White, Thelonious S. Monk, Jr., and Thomas W. Monk, Sr.
Courtesy of Marion Monk White and nephews

remember the day of the family's momentous migration, when her mother, who had never been out of North Carolina, dared to lead the children north and onto a trolley car in New York City.

People were jam-packed into the trolley during the evening rush hour. Her mother found a seat and told Marion, Thelonious, and Thomas to hold on tightly to her. The trolley started with a jerk, and the children fell on the floor. Everyone around them laughed at the sprawling kids. "It was fun for us," Marion remembered. "You know how kids are." After a short ride, the Monks got off the trolley and saw a familiar face. Their mother's cousin, Louise—her last name may have been O'Brian—had a small apartment on West 63rd Street in an African American neighborhood near the Hudson River. She took in the Monks to live with her that day.

The little Monk family noticed the lilting accents of their neighbors. It seemed as if everyone in that neighborhood, nicknamed San Juan Hill, had come from the West Indies. The Monks stayed with

Louise for a while—perhaps three months, Marion estimated—until they found their own apartment nearby on the same street, in one of the buildings the neighbors called the Old Houses.

Despite the shockingly different conditions from North Carolina, Barbara quickly found a job in a nursery. "Some people remember their parents didn't work, but I don't have that kind of memory," Marion recalled. "Our mother always had a job, and we always had food. She made enough to pay the rent and buy us clothes. So we never wanted for anything." Soon they acquired a radio, a Victrola, and an upright piano. The children missed their father and often asked Barbara if daddy would come to live with them. She didn't know. Soon Thelonious Sr. became a memory to the children, as they began going to school, where they earned passing grades in their schoolwork and good ones for their conduct.

Most of the time, the children were healthy. Marion had her tonsils removed. Once Thelonious became really sick. He had difficulty urinating and was in such pain that he was "climbing the walls," Marion remembered. A doctor told Barbara that Thelonious would have to be circumcised; the operation would help him. He was not frightened about it, because he was told he would go to sleep before the operation and wake up cured. He had no health problems after that, except for a tonsillectomy. Then Thomas had his tonsils out, too.

Around the time Thelonious was circumcised, the family had a happy surprise. Tall, dark, and handsome Thelonious Sr. walked in the door one day to live with them. It had been about four years since they had seen him. Marion, a lively, friendly girl with a mirthful face, was about ten at the time, Thelonious Jr. was seven, and Baby was five. Their father found a job working on a pier at the nearby Hudson River. Marion wasn't sure what he did, but she knew it was hard work. Then he found another, somewhat easier job as a fireman, tending and maintaining furnaces in apartment houses in a neighborhood to their north, on West End Avenue, where well-to-do, white people lived.

Only one unsettling incident stands out in Marion's mind about her early years in Manhattan. One day, her father and Thelonious Jr. were down in the dark cellar of the Old Houses, where her father may have been doing some work. A lid covering a hole in the floor had somehow been moved. Thelonious Jr. fell into the hole, which was filled with murky water. When he bobbed up, within his father's reach, his father instantly plucked the boy out. Together they hurried upstairs to the apartment. Marion noticed her brother dripping water in the house. Her father explained what had happened. "I got him out right away. I knew your mother would kill me if I came home without that boy," he said. Everyone was both amused and terrified by the story.

About this time, the family moved across the street to the Phipps Houses, at 243 West 63rd Street,' informally called the New Houses, where they rented a very small apartment with a bedroom for Barbara and Thelonious Sr. and a small kitchen combined with a living room, or family room, where the children slept. "It had three rooms and a bathroom," Marion would recall, "but it seemed big to us, because all the apartments were small in the Phipps Houses."

Marion and Thelonious Jr. often played together. "Thelonious was pretty cheerful and happy," Marion recalled. "We used to play games." Thelonious was very good at games and sports, and he was smarter than Marion in school, especially at math, she thought. She passed her courses in school, and so did he; she didn't recall his marks as being high, but she knew he was very smart. Quickly, it seemed, he grew taller than Marion. He would grow to six feet two inches tall, and Marion would reach a height of about five feet five, a little taller than her mother. Marion looked up to her brother Thelonious, while he admired his sister and trusted her to give him advice. Marion thought of the family as tightly knit, particularly "before our love lives came in. Thelonious was never too serious, and he wasn't wild. He got along with everybody. He was a nice kid." When the Children's Aid Society center in the neighborhood was converted to a community center, Marion and Thelonious went there to play checkers, pool, and ping-pong; Thelonious was good enough at basketball to play on the center's team. "And [above all] he could think," Marion recalled. "He was a good thinker."

Their mother insisted that they go to the dinner table at the same time every evening. Barbara was a skilled cook of heavy, Southern-style food; she seemed to love dinner time best of all the hours in the day, because she liked to talk during meals and invited the children to speak about themselves. Many of Marion's friends weren't allowed to talk at their dinner tables, but the Monk children knew that if they wanted anything, the time to ask for it was at dinner. "Seemed like Mother was always in a good mood then," Marion would recall for the rest of her life, with her eyes mirthful.

Raised as Methodists in North Carolina, the Monks sometimes went to St. Mark's Methodist Church on West 53rd Street on Sundays. After the church moved uptown to Harlem, they often went to an Episcopalian church that was closer to home, and they especially liked to visit the Union Baptist Church on West 63rd Street. "They did have good music in all those churches. The Methodists had a choir, and the Baptist church jumped, and the people shouted," Marion recalled. Their parents were not especially religious, but their mother insisted that the family go to church on Sundays. As the children grew up and wanted to go to parties on Saturday nights, Barbara told them they could go out to have a good time if they promised to get up and go to church the next day.

Barbara's friends in the neighborhood were West Indians. Marion recalled them as rather strict, ambitious people who looked down upon their American neighbors. But Barbara admired the values of the West Indians, most of whom demanded that their children be well-behaved, cultured, and good in school. Because her friends gave their children music lessons, she decided that Marion should take piano lessons. Barbara may have thought it would be a good idea for Thelonious to study the violin, but he had no interest in it. He may have had a touch of asthma that prevented him from trying the trumpet—another instrument that was suggested for him to play, and which he didn't like, either.

Thelonious preferred to listen to Marion's lesson on the family's upright piano, when the teacher came to the house. By ear, Monk, then about twelve, probably in 1930, learned to play the piano very well. Impressed, the teacher advised Barbara not to waste money on Marion's lessons. Marion had no interest in playing music, but

Thelonious seemed to have a prodigious talent, the teacher insisted. Marion remembered the teacher's name as Mr. Wolfe and thought he was connected to the Juilliard School of Music as a teacher (he may have actually been a student at the school).[2] Nellie Smith, who would become Thelonious's companion, believed that the teacher may have come from the neighborhood and taught many kids there.

Years later, Thelonious's nephews would recall that his father played the piano in the house, too. According to them, Thelonious's father played swing-era, big-band style music. As a prank, some neighbors—probably kids—hung a skull and crossbones on the Monk apartment door while the father was playing one day, and after that he played more softly.[3] He may have played the ukelele occasionally, too, and liked to dance. Barbara dabbled with the piano, and it's possible she sang in a church choir. The Monks respected music.

When Thelonious Jr. began taking lessons, his father became ill, unable to tolerate the cold winters in New York, and he decided he had to move back to North Carolina. "But my mother had come to stay, not to go back, because she could make a living up here in New York; she couldn't make it down there," recalled Marion. After that, the children asked their mother when their father was coming back. Without a telephone, the family received a letter saying that Thelonious Sr. was in the hospital for treatment for asthma. "He sent word that he couldn't come back to New York; the climate would kill him," Marion recalled. "He never left North Carolina again."

The family had very little contact with him after that. His side of the family didn't stay in touch with Barbara, and she didn't maintain a connection with her husband's relatives. Marion thought the North Carolina Monks might have been afraid that a woman alone with three children in New York would ask for financial help. So the relationship between Barbara and her husband ended. Eventually the Monk children learned that their father had died in 1964. The children in New York grew up knowing very little about their relatives.[4]

Thelonious Jr. was a good student possessing obvious intelligence. In Junior High School 69, he had an excellent record. He was late only nine times during several years, received one A and two Bs and 2 Cs for conduct, and had fair to good grades in written English, fair but passing grades in spoken English, and fair to good grades in algebra—with the exception of one term, in which he suddenly dipped down to a score of 47, a wildly erratic swoop down from his mark of 65 the previous term. After that, he climbed back up to 80, then dropped a little to 75. He squeaked by in history and failed badly in geography, where his top grade was 57. He also barely passed "shop cooking" and "science sewing"—whatever these classes were. But he shone in music classes, with an 87, two 80s, and two 90s for his five terms—his only As. His marks satisfied his music requirement for high school. That may be why he slipped through the cracks at Stuyvesant High School, which admitted only the brightest students in math and science from all over the city. The school was known to have a good music program, too. But Thelonious, who didn't have to take a music course in high school, didn't get a chance to impress any of his teachers there with his talent.

Thelonious is believed to have scored high on an I.Q. test, another reason for his admission to Stuyvesant High School. Altogether, his junior-high school work and native intelligence qualified him to enter Stuyvesant in 1932, where he spent his first year attending classes regularly for 88 out of 95 school days in the spring semester and earning passing marks. Suddenly, in 1933, his attendance record fell to sixteen out of ninety-two days. His marks swooped around from 75 to 90 to 20 in mechanical arts and plunged from 80 to 40 to 66 in English; he maintained an average of 70 in math. His mark in music was registered as 80, but that was simply a carry-over from his last term in junior-high school.

His son would later tell an audience gathered to pay tribute to Monk at the unveiling of an exhibition of his recordings in the lobby of Stuyvesant High School that Monk left school to concentrate on playing music in 1934. His son was under the impression that Monk hadn't been *allowed* to play in the school band, because he was African American and one of the few African Americans in the school at that time. Had anyone paid proper attention to Monk's musicality at that time, he might have been packed off to a conservatory. His profile was emerging as that of a genius—a person who concentrated only on his major interest at which he excelled.

It's certain that the only thing that could have kept him in school was music. If he couldn't play music in school, he wouldn't bother going there. He was already settling into the habit of staying at home, listening to music, and playing the piano. Friends who were musicians were beginning to come to visit him at the family's apartment. An area of the kitchen-family room was turned into a bedroom for Monk, where he had his piano, a narrow bed, and a dresser. Marion slept in the room with her mother, and Thomas slept in the family room with Thelonious.

In his midteens, Monk was playing in a trio with a trumpeter and another instrumentalist, possibly a drummer, working at little gigs in town, usually earning tiny amounts of money in fees or tips. Thelonious was probably too busy working late at night with his trio to bother getting up for school in the mornings. After the spring semester in 1934, he left school. The trio began to attend the Apollo Theater's Wednesday-night amateur contests, where, his sister Marion recalled, the teenagers won the $10 first prize so often that they were told not to come back. They had to give other kids a chance. Wryly Monk later quipped to a writer that the experience convinced him to leave behind his amateur status and become a professional.

Monk's school records had listed him only as Thelonious Monk, not referring to him as "Jr." He hadn't used a middle name for his school registration, either, but Marion recalled that, at about this time, Monk adopted the middle name "Sphere," his maternal grandfather's first name. No longer a "junior," he was asserting his individuality.

Although he still played ball games, he became known as the musician in the family. Marion began to think her mother favored him. He wasn't required to wash the windows or do other chores around the house. "He had to protect his hands," she recalled, while she and Thomas did the work. Monk's son would eventually pass along the legend that his father was "the apple of his mother's eye, her little darling."

Marion would not be surprised later on when her brother became famous. "I knew he was that good," she said. "It didn't surprise him, either. He always said he was good anyway. He knew he could do things, and he would do them. Any game he played, nobody could beat him. He used to say, 'He can't beat me. I can beat him.' It wasn't just at the piano but at anything. He was a perfectionist. He demanded a lot of himself. If he lost, it would have bothered him. But he wasn't self-centered or selfish. He was generous. He shared his things with us."

Monk studied the organ with the Union Baptist Church's regular organist, Professor Buster Archer. When the church moved up to 145th Street, the Monks didn't often go there anymore, unless the church scheduled a special event. In his late teens, Thelonious played as substitute organist there when Mr. Archer wasn't feeling well.

One of Barbara's friends, an evangelist who traveled around the country singing and preaching in various churches, asked Barbara if she could take Monk and his trio with her on the gospel highway. Sixty years later, a few older members of the Union Baptist Church still remembered this evangelist: Reverend Graham, whom they dubbed "The Texas Warhorse." She sang and preached at Union Baptist, although she was a faith healer, and probably not a Baptist. Nobody knew exactly what denomination she was; most likely she came from the Sanctified Church. Barbara trusted her and gave her permission to hire Thelonious. He would later recall for journalists that he had played jazz—sometimes he called it rock and roll, or rhythm and blues—while she tried to stir up excitement for religion with her singing and preaching. By rock and roll, Monk meant the rhythmic, spirited way gospel hymns were performed in African American Baptist churches.

And that's why, later in life, Monk frequently told journalists, he valued the experience of playing for the evangelist. He didn't specify how it helped him develop his mature style, but undoubtedly the benefit lay, in large part, in the steadiness of the rhythms and the groove, the way the rhythms combined.

Gospel music was especially popular after the Depression had overwhelmed the country, denuding many financially successful African

Americans of their money and acquisitions; people turned to churches for solace and inspiration. But Monk wasn't very happy with the gospel lifestyle. He missed New York, and the gospel highway was a bumpy one. The road between the refuges of the churches was often fraught with dangers for African Americans. The fees for gospel groups were usually tiny. Veterans in gospel groups liked to say they traveled in cars with Maypop tires—so called because they "may pop at any minute." Thelonious toured the south and southwest with the Texas Warhorse. "She preached and healed, and we played. And then the congregation would sing."[5]

In Kansas City, pianist and arranger Mary Lou Williams, a role model and teacher for many younger musicians, heard Monk for the first time when he toured as a teenager on the gospel circuit. She was very impressed with his playing, discerning in it the roots of his mature style and treatment of harmonies.[6] Apparently the evangelist had no quarrel with Monk's experiments with dissonance (if he was playing in this style when accompanying her), and she didn't tell him how to play the piano. More likely, he was simply working out his own ideas in jam sessions at night. Whatever freedom he did find to experiment on the road must have encouraged Monk to stay with the evangelist for a while. But within a couple of years, he returned to New York, which he loved, and moved back into the family's apartment, where he could write without interruption whatever music he was hearing in his head.

By that time, his younger brother Thomas had married his girl-friend, nicknamed Rita, with whom he would have four children, the twins Thomas Jr. and Marion, Thelonious Theo, and Charlotte, the youngest. Thomas's family stayed in the west sixties neighborhood. So now Thelonious had more room for himself in his mother's apartment. In New York, too, he had a girlfriend, Ruby Richardson, for whom he wrote a pretty, refreshing ballad, with a haunting melody and rich, romantic harmonies, called "Ruby, My Dear."

He met Ruby through his sister Marion, who had become best friends with the young West Indian girl at the neighborhood commu-nity center. Marion, a little older than Ruby and a grade ahead of her,

Thomas W. Monk, Jr., Alonzo White, Jr., and Thelonious Theo Monk, nephews of Thelonious Monk. Courtesy of Marion Monk White and nephews

had dropped out of school. Ruby had studied catering in high school, and a college down south offered her a job. Thelonious and Ruby cared for each other, but Ruby's parents didn't want her to marry an American. "Her parents wanted her to go down south so she could get away from Thelonious," Marion recalled. "Her mother didn't like Thelonious, because he wasn't a West Indian. All the West Indians around the neighborhood were our friends, but they didn't want their children to marry Americans. 'It's all right to fool around, but don't get married.' That was the attitude."

Ruby eventually took the job down south and, when she came back a while later, discovered a change in Thelonious. He was involved with a young woman named Nellie Smith, a slender, attractive neighborhood girl from 62nd Street whose family came from Florida. Marion was disappointed and so was Ruby. But Thelonious and Nellie were happy because Nellie was loyal and gave no sign that she would leave him to fend for himself and his music.

Monk was hardly a famous musician at that time. He knew his way around Harlem and played in little clubs there and all around the city. Other musicians noticed that he worked any place he could earn a bit of money. Drummer Kenny Clarke, who was becoming well known in Harlem musical circles, would later tell French jazz historian Maurice Cullaz that Thelonious in his late teens was playing gospel music and there was no hint of anything unusual in his style. Thelonious himself took as his idols and inspiration James P. Johnson—who lived and worked in the San Juan Hill and nearby Hell's Kitchen neighborhoods for a while—Fats Waller, and Duke Ellington, whose piano techniques were rooted in the well-known Harlem stride style. That was the reigning jazz piano style, although the modernity of Ellington's ideas, harmonies, and arrangements for his orchestra inspired young Thelonious in a special way and intimated the possibility for him to make even more fascinating experiments.

Monk earned pocket money in some dreary places. Many were well off the beaten track. He played for seven nights a week for seventeen dollars, and sometimes he never received the pay promised to him. Some things he could forget, he said, but not that, nor the hecklers, either. Bassist Red Callender saw him playing at a little Harlem spot, Mack's on 139th St., where cockroaches climbed on the walls. Monk simply ignored them. Thelonious himself later told Orrin Keepnews, when Keepnews was a writer for *Record Changer* magazine in 1948, that he worked everywhere; it didn't matter to him. Monk's mother supported his decision to be a musician. If he wanted to play music, that's what she wanted him to do. He

Thomas W. Monk, Sr., Marion Monk White, and Thelonious.
Courtesy of Marion Monk White and nephews

would say many times that she had stood behind him 100 percent of the time.

Monk formed his first documented group, the Thelonious Monk Quartet, in 1938 or '39, with Jimmy Wright on tenor sax, a man known as Masapequah on bass, and William "Keg" Purnell on drums; the group played everywhere for every kind of salary. With this group, Monk began experimenting with chords and rhythmic effects. "I never studied," Monk said. "I just experimented arranging. You learn most harmonics by experience. You fool around and listen. Most chord structure is practically arithmetic, anyway. You just have to use common sense." He had little interest in working with the big bands. "I wanted to play my own chords. I wanted to create and invent on little jobs."[7]

Before the 1930s were over, in the family apartment Thelonious had written many songs, including "Ruby, My Dear," and by 1940 or '41, his most famous tune, "'Round Midnight." His manager-to-be, Harry Colomby, who came into Monk's life in the 1950s, believed that Monk wrote it when he was nineteen—as early as 1936—and originally called it "Grand Finale." Harry saw the music paper in a box in Monk's apartment; Monk had written the song neatly in pencil.

Though Monk's sister, Marion, had been relieved that she didn't have to take piano lessons, she always liked to listen to all of the music—from church to jazz to classical music—that her family enjoyed. She liked hearing the songs that her brother was writing. "He used to play his songs for me to see how I liked them before he would go off with them," Marion recalled. When his brother, Thomas, came to visit, Thelonious would say, "Baby, listen to this," and Thomas, too, would hear the songs before Thelonious took them out into the world to his gigs. Thomas wasn't the slightest bit musically inclined, and didn't understand what Thelonious was doing. But Thomas listened respectfully and liked the music. For understanding of his experiments, Monk went to Harlem. Or anyway, he hoped he would find understanding in musicians' circles there.

Pianist Billy Taylor met Monk in 1940, when Billy was a junior at the Virginia State College, working toward his bachelor's degree in music. In love with the piano style of Teddy Wilson that he had heard on recordings, Billy decided to visit New York and hear his idol play in person. Billy's father "didn't take kindly," Billy recalled, to his plan to visit New York on his own. "So he made me check in with a friend of his who owned a club in Harlem." It was probably the Yeah Man, which would soon become known as Jock's Place, a popular Harlem hangout.

When Taylor arrived at the club, a trio was playing. Billy decided to sit in and play his favorite song, "Lullaby in Rhythm." Billy played everything he knew in the first eight bars! Everyone applauded him. The trio's piano player gave Billy a funny look, then played another tune himself, and joined Billy at the bar. "Nice," the piano player told Billy, who was very proud of his performance. Billy was classically trained, and he thought he was playing like Art Tatum and Teddy Wilson all wrapped up in one. "I've got some friends whom I'd like to hear you," the pianist in the house trio said.

He took Billy around the corner to a brownstone, where they found a group of men in a room with a piano. "I played eight bars of something, and then Willie the Lion Smith played," Billy recalled. "They were all piano players in that room. And the guy who brought me there turned out to be Clarence Profit, who wrote the song 'Lullaby in Rhythm.'" (A leader of his own popular trio playing in the style of Nat King Cole's, Profit had thought Billy had deliberately played that song to make an impression.) "James P. Johnson was in the room that night. It might have been his house. Every one of them was a really good stride piano player. I went back to the woodshed. I was the youngest person there. And there was one other my age, who played like Art Tatum. He impressed me especially because he was about my age. That was Monk." He was four years older than Billy. "He later told me that the older guys encouraged him. They thought he had his own thing. Especially Willie the Lion Smith was encouraging to him. Monk sounded wonderful."[4]

NOTES

Much of the material in this chapter was based on personal interviews with Monk's family, most prominently his sister, Marion, and his nephews.

1. Later, Marion Monk rented an apartment with her family at 235 W. 63rd Street, and Thomas moved to 239 W. 63rd Street with his family.

2. Nobody named "Wolfe" taught on the Juilliard faculty before Stanley Wolfe began teaching there several decades after Monk started piano lessons. However, Stefan Wolpe, a highly respected European-born composer who wrote twelve-tone music—whose German last name could be pronounced as "Wolfe" in English—arrived in the United States in the late 1930s; although he was well-known to Juilliard teachers, he never taught at that school. It's likely that Monk met Wolpe in Wolpe's early years in the U.S. This might be the person that Marion remembers as a teacher of Monk's, although again it would have been at a later date than his first lessons.

3. Monk's nephews treasured this tale as part of the family's legend and lore.

4. The New York Monks had no contact with their North Carolina relatives until Monk's son visited Rocky Mount and started to learn about the family history after his father died. Past generations had been very creative in the names they picked for some of their children. One relative was named simply Jack Monk. But Monk's grandfather, who was named either Hinton or Arthur Monk, and his wife named one of their children Squalilian; another may have been Cleo, and another Thelonious—Monk's father, the first Thelonious in the family, misspelled on the pianist's birth certificate as "Thelious." The pianist's mother's name, Barbara, says her daughter Marion, was misspelled as "Barbra" on Thelonius Jr.'s birth certificate. One branch of the Monk family moved to Connecticut and gave rise to a well-known gospel group.

5. Quoted in Hentoff (1956).

6. Mary Lou was playing with Andy Kirk's band when Monk passed through town. "He was one of the original modernists all right, playing pretty much the same harmonies then that he's playing now," she told Max Jones, jazz writer for the English magazine *Melody Maker* in 1954. "Only in those days we called it 'Zombie music' and reserved it mostly for musicians after hours." The interview is quoted by Chip Deffaa (1996), p. 142.

7. Quoted in Simon (1948).

8. Taylor's story was told in a personal interview with the author. To critic Martin Williams, Willie "the Lion" Smith seemed to play the most interesting harmonies of all the Harlem stride players. In the stride piano style, a two-handed technique, the left hand alternated between playing chords and distant, single, sharply sounded notes, making rapid strides between the chords and the notes. The sleight of hand gave the stride pianists a great, proud bounce. The right hand played blues and ragtime variations, but also explored other musical ideas and brought European themes into the music. The European influence gave stride players an airy, thoughtful, cultivated sound. When Harlem players combined European ideas with stride rhythms, the swinging music sounded sweet and athletic, whimsical and exciting. An important stride player beginning in the 1920s, "Little" Joe Turner, said of stride, for a simple explanation, "You have your own accompaniment, like the bass and guitar, going with your left hand, and the melody is improvised with your right hand." He thought that James P. Johnson called the style "stride" because it sounded like a man striding proudly down the street.

Thelonious, Howard McGhee, Roy Eldridge, and Teddy hill in front of Minton's Playhouse, 1948. Courtesy of the Institute of Jazz Studies, Rutgers University.

2 House Pianist at Minton's Playhouse

In 1940, Monk's first break came when he was hired as the house pianist for a small Harlem nightspot called Minton's Playhouse. Today, the club is remembered in legend as the place where bebop was born; in after-hours jam sessions, musicians congregated and experimented with new musical ideas. Monk's presence at these jam sessions introduced many soon-to-be-prominent musicians to his compositions and musical style. Even though Monk would remain somewhat obscure, by the early fifties his music was well known in the jazz world thanks, in part, to this association.

Kenny Clarke, who was already the house drummer at Minton's Playhouse when Monk was hired, would later tell an interviewer for a French jazz publication that he wasn't happy about the prospect of Monk coming to work there. Clarke was already playing in a modern style, keeping time on the cymbals or the snare drums and using off-beat accents on the bass drum. Recalling Monk's work with the Texas Warhorse, Kenny thought Monk was still playing in a "rock-and-roll" style. But Kenny was delighted when he heard Thelonious again. Thelonious was working aggressively, with great originality, on dissonant harmonies and modern phrasings, along with his individualistic rhythmic sensibility. Together, they began modernizing the music of the swing era that both had played earlier. Their accents, phrasing, and harmonies changed.

Minton's was a popular spot for musicians. It was located in two rooms off the entrance of the Hotel Cecil at 210 West 118th Street and Seventh Avenue, not very far from the Apollo Theater on 125th Street. Minton's bar was right inside the door, with rose-colored lights shining down on the customers. On Monday nights, when musicians usually didn't work, they lined up at the bar, waiting for their turn to sit in and jam on the bandstand against the rear wall in the back room. In front of the bandstand were tables for dining with a dance floor in the middle.

Minton's became known for its Monday night jam sessions. Entertainers from the Apollo Theater showed up to enjoy the music and eat the free food provided by the Apollo Theater's owners, the Schiffmans. They wanted to treat their performers to soul food—such traditional delicacies as fried chicken, ribs, grits, and collard greens—after the rugged week they had put in doing countless shows at the Apollo. Years later, a surviving musician, drummer Roy Haynes, remembered the biscuits had been made from scratch, not whipped up from a prepared biscuit mix. And there was free whiskey.

Minton's was owned by Henry Minton, a former saxophonist and one of the first African American delegates to the musician's union. So, even though musicians weren't supposed to play unless they were paid, at Minton's they could jam without the worry of getting fined. Everyone became familiar with Thelonious there. He had developed a very unusual, amusing, eccentric melodic style based on stride, with surprising harmonies, angular, pointed chords, and twists and turns, stops and starts, and unusual rhythmic play and elasticity.

Joe Guy, a trumpeter, led the house trio—the nucleus of the house band—including Monk and Clarke. Nick Fenton and others played bass at different times. Henry Minton hired the former bandleader Teddy Hill to manage the club and make the music program successful. It was probably Teddy Hill who instituted the Monday night jam sessions and feasts paid for by the Schiffmans. Guitarist Charlie Christian, though only in his twenties, had become a legend among swing-era musicians, and he jammed at Minton's occasionally, using an amplified, electric guitar. Monk loved listening to Charlie play solos with fluid lines and interesting harmonies; they hinted at the developing revolution in jazz.

In 1941, the Minton's jam-session group, including Christian, was recorded in performance at the club. The recordings were technically rudimentary, done by a man named Jerry Newman, then a student at Columbia University.[1] The musicians, who weren't paid extra, allowed Newman to make the recordings because they liked to hear themselves play so that they could learn from listening to themselves.[2] On these recordings Monk has a modern, fluid sound, when he could be distinguished playing in the background of "Stomping at the Savoy" and "Charlie's Choice"—also called "Swing to Bop"—and "Topsy" and "Sweet Lorraine." Some people recognize Teddy Wilson's influence in his playing, which on these numbers feature more notes and more fluid lines than Monk would use for his mature, hesitating, spikey, percussive, succinct style. Joe Goldberg, in his 1965 book, *Jazz Masters of the Fifties*, noted that these recordings revealed Monk was hardly a primitive pianist: "[Monk] can be heard . . . blithely making runs that many writers have for years assumed were beyond his technical grasp." Monk wasn't featured on these recordings and took brief solos on only a few numbers. Not only that, but the recordings weren't released until 1947.[3] Altogether, they did little to further his career.

However, Jerry Newman used his Wilcox Gay disk recorder to record many other performances at Minton's. He took the recordings to Columbia University's radio station, then CURC, located in Ferris Booth Hall on the campus, and broadcast at least four shows, each about fifteen minutes long. Monk played brilliantly on his own tunes, such as "Epistrophy," then called "Joe's Tune," his mature style ringing with originality.[4] On other recordings, on which some people believe that Monk was included, tenor saxophonists Don Byas, Al Sears, and Herbie Fields and trumpeters Roy Eldridge and Hot Lips Page, all well-known players in the jazz world of the era, perform. Singer Helen Humes, who had been discovered by Count Basie and traveled with his band after Billie Holiday left it, sang on one recording. Saxophonist

Kermit Scott from Texas, can also be heard on some of Newman's recordings; Monk would later work in a group led by Scott, nicknamed "Scotty," at Minton's. Many other musicians sat in. For the most part their repertoire consisted of popular tunes of the swing era such as "Indiana," "Stardust," and "Exactly Like You."

By 1942, most young lions of jazz began making a habit of going to Minton's and sitting in. Charlie "Bird" Parker, pianist Ken Kersey, and trumpeters Benny Harris and Idrees Sulieman, all out of big bands, stopped at Minton's to see what was happening and to help make it happen. "Monk liked the way I played and told me to come by and bring my trumpet," recalled Sulieman. A new spirit for playing music was in the air. Though Monk would say, in one interview, that he never liked Charlie Parker's style, he appreciated the value of Bird's music. There's a tale—probably apocryphal—recounted in *Blue Monk* that Monk and Kenny Clarke, who was nicknamed Klook, asked Teddy Hill to hire Bird for the house band. When Hill refused, Monk and Clarke gave Parker a little of their salary to play with the group.

On October 24, 1941, Monk got the first hint that he might have a steady paycheck from the United States Army. A Selective Service questionnaire arrived at his apartment, and Thelonious S. Monk, as he was officially known by then, returned it on November 7. At first he was classified 1-A: available to serve, the highest classification and the one nearly everyone received to start. Then he was reclassified as 1-B: available to serve on a limited basis. Army records about what his limitations were have since been destroyed.

Both he and his sister, Marion, had suffered from bronchial trouble when they were young. "When my mother shook the sheets out to cover the bed," Marion would recall, "I would nearly strangle. I struggled for breath. Thelonious had the same trouble." It never developed into diagnosed asthma or tuberculosis, and both of them outgrew the problem. That was so far in Monk's past that it may have had nothing to do with his limited qualification for army service. He was instructed to report for induction on April 12, 1943, at which time he was reclassified again, this time as 4-F, rejected for service. Army records more than fifty years later reported only that the classification meant he was found physically, mentally, or morally unfit for service, without further explanation. The classification was quite common for prospective soldiers. During the next few years, Monk was reclassified several times, as 1-B, then 4-F, and finally as over the age qualifying him for service. By then the war was over.

No recordings were made of the Minton's Playhouse band in 1942 and 1943; Jerry Newman was simply not recording at Minton's at that time. During the mid-1940s, trumpeters Fats Navarro and Miles Davis, saxophonists Dexter Gordon and Lucky Thompson, drummers Art Blakey and Max Roach, bassist Tommy Potter, trombonist and arranger Jerry Valentine, and scores more musicians, including, of course, Dizzy Gillespie, dropped into Minton's. Some went just to listen. Others played for the joy of experimenting, improvising on the chords of songs already written and, in effect, writing new lines. Mary Lou Williams, recalling Minton's as a testing ground for new talent, said that "Monk, Charlie Christian, Kenny Clarke, Art Blakey, and Idries [*sic*] Sulieman were the first to play bop. Next were Parker, Gillespie, and [pianist] Clyde Hart."[5] From time to time, the question arose about who were the first musicians to modernize jazz; the most reasonable answer was that several musicians began experimenting independently at the same time and crossed paths at Minton's, where they developed the new style further. About himself, Monk said he was not really a bebop player. His style was "more original," he told writer George Simon.[6] Monk had always had a strong sense of his own originality.

Minton's became known as a hangout for a varied crew: pimps, prostitutes, hustlers of all kinds living on the fringe of society, neighborhood people relaxing for a night, young people looking for a place to dance and hear some of the hippest jazz sounds in town, and musicians and singers seeking an exciting way to spend an evening showing off their talents by sitting in and trying to win cutting contests among their colleagues.

Monk, who as the house pianist provided the foundation for the music, had more to teach than any of the others at Minton's. When he heard a young bass trombone player, Ted Kelly, Thelonious told him, "Man, come by the house tomorrow, because you don't know what the hell you're doing." Kelly, who lived near Monk, started going to Monk's apartment everyday. Monk turned him into a competent player and asked Dizzy to hire him.

Monk later discussed his role in the new music of the day with Bill Gottlieb: "Bebop wasn't developed in any deliberate way," Monk said. "For my part, I'll say it was just the style of music I happened to play. We all contributed ideas, the men you know plus a fellow called Vic Coulson [a trumpeter] who had been with [Charlie] Parker and Al Hibbler in the [Jay] McShann band [out of Kansas City]. Vic had a lot to do with our way of phrasing." By the end of the century, older musicians who recalled Coulson at all remembered him as a swing-era trumpeter, not a modernist. But he obviously appealed to Monk. In a review in the October 1944 issue of *Metronome*, critic Leonard Feather noticed that Coulson played a "Dizzy Gillespie-ish trumpet."

"If my own work had more importance than any other's, it's because the piano is the key instrument in music," Monk told Gottlieb. "I think all styles are built around piano developments. The piano plays the chord foundation and the rhythm foundation, too. Along with bass and drums. I was always at the spot [Minton's] and could keep working on the music. The rest, like Diz and Charlie, came in only from time to time, at first."[7]

Dizzy Gillespie, one of the most ambitious and artistically curious jazz musicians of the era, made Minton's a regular stop when he wasn't working elsewhere or when he finished his jobs in other clubs. Dizzy recalled first meeting Monk in 1937 and 1938 at the Savoy Ballroom— Dizzy thought Monk had played with trumpeter and bandleader Cootie Williams there—and they met again at Minton's. Dizzy credited Monk for valuable lessons in the new jazz harmonies. "I learned a lot from Monk," Dizzy said in his autobiography, *To Be or Not To Bop*:

> It's strange with Monk. Our . . . music is so closely related that Monk doesn't actually know what I showed him. But I do know some of the things that he showed me. Like, the minor-sixth chord with a sixth in the bass. I first heard Monk play that. It's demonstrated in some of my music like the melody of 'Woody 'n

You,' the introduction to 'Round Midnight,' and a part of the bridge to 'Manteca.'

There were lots of places where I used that progression that Monk showed me. . . . The first time I heard that, Monk showed it to me, and he called it a minor-sixth chord with a sixth in the bass. Nowadays they don't call it that. They call the sixth in the bass, the tonic, and the chord a C-minor seventh, flat five. What Monk called an E-flat-minor sixth chord with a sixth in the bass, the guys nowadays call a C-minor seventh flat five. C is the sixth note of an E-flat chord—the sixth in the bass—the bass plays that note. They call that a C-minor seventh flat five, because an E-flat minor chord is E-flat, G-flat, and B-flat. So they're exactly the same thing. An E-flat-minor chord with a sixth in the bass is C, E-flat, G-flat, and B-flat. Some people call it a half diminished, sometimes.

So now I extended that into a whole series of chords. B minor, E seventh, B-flat minor seventh, E-flat seventh, and into C. We'd do that kind of thing in 1942 around Minton's a lot. We'd been doing that kind of thing, Monk and I, but it was never documented because no records were being made at the time. There was a recording ban.

Dizzy recalled showing Monk some things on the piano, but Dizzy knew Monk to be traveling along his own path: "Monk is the most unique musician of our crowd. He was the one least affected by any other musician, unless he's affected by piano players like James P. Johnson and Fats Waller or Duke Ellington. I never heard him play like Teddy Wilson . . . . When I heard him play, he was playing like Monk, like nobody else."

Dizzy also recalled how Monk's playing influenced his most famous song, "A Night in Tunisia." He had been sitting at a piano one day. "And after hitting this chord, a D minor, I said to myself, 'boy, that's a nice chord change.' And the melodic line of 'A Night in Tunisia' was in that chord . . . I had to write a bridge for it, of course, and I didn't have a name for [the song]." Dizzy said the bridge used a chord progression that Thelonious Monk had showed him during a jam session at Minton's; then Dizzy added a Latin rhythm.[8]

Dizzy was proud that Monk used to point him out as the best trumpeter in the world. Monk told trumpeter Roy Eldridge, originally Dizzy's role model, "He'll eat you up." Dizzy said, "Monk would tell anybody how he feels about his playing. Monk'll tell you the truth, whatever he thinks about it. He's not diplomatic at all."

When questioned about Dizzy in an interview for Gillespie's autobiography, Monk said he first met Dizzy at the Rhythm Club on West 133rd Street and Seventh Avenue in Harlem and thought Dizzy sounded good, original, with an amusing stage presence and fine musicianship. Monk made the interviewer question him repeatedly until that little bit of information emerged.

On the other hand, the gregarious Dizzy loved talking about music to everyone—writers, students, protégés. "Monk's contribution to the new style of music was mostly harmonic and also spiritual," Dizzy said, "but Kenny Clarke set the stage for the rhythmic content of our music. He was the first one to make accents on the bass drum at specific points in the music. He'd play 4/4 very softly but the breaks, and the accents on the bass drum, you could hear. Like, we called them, dropping bombs."

Dizzy paid Monk the ultimate compliment: when Dizzy played the piano to compose, arrange, or teach other musicians, he sounded like Monk. He imitated Monk's style. Monk was doing more than making a harmonic and spiritual contribution to modern jazz. He was creating an entire direction or school of modern jazz, a separate entity —in effect a unique sound—just as Louis Armstrong and Duke Ellington had created their characteristic sounds. And it was, to a degree, more of a convenience than an accurate description to call Monk's music bebop, lumping it under an umbrella genre to try to make it seem identical to the sometimes frenetic, souped-up music played by Dizzy or Bird and their coterie.

Dizzy could analyze and explain what he and other modernists were doing. Monk taught the seductive sound of his own creative imagination primarily by example. It would take a long time for Monk's compositions and his style of communicating them to make themselves plain as extraordinary art music with a timeless sound. Early in his career, Monk was, in effect, assigned a slot by Dizzy, the most loquacious and outgoing modernist leader.

Johnny Carisi, a trumpeter, was one of the few white musicians welcomed onto the bandstand to play the new music at Minton's because he had the ability to do it. The beboppers liked to play such complicated music that lesser musicians found themselves run off the stage. Joe Guy got drunk one night and blamed Carisi for going to Minton's and adopting the new creation. Carisi knew he had good instincts, if not polish, for what to play. Monk appreciated his talent and invited him to go to the bar for a drink. "I'd say, 'Monk, I don't drink much,'" Carisi recalled. "He insisted. He'd say, 'What? Call yourself a jazz player . . .' And the next thing you know he had me drinking double gins. It was very funny."

According to some members of his family, when Monk had returned to New York in 1937 or '38, he had studied theory, harmony, and arranging with a professor at Juilliard, although Monk wasn't officially registered at the school. And no teacher at the school at that time left any record of ever having taught Thelonious. It's certain, however, that by the time he began playing at Minton's Playhouse in 1940 he had developed his characteristic style and progressed a long way from "'comping" for an evangelist. And the musician with the greatest obvious effect on Monk's compositions was Duke Ellington.

Clarinetist Tony Scott thought that Monk had never studied with anybody. "That's why he was so great," Scott quipped. Nevertheless, there's a chance that Monk heard some very inspiring music from a European refugee. In 1938, Professor Stefan Wolpe, a refugee from Hitler's Germany, arrived in the United States by way of Palestine. A significant composer enthralled with twelve-tone music, he had studied at the Berlin Hochschule für Musik and then with Anton von Webern in Vienna. And von Webern's music was influenced by the great atonal modernist composers, including Arnold Schoenberg and Alban Berg.

Arriving in New York late in 1938, Wolpe made that city his home base in the United States. A year later, he found a teaching position two days a week in the Settlement Music School in Philadelphia. He never taught at Juilliard, though eventually he became well known to his colleagues there. From the first he began teaching students privately in New York, trying to rebuild his life. It's conceivable that Thelonious Monk may have studied with Wolpe at this time. Nobody at Juilliard, including Bertha Melnik, who studied there from 1934 to 1941, and later taught there beginning in 1955, knew of anyone whom Thelonious had studied with at the school. But familiar with both Wolpe and Monk, she thought it was a tantalizing idea that the paths of the jazz composer and the European experimentalist who needed to earn a living had crossed in New York.

It was particularly possible that Stefan Wolpe met Thelonious sometime between 1938 and the early 1940s, because Wolpe had several jazz musicians for students. One of them was Tony Scott, who met Wolpe through Harry Marks of the Marks Music Publishing Company. Scott invited other jazz musicians to his house, where he introduced them to Wolpe. Among them was pianist Bud Powell, a probable connection between Monk and Wolpe, for Bud and Monk, along with pianist Elmo Hope, were best friends. They were so close, they were like "triplets," said tenor saxophonist Johnny Griffin, who met them in the late 1940s, when Elmo played in his band.

Monk, Bud, and Elmo didn't talk to each other about music; they played the piano for each other. Tony Scott sometimes sat in with Monk at Minton's but never spoke to him. "He had his own little world," recalled Tony, an extremely talkative man. "[Wolpe] was white shit. We [jazz musicians] laughed because Monk played with such unorthodox fingering, so silly and childlike but so swinging, and it came out so well. He was out of the black African tradition; the elders teach the kids."

It's certain that anything Bud Powell learned, he told to Monk and Elmo. Monk was experimenting with the beauties of dissonance suggestive of atonality even before Bud met Wolpe. But Monk would have had his ideas reinforced, and he may have been intrigued enough to talk to Wolpe himself and show Wolpe his compositions. Wolpe gave many jazz musicians and arrangers the benefit of his critiques.

In 1942, Monk first met Bud Powell, who was then eighteen years old, and befriended him and took him to Minton's, where, as Monk recalled, he tried to modernize Powell's style. Powell was a classically trained, very gifted young pianist. In a personal way, Monk defended young Bud, too. Once Bud put his feet on a white tablecloth. A waiter was getting ready to throw Bud out of Minton's, but Monk stopped him, saying, "Don't do that. The kid's got talent."[9] Monk used to insist that Bud get a chance to play at Minton's. At first Bud struggled to play the modern style. Soon he became the most popular pianist of the bebop era. He played with a blazing technique that was ideally suited to the aesthetic goals of the groups led by Dizzy and Bird. Young pianists around the country heard Bud's work on recordings, and everyone wanted to play with the explosive, fast, complicated technique and power of Bud Powell.

Monk didn't begrudge Powell his fame at all. Instead Monk, who always played his own ideas on the rare occasions when he was hired as a sideman, kept on working at his own compositions, many of which he wrote specifically for Bud to play. Bud recorded "'Round Midnight" with Cootie Williams's band on the Hit label in 1944, before Monk ever put it on a record himself.[10] Among Bud's many important recorded interpretations of Monk's compositions was the classic "52nd Street Theme" (with a bridge derived from Fats Waller's "Honeysuckle Rose"), which Monk wrote in 1940 at Minton's and never recorded himself, and "Off Minor" in 1949. Monk dedicated "In Walked Bud"—written on the chords of "Blue Skies" with such certainty in its groove—to his protégé and took pains to teach his compositions to Bud. Bud worshipped Thelonious's music and learned the songs note for note. That pleased Thelonious a great deal.

Unknown to Bud and almost everyone else, Monk learned to imitate Bud's style too. Years later, Monk was hanging out with a younger pianist, Walter Davis, Jr.—just the two of them in a room with a piano. Thelonious pushed back the cover on the piano and started to play, sounding just like Bud Powell. Walter's mouth dropped open. All of a sudden, Monk stopped, put the cover down, looked at the flabbergasted Walter, and said, "Don't tell nobody."

Monk struggled to find work while Bud's career took off. There are conflicting reports from this period about Monk's style. A long time before George Wein opened his own Boston jazz club, Storyville, and then founded the Newport Jazz Festival in 1954, he heard Monk play at a place called Irving Plaza in New York—probably in 1943. George paid attention because he was an amateur jazz pianist, and the odd name Thelonious Monk was unforgettable. George didn't think Monk played very well at that time. It sounded like "a bad imitation between Teddy Wilson and Earl 'Fatha' Hines," George thought, two of the most important jazz pianists of the era. His idea could surprise anyone who hadn't heard Monk in those days, since both Wilson and Hines played long, flowing lines—Wilson known for his elegance and touch, Hines the originator of the trumpet style of piano playing, an imitation of the long lines of the horn players—while Monk was devising a percussive approach to the piano, and his style would become choppy and angular. At the risk of overstating the case, he was, at times, the Anti-Horn. Perhaps that alone was enough to unnerve, confuse, or discourage a new listener at that time. Or perhaps George Wein was hearing exactly what others, Martin Williams for one, thought Monk was doing in that period—playing under the influence of Teddy Wilson—and not clearly projecting Monkian harmonies.

However, another musician detected Monk's developing style. Classically educated jazz pianist Herbie Nichols, writing about a year later for the *Music Dial* in August 1944, made several tantalizing and curious observations about Monk:

> Thelonious Monk is an oddity among piano players. This particular fellow is the author of the weirdest rhythmical melodies I've ever heard. They are very great, too. (Don't ever praise Monk too much or he'll let you down.) But I will say that I'd rather hear him play a "boston" than any other pianist. His sense of fitness is uncanny. However, when Monk takes a solo, he seems to be partial to certain limited harmonies which prevent him from taking a place beside Art [Tatum] and Teddy [Wilson]. He seems

to be in a vise as far as that goes and never shows any signs of being able to extricate himself.

A young alto saxophonist, Lou Donaldson, who would arrive in New York in the 1950s and who eventually played and recorded with Monk, thought Nichols, more than anyone else, sounded like Monk. "Monk was the only one playing that way at that time. We didn't have anybody else like that then."

NOTES

Personal interviews: Brooks Kerr, Marion Monk, Dan Morgenstern, Tony Scott, George Wein, Lou Donaldson, Dizzy Gillespie.

1. Jerry Newman has been generally acknowledged as having recorded these performances, included in a Monk discography compiled by jazz historian Dan Morgenstern, who says that Newman recorded with a portable disk cutter.

2. From Ponzio and Postif (1995).

3. Recordings of Monk playing with Charlie Christian were released on 78 rpms on the Vox label in 1947. According to jazz historian and pianist Brooks Kerr, Dizzy Gillespie managed to acquire the recordings and make them available to Vox. None of the musicians on the recordings were paid for their work. From Brooks Kerr comes the information about the Wilcox Gay machine used by Jerry Newman. These are the only recordings Monk made with the guitarist. Christian contracted tuberculosis in 1941, and he died a year later. Monk would always say that he had never heard anybody play the guitar better than Charlie Christian.

4. These recordings, with details here supplied by Brooks Kerr, seem never to have had a commercial release, but jazz historian and jazz radio personality Phil Schaap broadcasts them every October 10 for the Thelonious Monk birthday anniversary show on WKCR, Columbia University's present-day station.

5. From an interview with Max Jones, *Melody Maker*, London, England, 1954, cited by Deffaa (1996).

6. Simon (1948).

7. Gottlieb (1947).

8. From a 1987 radio interview on WKCR, starring Dizzy Gillespie with Phil Schaap, host, for the fiftieth anniversary celebration of Dizzy's recording career.

9. Gitler (1966).

10. In 1941, Cootie's band, with Ken Kersey as pianist, had already recorded Monk's tune "Epistrophy" under the title "Fly Right." Monk wasn't listed as the composer on the recording's credit line. The tune had several other titles before it became known as Monk's classic tune "Epistrophy." When Monk played it in his distinctive style, it was like a sculpture in sound. Monk and Kenny Clarke collaborated on "Epistrophy," and both were credited for it.

Finding His Voice in the 1940s

Some sources say that Monk stopped working regularly at Minton's in 1942. However, Monk continued sitting in through at least the mid-40s. Idrees Sulieman recalled Thelonious playing there nightly from 10 P.M. to 4 A.M., when Idrees was living on 114th Street around 1943. After Minton's closed for the night, they went to play at an after-hours club next door. Monk also played at Kelly's Stable and other clubs on Manhattan's West 52nd Street, a street filled with wall-to-wall little jazz clubs. It would become revered as "Swing Street" in jazz history.

Monk played with Lucky Millinder's band at the Savoy Ballroom in Harlem in 1943—but not for long. Typically, Monk played in his individualistic way with Millinder's swing-era band for dancers. Monk had never been satisfied with what he heard played by other jazz pianists, and he had been working passionately on his unusual harmonies. Monk himself told Leonard Feather that he worked with Millinder for a week, although Millinder's drummer, Panama Francis, said that it only took one set for Monk to get fired. (Panama Francis, a very opinionated man, thought Monk was never a good player and couldn't read well enough to play Millinder's arrangements; Panama also believed that bebop was invented and popularized by record companies, not musicians—a novel view. And some of Monk's recordings would never make sense to Panama.)[1] Monk's son heard that his father had actually quit the job, saying "I'm no dancer." Monk himself would later contradict Panama Francis's tale and several other stories told by his friends when he told writer, jazz critic, and historian Nat Hentoff for an article in *Down Beat* in 1956, "I've always been told way back that I was unique, but I never lost a job on account of that."

After leaving Millinder's band, Monk returned to Minton's in 1943 in Kermit Scott's band, with Nick Fenton on bass and Harold "Doc" West on drums.[2] In 1944 Monk played alternately with pianist George Wallington in a group led by Dizzy Gillespie and bassist Oscar Pettiford, with Lester Young on tenor sax, and with Doc West (who was replaced by Max Roach for a while) at the Onyx Club on West 52nd Street. But it was Wallington, not Monk, who got the opportunity to record with Dizzy's band there.

Wallington was regarded as more important than Monk in the early bebop groups on 52nd Street for two reasons. Monk, with his customary succinctness, summed them up himself for several writers: he didn't socialize enough; and he was difficult for other musicians to play with. He sounded best with bassists and drummers in a rhythm section. But the front-line soloists, such as Gillespie, had to contend with Monk's enormous individuality. Gillespie, for one, was quick to admit that he liked pianists who stayed out of his way. Monk's distinctive style and personal shyness—his mind was always on his music, not on socializing in a political way to popularize himself—hampered his commercial progress.

As if to compound his difficulties, the rights to his moody ballad "'Round Midnight" slipped through his fingers for a while. Trumpeter Cootie Williams, who left Duke Ellington's orchestra and led his own small groups beginning in 1940, became friendly with Thelonious through Kenny Clarke. Monk later told Harry Colomby that Cootie offered Monk $300 as an advance for "'Round Midnight"; Cootie wanted to record and publish it in 1944. In return, Monk would give Cootie credit for having collaborated on the song. Monk accepted the deal. On the recording on the Hit label, Monk and Cootie were listed

Coleman Hawkins, unknown woman, Thelonious; foreground Eric Dolphy, photographed at Nola Studios, New York. Photo: Raymond Ross

as co-composers. But according to Monk's son, Cootie received all the money for the composition at first. In those days, the record companies simply registered the performer as the composer and shared in the revenues or royalties from the songs.

Monk waited about four years to claim his rights. It's not clear who helped him secure his share of the money for the song he alone had written, but it might have been Alfred Lion, an owner of Blue Note Records; Monk made his first recording of that song for Lion. (Lyricist Bernie Hanighen wrote the lyrics that became popular for the music, and his name would appear whenever the lyrics were used. Singer Jon Hendricks wrote lesser-known lyrics for it, too.) Monk's son recalled his father's bitterness about how his business dealings were handled, "I sat home with him when he was talking about being fucked over. There's an emotional dynamic involved for me."

Monk found a loyal champion, however. Coleman Hawkins, the tenor saxophonist, had become a legend in the jazz world for his recording of "Body and Soul" in 1938 and commanded respect as the greatest living tenor player. In 1944, although many musicians didn't think Monk was a very good pianist, Hawkins hired a sextet that included Monk to work at Kelly's Stable on West 52nd Street.

Hawkins actually had to defend his choice of Monk, because other musicians criticized the pianist so roundly. Hawkins had come back from Europe in the late 1930s and was distressed to find so little had changed in jazz during his absence. He himself played in a traditional, swing-era style, which he had essentially helped create, but he loved to be around young musicians who were trying to modernize the music. They excited him. Monk was one of his favorite younger players.

Hawkins's co-leader at Kelly's Stable was tenor saxophonist Don Byas, one of the most important stars on his instrument at the time, and the group was rounded out with trumpeter Benny Harris, drummer Stan Levey, and bassist Eddie Robinson. Levey was replaced by Monk's friend Denzil Best and Robinson by Selwyn Warner when Hawkins took the group to a club in Toronto, Canada. On the way back to New York, the men stopped to play in Boston. Warner would later say, "Thelonious Monk was coming along in those days, getting his [chops] together. He was very bright, quiet and cool, but not eccentric."[3]

Arriving back in New York, Hawkins took his group, with Eddie Robinson on the bass again, into the Downbeat Club on 52nd Street in May 1944. Billy Taylor, who was living in town by then and playing at the Three Deuces on West 52nd Street, recalled John Simmons as the bassist and Shadow Wilson on drums. They may also have played with the Hawkins group at that time, since it had some personnel changes during its booking there until mid-August. (They definitely played with Monk on a Blue Note recording that would be issued in 1948.) Monk stayed in Coleman Hawkins's group, but even he may have been occasionally replaced by others—John Malachi, a Washington-based pianist and a friend of singer Billy Eckstine, for one. Malachi played in Eckstine's big band in the 1940s. In those days the Street was swarming with talented young musicians. Hawk's group appeared opposite singer Billie Holiday at the Downbeat Club, as Billy Taylor remembered.

"Monk asked me, 'What have you got?'

"I said, 'A Steinway.'

"He said, 'I'd like to try it sometime.'

"I said, 'Okay.' It was about 5 A.M. We finished breakfast, and I went home to sleep. The doorbell rang at 6:15. It was Monk.

"'I want to try the piano,' he said.

"I said, 'I don't mind, but the people in the apartments around here work. They get up at seven o'clock. These people might beat me up if I wake them up before then.'

"Monk said, 'Okay, mind if I wait?'"

Billy was half asleep, and he dozed off and left Monk in the room. "I was awakened by his playing at 8 A.M. The thing I liked about him—he was a searcher; we called them searchers in those days. He said, 'What if I did this? If I did this with that, will it work?' For the interval of a seventhth, instead of using or playing C–B, a major seventh, he'd invert that and put the B on the bottom and the C on the top, and it was weird"—dissonant. "But if you put E and G in there, it doesn't sound too bad. And what he would do is ask what would happen if he left out these notes, E and G."

Billy wrote and recorded his own tune, "The Mad Monk," on the Savoy label in 1943, trying to compose in a bebop, Monkian vein. Monk told Billy he didn't sound like Monk at all. But with his effort, Billy knew, he had complimented his friend.

There were virtually two camps about Monk at that time: the jazz world insiders and fans who admired his playing, and those who couldn't stand it. The young Brooklyn-born pianist Randy Weston, not yet really a professional musician, was still in the army when he went to hear his idol, Coleman Hawkins, playing on 52nd Street. Randy felt very close to Max Roach, Dizzy Gillespie, bassist Tommy Potter, and Miles Davis, and the whole bebop movement. "And Monk wasn't in it," he recalled. Furthermore, the first time he heard Monk with

Billy Taylor, 1946. Photo: Charles B. Nadell. Courtesy Frank Driggs Collection.

Coleman Hawkins playing "Ruby, My Dear," Randy "couldn't understand what Hawkins was doing with this guy who didn't play much."

Nevertheless, Hawkins recognized Monk's gift and kept him in the
group, taking him to the Bali Club in Washington, D.C., from August 25
to September 8, 1944, back to the Down Beat on 52nd Street, still on a bill
with Billie Holiday, along with vibraphonist Red Norvo, and the zany
singer and pianist, Harry the Hipster. Then the group went for a one-
night stand playing for dancers at Hartford, Connecticut's Footguard Hall
in the autumn of 1944. Hawkins was reportedly very well-paid for the
Connecticut gig, though there's no record of what he paid his sidemen.
He also took Monk in the group into the Apollo Theater, where Monk
actually was given a good review by Leonard Feather.

According to Monk's son, Feather had previously written very critical articles about Thelonious. Monk was extremely upset. One day the big, intense pianist grabbed Feather, a slender, almost reedy-looking man, by the collar—or the "neck," as one person recalled it—and threatened to throw him over a guard wall at Rockefeller Center. There was a big drop to the ground below on a level that was a popular, sunken ice-skating rink. "You're taking the bread out of my mouth!" Monk said. At that time, Leonard, who played piano a little, was a rising songwriter, producer, and especially critic for *Metronome*, and he had only recently begun to pay attention to, understand, and support the modernists.[4] Still learning about the new music at the time when Hawk took Monk into the Apollo, Feather wrote in October 1944, that Hawk sounded "great," and "Monk's piano always covers fertile ground." But Feather was never completely won over by Monk and would hurt him deeply as late as 1949, when Feather published his book *Inside Bebop*. Dismissing Monk as a colleague of Dizzy and Bird, Feather wrote: "[Monk] has written a few attractive tunes, but his lack of technique and continuity prevented him from accomplishing much as a pianist." Feather thought Cootie Williams's recording of "'Round Midnight" was "vastly superior" to Monk's own interpretation. Feather granted only that "Monk is an original thinker" but denied that Monk's solos had "any of the mystical qualities attributed to them by non-musical admirers." And Monk was not among the musicians Feather credited with bebop's development.

Even in his introduction to the revised version of this book retitled *Inside Jazz* in 1977, Feather barely apologized, writing, "Thelonius, by the way, was given rather short shrift in the book; on the other hand, he was later overpraised by fanatical supporters. The truth about Monk lies halfway between the unjust early derogation and the subsequent cult-like hero worship."

On October 19, 1944, when Monk was twenty-seven years old, he made his first recordings, with Hawkins leading his quartet at New York's Empire Studios on four songs—two uptempo and two slow—on the Joe Davis label. For the slow ballads, "Drifting on a Reed," and "Recollections," Monk played in the background. But on the uptempo tunes, "Flyin' Hawk" and "On the Bean," Monk clearly played passages with his own distinctive sense of harmony, if not his trademark angularity. (Listening to these recordings years later, it's puzzling to try to figure out what other musicians didn't like about his style. But by that time, his harmonies had become familiar and universally respected in the world.) In 1944, when Hawkins took a group to Los Angeles, California to play at a nightspot owned by a well-known jazz club owner, Billy Berg, Monk was supposed to go. But the gig was postponed for a while; when it became a firm date in 1945, Monk decided to stay in New York.

One of Monk's nephews, Thelonious Theo, recalled that Monk played with the bandleader Andy Kirk at the reopening of the Cotton Club on Lenox Avenue between 141st and 142nd Streets in 1945. At the end of all the songs, Monk added his own unusual notes. Kirk told him, "You can't do that." Monk said, "Okay." But he kept doing it. Finally Kirk told him, "This will be the last session for you. You're good, and it looks like you have future hopes, but you just can't make it in this band." Kirk believed that Monk was a genius, but not for Kirk's music. Monk's mind "was going someplace else," Kirk later told one of Monk's nephews, who added "Kirk always respected my uncle for that." (It's clear that Monk's own family thought that his style had lost him jobs, despite his statement to the contrary.) Another possible explanation is that he wasn't fired from Andy Kirk's band at all but quit to take a better paying job in Coleman Hawkins's group. That story supports Monk's contention that he was never fired because of his style.

For his West Coast gig that year, Coleman Hawkins used pianist Sir Charles Thompson, composer of a jazz classic, "Robbins' Nest." Even without Monk, Hawkins kept playing Monk's songs as part of the band's regular repertoire, including "Hackensack," first called "Rifftide," based on the chords of the standard "Oh, Lady Be Good!" It became a bop classic, and shows a joyous blending of Monk's harmonic, melodic, and rhythmic genius. Hawk recorded it under the "Rifftide" name on a record date with Mary Lou Williams at the end of 1944. Hawk got the composer's credit for "Rifftide," and later Monk was credited with the same tune under the name "Hackensack."

Riffs traveled up and down 52nd Street; musicians heard something they liked as they passed the door of one club and took the phrase into their own gigs. Sometimes they knowingly pilfered each other's inspirations, and sometimes the borrowing was completely innocent. Many musicians played Monk's "52nd Street Theme" on the Street. Monk would eventually find that critics chose one or another of his songs as their favorite and declare it Monk's greatest composition; "Hackensack" would number among them. ("Crepuscule With Nellie" yet to come in the 1950s, would become another of the critics' choices.)

In the spring of 1945, Monk may have been playing with Skippy Williams's band.[5] Williams, a tenor saxophonist, led a big band of seventeen musicians, which went into the Lincoln Square Center on Mondays and Tuesdays in August 1945. At that time, Monk was fired for his tardiness for performances. There would be long stretches in his career when musicians working with him never saw Monk arrive at work late once, and there would be instances when he showed up very late. He was even rumored to skip engagements altogether, but that happened primarily, perhaps only, when his name had been used to promote a performance, and he had never even known about it. When he was delayed, or waylaid, it was usually because he had found something more important to do—something connected, even if only in a tangential way, with his own composing. Once in a great while he was actually sick and couldn't work. And at times his tardiness or absence may have been a value judgment: He simply may not have wanted to play the sort of music confronting him. Later on in his career, he may have thought occasionally that his own group had reached a point of serving his own music very well without his participation. But his attitude toward punctuality, whatever the cause at any particular time, so inconvenienced others that it added to his growing reputation for unreliability. In this case, he may have decided that it was not very important to his own music to show up on time for the gig with Williams.

And he was probably correct. Finding it easier to get work than he had previously done in the 52nd Street clubs, he soon went to play at the Spotlite, where he remet Coleman Hawkins and joined his defender's group at the Downbeat club.

Miles Davis joined the pro-Monk camp in 1945. Arriving in New York City to study at Juilliard, Miles fell in love with Monk's music and began to try to play on his trumpet whatever he heard Monk do on the piano. Miles would later say in his autobiography, "If I hadn't met him in 1945 when I came to New York, I wouldn't have progressed so well."[6] Charlie Parker kept taking Miles to hear Monk in clubs and urging him to play with Monk. Monk influenced not only Miles's voicings and chord progressions but also his use of space for solos, Miles said. Bassist Al McKibbon joined Hawk's group at the Downbeat and noticed Miles sitting on the bandstand and digging Monk. "Sometimes Monk would hit something strange, and Miles would figure it out on his horn, but he'd never play. He would just sit and listen and laugh to himself," McKibbon said.[7]

That same year, Monk went to play in Philadelphia with Hawkins in an all-star concert, along with Art Tatum, Dizzy Gillespie, and guitarist Mary Osborne. After this concert, a reviewer for *Metronome* made fun of the way Monk played.[8] Hawkins defended Monk, telling a writer for *Down Beat*, "That's originality."[9] And reviewers didn't discourage Hawkins from keeping Monk in the group.

In 1945 in Philadelphia—probably during Monk's engagement with Hawkins there—Bud Powell experienced a nasty, traumatic beating by the police. According to one version of the story, the beating may have stemmed from his loyalty to Monk. Bud was working with Cootie Williams in a club; after his gig ended, he went to hear Monk play. Bud saw the police harrassing Monk and rushed to his defense. A fight broke out. The police arrested Bud for disorderly conduct, took him to jail, and beat him on the head. He was so badly injured that he couldn't get home under his own power the next day. His mother had to go to the jail and fetch him.

Another version states that Bud was drunk and became disorderly in Philadelphia's train station, and the police fought with him there. (Philadelphia had the reputation for being a very scary place for jazz musicians in those days; in part because of several racial incidents, it became the first city to have a civilian review board to review police actions in the '50s.) That's probably the true story, since Bud's gig with

Cootie Williams ended early in 1945, and Monk played in Philadelphia with Hawkins later in the year, most likely in November. But Bud's reverence for Monk was so well-known that the tale of his rushing to Monk's aid gained a foothold in jazz lore. After the beating, Bud, who had always been psychologically unstable, became permanently unhinged, and he was subsequently hospitalized frequently for long periods.

Firmly supported by Hawkins, Monk next traveled in Hawk's rhythm section, with drummer Denzil Best and bassist Al McKibbon, and with trumpeter Roy Eldridge in the front line, on a North American tour with Jazz at the Philharmonic, the jazz concerts organization produced by impresario Norman Granz. Granz had been encouraged by his successes with jazz productions in Los Angeles to organize a touring group under the name "Jazz at the Philharmonic" in honor of the theater, Philharmonic Hall, where he had produced his first concert. This time Hawkins had no trouble in getting Monk to leave New York and fly to California to join the tour.

The star-studded tour began at its namesake hall in Los Angeles on November 26, 1945, attracting an audience of over 2500 people. For the rest of the tour, which included Canada, Monk enjoyed the protection of Norman Granz, who never permitted his concerts to be staged for segregated audiences, writing his stipulation about integration into all of his contracts. The tour was supposed to last four weeks, but some managers in the South cancelled when they read Granz's contract prohibiting segregation in the audiences, so it was cut short to only three weeks. Naturally Monk and all the musicians enjoyed the first-class treatment they received. Among the other African American musicians traveling with Monk were alto-saxophonist Willie Smith, trumpeter Howard McGhee, tenor-saxophonist Lucky Thompson, pianist Meade Lux Lewis, and singer Helen Humes, along with the white musicians, tenor saxophonists Corky Corcoran and Vido Musso, guitarist Barney Kessel, and pianist Arnold Ross.[10] It was Hawk's support of Monk, despite Monk's detractors, that led Monk to be included in the historic, first Jazz at the Philharmonic tour. (Audiences responded to it so well that Norman Granz made his tours a tradition for many years.) For the rest of Hawk's life, another quarter century, the grateful Monk always showed him the greatest respect and affection whenever their paths crossed by chance, for gigs, or for a record date led by Monk.

Back in New York in December 1945, Monk was resting, when Dizzy Gillespie began organizing a big band to open at the Spotlite club on 52nd Street. For Dizzy, it was a great opportunity. He always loved leading a big band. His previous attempt had foundered on a tour of the South. Exuberant about the Spotlite engagement, Dizzy hired Bud Powell to play for the band; Bud was tremendously popular. But Dizzy couldn't contend with Bud's pronounced mental problems, and so he replaced Bud with Monk. Pianist Sadik Hakim, then on the scene, would eventually tell the tale that Monk used to play a wrong chord every time he got to it in a song. Dizzy would say, "Damn, Monk, don't you know that's the wrong chord?" Monk would point to the music where the wrong chord was mistakenly written; Monk wouldn't change it until Dizzy corrected it on the music. "Monk was that way," explained Paul Jeffrey, who much later played tenor for Monk and passed along this story. "He expected you to do things for yourself, correct yourself."

Monk infuriated Dizzy by never showing up on time for performances. "I had no trouble outta Monk, not too much, but Monk wasn't showing up on time either. It was against the law to show up on time," Dizzy said ironically.

Monk, who was officially with the band in May, June, and July of 1946, recorded with it. Dizzy's music director and arranger, Walter Gil Fuller, didn't think Monk was the best pianist in the world, certainly not on a par with Oscar Peterson. That was Fuller's frame of reference, the standard set by the great mainstream pianist who would emerge as a star under Norman Granz's personal management. Years later, it would dawn on everyone that Monk's style was perfect for his own music and stamped other people's songs with his characteristic edginess, suspense, and uplift. But Fuller loved Monk's compositions, recognizing them for the great works they were, and he wanted them for the band's repertoire:

> Monk never would show up on time, but I didn't want Monk in
> the band for the sake of showing up, as much as I wanted to get
> Monk's things. Because Monk was a freak for tunes. He had all
> kinds of strange shit going on . . . but I never did have a chance to
> write the arrangements on the things because everything was
> happening. I was writing for six or seven other bands at the same
> time . . . Anyway, we had Monk for . . . 'Ruby My Dear,' and all
> that stuff . . . Dizzy's mad because Monk don't never show up on
> time. Anytime we got ready to hit, we'd hit without a piano player.

Dizzy became so upset that he finally fired Monk, replacing him
with a young, classically trained pianist, John Lewis, a friend of Kenny
Clarke's, just out of the army. Lewis knew about Monk's problem and
told Dizzy and his wife, Lorraine, "I can play better than Monk." The
change of pianists evoked all the considerable irascibility that Gil Fuller
could possibly feel. He had wanted to arrange Monk's tunes for the
band so much that he could taste it. After Monk left, the band kept
"'Round Midnight" in its repertoire, but that was just a fraction of
what Gil had dreamed of arranging. "I never forgave Dizzy for that,"
he reminisced later."

Monk—who often became distracted while thinking about his
music (which he either wrote on paper or composed in his head or at
the piano at home), and who often took naps at odd hour to rest
between compositions—simply couldn't keep track of the moments
when he was supposed to "hit," as musicians referred to the hour when
a gig started. But Monk's attitude toward Dizzy's band wasn't cavalier
or deliberate. He was very unhappy about his dismissal and saddened
in general because he wasn't receiving credit for the work he had done.

Budd Johnson, a tenor saxophonist who sometimes played with
Dizzy (even though Budd wasn't a modernist), used to visit Monk at
his family's apartment on West 63rd Street. He recalled:

> Monk's feelings got hurt because Dizzy and Charlie [were]
> getting all the credit for this music, this style—I used to go over
> to Monk's house with him, drink some wine with him. "Come

on, I want you to hear what I'm doing," he said. "I'm gonna let them take that style and go ahead, and I'm gonna get a new style." His mother would fix some food for us, and he would just play for me. All this funny-type music that he was playing. And he had gone altogether different from what he had been doing. I said, "Hey, man . . . that's outtasight! What're you doing; whaddayou call that?"

"I don't know, man, it's just—you know." He couldn't explain it to me. And I never thought of Monk as a great piano player. But he would fumble on that piano and get these things out and make all the dissonant chords, and major seconds, and minor seconds.

And I said, "Hey man, that's outtasight."

"Well, I'm going on now with my new music," he said. And he did. He did go right along with his new music."[12]

By new music, Monk seems to have primarily meant new compositions, for which he usually favored slower tempos than other beboppers used. He didn't do anything radically different from the music he was already writing and stylizing in performances.

In 1946, Kenny Clarke recorded Monk's tunes "52nd Street Theme" and "Epistrophy." Clarke maintained that he was actually the composer of these songs, and he had shared them with Monk to help the pianist survive. But only "Epistrophy" is registered with Broadcast Music Inc. (BMI) as a collaboration between Monk and Clarke, while "52nd Street Theme" is listed under Monk's name alone. Thelonious never argued with other people's claims to have collaborated with him on songs. Drummer Denzil Best, for example, cowrote the driving "Bemsha Swing" with his good friend and admirer. However, Monk's manager Harry Colomby heard Monk complain about not getting the credit for having written the bridge to Dizzy's most famous song, "A Night in Tunisia"—the bridge that Dizzy himself said he learned from Monk. "Where are the royalties for that?" Monk said.

But by 1946, Thelonious—the titan of the bebop era's composers—was unemployed, except for his own commitment to composing. Even though he was becoming better known, he had maintained an uncanny knack for ignoring the niceties of professional etiquette. He knew that everyone regarded him as an eccentric, and he hadn't yet learned to use that image to his advantage. He didn't seek out the press, yet he hated to be misconstrued and misquoted. His feelings were often very hurt, and he was a lonesome figure. Several friends recalled that he was collecting unemployment compensation checks for a while in the 1940s; they may have been owed to him from his gig as the house pianist at Minton's.

NOTES

Personal interviews: T. S. Monk Jr., Billy Taylor, Randy Weston, Thelonious Theo Monk, Paul Jeffrey, Harry Colomby.

1. From Ponzio and Postif (1995), and from an interview by the author with Panama Francis in 1996.
2. Ponzio and Postif (1995).
3. In Chilton (1990).
4. Later, in the 1940s, Feather, who was developing into one of the best, most influential jazz critics of the century, would publish his book Inside Bebop (eventually retitled Inside Jazz), the first book to take the new music seriously and attempt to explain its genesis and accomplishments.
5. From Ponzio and Postif (1995), who also said that Williams was best known for having replaced tenor saxophonist Ben Webster—probably briefly, if it ever happened at all—in Duke Ellington's band.
6. Davis with Troupe (1989).
7. Cited in Davis with Troupe (1989).
8. Chilton (1990).
9. Ibid.
10. Ibid.
11. Gillespie with Fraser (1979).
12. Ibid.

Along Came Blue Note

Monk was thirty years old in 1947, when Blue Note, a small, important jazz recording label, invited him to record under his own name. These recordings would do a great deal to disseminate his music and unique style and establish him as one of the most important jazz players of the day—at least among many of the jazz cognoscenti.

Ike Quebec, a saxophonist who played for Cab Calloway's band and did a great deal of recording for Blue Note, brought Monk to the attention of Alfred Lion and Francis Wolfe, the owners of the label; singer Kenny "Pancho" Hagood may have passed the word, too. Lorraine Gordon—who was then Lorraine Stein Lion, married to Alfred—remembered those exciting days: "Ike Quebec was a very good friend of ours. He was more than just a musician in our lives; he became our pal, and he introduced us to Thelonious. We may have known something about him because he had a record out from Minton's, which I still have, with Joe Guy on trumpet, and Thelonious muffled in the background, not shown off, and Kenny 'Klookmop' was on it." (Kenny Clarke earned his onomatopoeic nickname, Klook, in imitation of the sounds of the accents he played.)

Lorraine, Alfred, and Frank—and sometimes Ike Quebec and Art Blakey—visited Monk to talk to him about recording for Blue Note.

"It was as simple as that," Lorraine recalled. They went to his apartment, where he lived with his mother, and sat with him in his bedroom. Though Lorraine didn't see Nellie Smith anywhere around Monk in those days, Nellie, who would become his constant companion, was actually already a part of his life. "Monk had an upright piano in his narrow room, which looked to me like Vincent Van Gogh's room in Arles, with the bed and the dresser, except there was a piano and a bed there along the wall," Lorraine said. The bed was the only place for them to sit, with their backs against the wall and their legs sticking out.

Lorraine recalled:

> Thelonious with his back to us played various numbers we had never heard before. They were all originals. Everyone of them, "Ruby My Dear," "'Round Midnight," "Straight No Chaser," "Well, You Needn't," every single thing that I ever heard there, he just spun out, one after another. And I thought: Is he a great blues pianist! So I fell in love with him. I just heard his bluesy sound. It didn't seem so revolutionary to me. That's why I liked him so much. In those early days I couldn't listen to a lot of avant garde musicians. I was steeped in Sidney Bechet and Duke Ellington. But Monk made the transition for me, because I was hearing his great stride piano style from James P. Johnson and the blues and his great left hand. I heard all those things plus some fascinating melodies that I had never heard before.

She didn't remember if she had ever seen him move his left hand over his right to play the melodies. Monk would become well known for crossing his hands to play his songs. "It's possible. I don't know. He was full of quirks," she said. "He had a style. His fingers would stay above the keys for a split second, and I would wonder when they were coming down. I could hear the wheels going in his head. 'Where shall I put them, these hands, these fingers?'—and flat, not an arched hand, flat, wham."[1]

Lorraine recalled that she, Alfred, and Frank became very involved with Monk's music and what he was going to play for Blue Note. They didn't go dancing or to the movies with him, but Lorraine, in particular,[[Au/? sense OK?]] became friendly with him. "It was a very businesslike relationship," she recalled:

> But I liked him a lot. We had birthdays close together, and so we talked about that. Alfred and I had a car, and I used to chauffeur Monk around. We lived down in the Village on Grove Street, and he used to call me up and say, 'Will you take me here? Will you take me there?' So I kind of pampered him in that way, because I did feel he was very special even then. And I didn't feel that way about anybody else in that style. Well, nobody had his style. But I didn't feel that way about modern musicians.

"I took him to Minton's. I did it alone." She drove him many places. "I don't remember where all the time. I was there, the errand lady."
Still, Lorraine discovered Monk's unique sense of humor:

> We had silly conversations. One would be, I would say something indirectly: "Nothing is nothing." He would say, "Nothing is something." I would say, "Naaa, nothing is nothing." He would say, "You're wrong. Nothing is something." And this could go on for an hour. "One is one, two is one, nothing is something," he said. Well, go figure that out. We just played around with these words. These were the kinds of conversations we could have. He was very close-mouthed about himself.

Blue Note was an active jazz label before Lorraine met Alfred Lion, but she felt as if she was a pioneering part of the company. "I liked jazz as a young person." She and her brother had been members of the Newark Hot Club, a club of fervent jazz lovers and record collectors. She fell in love with the early Blue Note records:

> I used to hear a WNYC disk jockey who played fantastic, 12-inch [78 rpm] records of improvisation by Meade Lux Lewis. To me that was the most advanced kind of jazz. That was something

outside the realm of ordinary jazz piano players. Boogie woogie with Meade Lux Lewis, Pete Johnson, Albert Ammons, just gorgeous records that I kept hearing on Blue Note. They were very expensive then, 50 cents for a small one and a dollar for a 12-inch. I thought: "Whoever is producing these records is a genius." It was a completely different area of jazz, not Dixieland.

With her brother, who was three years older than she, she used to collect stamps intensely, and then jazz records even more intensely. "We had complete Bessie, Louis, Duke, all the great Blue Note artists. You had to have the complete collections. And if it had a scratch on it ..."

She had met Alfred Lion through friends, when she was about eighteen or nineteen and he was about thirty. "He invited me up to his office one day, and he gave me a complete set of all the Blue Note records available at that time, and two albums. I was so thrilled by this. The original label was chartreuse and blue, not blue and white. We started to see each other. Then the war began. He got drafted, sent to Texas, and that's when I went to Texas. We got married in New Mexico," she said.

Thelonious went into the studio in October 1947 to cut his first Blue Note sides:

> He was happy to play for us. We went into the studio and recorded and recorded and recorded. And we were excited. Every day we listened to the takes. We used to meet in our little apartment with a little record player in Grove Street all the time. When I think of the equipment we had. All the musicians came there. It was a hangout for Art Blakey, Sidney Bechet, Ike Quebec, [Roger] Ram Ramirez. I have some pictures of us in those days. Musicians would come to talk about recordings, to visit us, to eat, to listen to the tests, the playbacks, the test pressings. We chose what we wanted, what was the best, what we thought was the best. I ate, lived and drank the records, I breathed them. That was my life with Alfred.

Lorraine Stein Lion and Alfred Lion on their wedding day in New Mexico.
Courtesy of Lorraine Gordon.

She had gone to the Village Vanguard as a kid to jam sessions, but she
hadn't gotten to know the owner, Max Gordon, a charming man
considerably shorter and older than she. A slim, tall, very attractive young
woman, she had long dark hair, "a huge mane of black hair," she recalled.

She was very well dressed the day she met Max Gordon. Guided by
her mother, she had always had good taste in clothes anyway. And her
husband, Alfred, was a handsome, elegant, debonair man, who had fled
his native Germany before World War II. He had understood what was
going to happen and left the country, then convinced his friend
Francis, a photographer, to come to the United States, too. Alfred had
excellent taste in clothes and bought Lorraine the best clothes they
could afford—a suede jacket from Sport and Travel on Madison

Avenue, for one thing. Their apartment was decorated with collector's items purchased at a time they were on display at the Museum of Modern Art, Lorraine recalled.

Lorraine was staying on Fire Island in the summer of '48, after the first recordings were done. She saw Max Gordon sitting alone at a table and went over and introduced herself to him. He said, "Sit down and have a cup of coffee, a toasted bagel." She laughed at the memory. "I told him about Thelonious," she said. "And he had never heard of Thelonious in his life. But I guess he thought I was kind of cute. Anyway, he had an opening in September of that year. And he said, 'Yeah, well, come on, we'll book him.'"

Nobody knew who Thelonious was, and the Vanguard was empty during his initial performances. Lorraine recalled, "Max said to me, 'What are you doing? You're ruining my business.' I said, 'Be quiet. He's a genius.' Of course that's all Max ever said afterward: Monk is a genius. But he didn't take off the minute he was at the Vanguard. It was nothing. Art Blakey was on drums, Sahib Shihab was on saxophone. Nobody was there but me and Alfred and Max. And that was it."

Max Gordon had hired Billy Taylor to play for a singer at the Vanguard that week, because Max liked the way Billy accompanied singers. Billy remembered that Lorraine had convinced Max to hire Monk:

> Max was buying anything she was selling. She was very attractive. And the booking was truly wrong for that room at that time. She said to Max that Monk was a genius. Max said, "Right."
>
> Usually there was a little show, and then Monk's group would play, with Sahib Shihab on sax, and Denzil Best on drums, and Al McKibbon on bass, and sometimes Art Blakey sat in. There was a dance floor, which is now covered by tables. I'd play for my singer, and Monk played. People couldn't dance to his music. You had to be a very hip dancer to dance to Monk's music. Someone would always ask Max: "Who's that?" "Monk," Max would say. "He's a genius." Those people, one or two of them, might come back later in the week, and they would bring others. And they would try to

dance. They were told, "It's Thelonious Monk, he's a genius. You're not supposed to dance to it."

Billy was very amused: "All the musicians came down to the Vanguard. Max was happy about that part. It was exciting."

Lorraine recalled:

> Monk was playing around other places, but the Vanguard was his first major, if you want to call it major, booking in the jazz world. And he didn't play anyplace else of note [in New York] except for Minton's [and on 52nd Street with Coleman Hawkins and others] in those days. And this was his first opening [as a leader] into the club scene, his first actual confrontation with customers, his first real club date. It was at the Vanguard with an all-star lineup. But nobody knew Art Blakey then, either. They were all future stars more or less. At the time Monk was not the most popular pianist. Bud Powell was more popular.

Lorraine went all over the country with a little case of Monk's Blue Note records to sell. "I went to Philly, Baltimore, a whole lineup, Cleveland, Chicago. I was a kid, doing all this for him and for my belief in the records and other Blue Notes. I went to Harlem to try to sell Monk in Harlem. And the guys in those record stores would say, 'He can't play. He has two left hands.' I had to battle all the way to get them to buy a Monk record and listen to him. The [other artists] on Blue Note sold more easily." Lorraine knew she was having trouble marketing the Monk recordings because they were so different. People weren't used to Monk's sound.

Lorraine sat in the Blue Note offices—at 767 Lexington Avenue, on the sixth floor of the Lambert Building, right across from Bloomingdale's—trying to think of ways to promote Monk. She wrote to Ralph Ingersoll at *P.M.*, a popular newspaper focusing on New York's nightlife, saying that Monk was a genius living in New York; Ingersoll should send someone to write about Monk. Lorraine described how Monk looked: a big, intensely serious, powerful dark man; even when he smiled, one had a sense of the authority in his expression. It reflected his intelligence and his sense of self-worth as a creative genius, but anyone who didn't know how superbly gifted he was might simply have perceived his presence—his size and mien—as awesome. He didn't wear many hats in those days, only little caps— none of the elaborate, varied hats he would sport once he became better known.

Ingersoll called Lorraine and said he would send Ira Peck, a writer for the newspaper, to write a feature on Monk. Lorraine picked him up and took him to Monk's house, parked the car, and prepared to go in with him.

Lorraine said, "Come, I'll show you. I'll go with you."

He said, "No, you can't go with me. I'm going to go in alone."

Lorraine said, "Wait a minute, you can't do that. Monk's not going to talk to you. He'll barely let you in the door."

He said, "Well, I don't need you to come with me."

Lorraine was intimidated. It would take her many years to become outspoken, she would reflect nearly fifty years later—"to have the big mouth I have now," as she described her authoritative contralto speaking voice. But then, she simply said, "Okay, you don't know what you're doing."

Sure enough, he came back in ten minutes and said: "There is no story there. This man doesn't talk."

Lorraine said, "I told you. You cannot go in alone with him. He doesn't know you, and he doesn't talk to strangers. You have to trust me. I'm not going to go in and talk for him; it's just that, if I'm there, you'll have an easier time."

Ira Peck said, "No, there's no story. Goodbye."

Lorraine was extremely disappointed, not only because of Blue Note's interests but because of Monk's situation. She returned to the Blue Note office after the fiasco with Ira Peck. Sitting in her office, she called Ingersoll again, and told him what had happened:

> And whatever I said, he said, "That's not right. And you are going to go back with him, and I will see to it." And indeed he

did. And I was there. What resulted was a double-page Sunday inside spread of Monk, one picture with the piano, and on the ceiling a picture of Billie Holiday, and a picture of the kitchen, and the Frigidaire. Ira Peck wrote about the Frigidaire, calling it a big white Frigidaire. Monk's mother was furious with me because she thought talking about that refrigerator denigrated the Monks.

I said, "Mrs. Monk, You don't understand. Your son is going to be very famous someday, and they are going to write all kinds of things, and most of them are going to be good, and there's nothing terrible about your house. It's just wonderful." But she disliked that a reporter wrote about how Monk lived. The room was dominated by a refrigerator. She resented that. She thought she was being put down. How do I know what she was thinking? I wasn't thinking of her or the refrigerator.

Actually, Peck was genuinely curious about bebop and this enigmatic figure who represented it. In his article, he repeated a then common definition of bebop as being aligned with surrealism, cubism, and modernism in general, comparing it with the paintings of Picasso and Dali and the music of Stravinsky.[2] Peck interviewed several jazz players to get their reactions to the new music; he mentioned that New Orleans-style guitarist Eddie Condon said it was weird, about as musical as "tonsilitis," while Duke Ellington felt sympathetic toward bebop. "Why be surprised that bebop is ridiculed?" he said. "Jazz and swing got the same treatment in their early days, too. Anything that's alive must progress, and music is alive. This is 1948, and there are young minds, wonderful minds, working on fresh musical ideas. Those ideas have spread and some part of them will certainly survive and become incorporated into the music of tomorrow."

This view of bebop in general had inspired Lorraine's original letter to *P.M.*, which said that the Blue Note label had "actually found the one person responsible for this whole new trend in music. The genius behind the whole movement—and we have had the privilege of being the first to put his radical and unorthodox ideas on wax—is an unusual and mysterious character with the more unusual name of Thelonious Monk. Among musicians, Thelonious's name is treated with respect and awe, for he is a strange person whose pianistics continue to baffle all who hear him."

Peck described the Monk family living in the apartment on West 63rd Street between Eleventh Avenue and the West Side Drive—Marion, her husband Alonzo White, their son Alonzo White Jr., Thelonious Monk, and their mother—although in fact Marion's family lived in a nearby apartment house. Thomas, who had already left behind his fledgling career as a prizefighter, lived with his wife and children in a nearby apartment.

Peck noticed that Monk seemed to have little interest in girls except for one—a neighborhood girl who liked to come to the apartment, clean Monk's room, and wash his clothes. Peck didn't mention her name, but it was Nellie Smith. "The girl idolizes him," Peck wrote. "He sits there and she puts cigarets in his mouth and lights them for him. Yet he hardly speaks to her. He tells me that women are 'a heckle' sometimes. *He doesn't want to be tied down to anything except his music* [emphasis added]."

Peck believed incorrectly that Monk was Barbara's youngest child. But Peck accurately surmised that Monk was "his mother's favorite." Peck wrote,

> He depends on her for a great many favors. He frequently says, "My mother will take care of that for me" or "Leave the message with my mother." . . . Monk holds jobs only infrequently, and it is doubtful whether he could get by financially if he did not live at home . . . . He has turned down work for a variety of reasons. For one thing, he does not like to play "commercial" jazz. He has also refused to play at clubs simply because he felt the piano was out of tune.
>
> Once he got up and walked out of a club in the middle of a gig, saying that the B note rang. "It disturbs me," he says.
>
> Monk's eating habits are equally erratic. On waking up, he usually plays the piano for a couple of hours, then has a couple of

beers, and later on, when he gets hungry, a sandwich. He eats a
meal only when he feels like it.

A friend of Monk's told Peck, "I honestly don't believe that food
means a thing to him." In fact, when Monk could finally afford it, he
would prove how much he appreciated good food, clothes, and
symbols of wealth and influence, but not if they interfered with his
music. According to Peck, Monk slept about five hours a day—or
night—it wasn't clear which, "and has occasionally gone as long as
three days without any sleep at all. During that time he wanders
around from one friend's house to another, or from one club to
another, working out his ideas on the piano. Apparently nobody says
no to him," wrote Peck. So Monk was already having periods of
exceptional excitement connected with his music—perhaps inspired
by the stimulant Dexedrine.[3]

"He'll go to Mary Lou Williams's house at four o'clock in the
morning, and she'll just say, 'Come in, there's the piano, go ahead,' and
go back to sleep. At the end of one of these periods, Monk is so
exhausted that he is likely to sleep straight through three days. Then he
sleeps so deeply that it is almost impossible to wake him."

More often than not, Mary Lou stayed awake for the visits. Her apartment at 63 Hamilton Terrace in Harlem served as a salon for jazz
pianists. Erroll Garner, Phineas Newborn, and Art Tatum went there,
too, to play and exchange ideas in the wee hours of the morning. And
during Monk's visits to Mary Lou's apartment with Bud Powell, Elmo
Hope, and trumpeter Idrees Sulieman, she told each of the pianists that
they had a terrible sound on the piano, because of their touch on the
keys. She decided to help them work on their touch. "She told me
herself that she did it," Billy Taylor recalled. "And I heard the difference."
Billy thought that Monk became more musical while losing nothing of
the effect and expressiveness of his percussiveness. Idrees Sulieman
thought that sometimes it was hard to tell who was teaching whom.

"Monk listens to records almost as much as he plays the piano and
is extremely uncomfortable unless there is a phonograph or a piano
wherever he is," Peck continued.

Peck described Monk's home in a somewhat condescending manner: "It was a typical tenement flat—dark, tiny, and dilapidated. The central room was the kitchen, into which an old cot had been placed to provide extra sleeping quarters. A tin ceiling, walls darkened by stove soot, linoleum worn through to the floor boards in places contrasted incongruously with a large, new, shiny, white refrigerator and, next to the cot, an expensive-looking console model radio and phonograph."

Peck thought Monk "was a tall, well-built, gentle-mannered chap, unusual looking only in that he wore green-tinted horn-and-gold rimmed glasses and a small goatee. These, I learned later, are standard equipment among bebop musicians."[4]

Monk invited Peck into his room—or his area—with its small upright piano, a cot, a dresser, and a chair. "It had only one window which, because it faced an alley, admitted very little light; a feeble lamp on Monk's dresser provided most of the light in the room. There were several pictures around the room. One of Billie Holiday was pasted on the ceiling next to a red bulb. Monk said he liked to lie back on his cot and gaze at it. On the wall near his cot was a picture of Sarah Vaughan and, above the piano, one of Dizzy Gillespie. This was inscribed, 'To Monk, my first inspiration. Stay with it. Your boy, Dizzy Gillespie.'"

Peck found Monk to be enigmatic. "Although polite, he maintained a stone wall reserve throughout the interview. To most of my questions about himself, his answer was 'I don't know.' He seldom spoke two consecutive sentences. About his music he was almost as uncommunicative. He defined bebop only as 'modern swing music' but would not elaborate.

"I was able to gather, however, that he first began experimenting with bebop about six or seven years ago while working with a quartet at Minton's Playhouse ... He and the other musicians, Kenny Clarke, drummer, Nick Fenton, bass fiddler, and Joe Guy, trumpeter, 'started making up melodies. In order to play what we wanted to play, we had to make up our own tunes, just like Duke Ellington had to make up his own music and sounds to express himself,'" Monk told Peck.[5]

"Bebop," Monk said, "just happened. I just felt it . . . it came to me. Something was created differently without my trying to." Monk stated that the bebop style that he had originally worked out at Minton's had been further refined by Gillespie and Parker into something entirely different. He felt that Gillespie, who used to engage in after-hours jam sessions with him, improvised on the original and then turned out his own version of bebop.

"Monk went into the kitchen and put on a recording of one of his piano solos," Peck continued in his article. "It was more subdued and slower than most bebop I've heard; but the principles were the same; there was no melody pattern—one never knew where the music was going next—a lot of unharmonious chords and a steady, insistent rhythm. It was imaginative, interesting music and it was plain that Monk was striving for something different.

"Monk felt that one of the reasons he has not achieved the fame and commercial success of Gillespie and Parker is his reticence. 'I don't get around as much,' he said. 'People don't see me as much. I'm sort of underground in bebop.'" Peck didn't mention that Parker had his own problems, because of his heroin addiction, and really wasn't faring as well as he could have, if he had been healthy. He, too, was more of an underground figure than Dizzy.

Peck wrote, "Another reason, Monk felt, for his lesser fame is that most musicians have difficulty playing with him. The exceptions are drummers and bass fiddlers 'because they have more beat.'

"Most people, [Peck] mentioned, have found bebop pretty weird."

Monk replied: "They don't know what it's all about. They don't understand the music and in most cases never heard it. Weird means something you never heard before. It's weird until people get around to it. Then it ceases to be weird."

Monk never liked the word *weird* applied to himself or his music. It hurt his feelings, and he was sick of it—although he started using it himself, often in a satiric way. "That was all I could get from Monk," Peck wrote. Actually Monk had gone right to the heart of the matter and said all that needed to be said on the subject of weirdness in music or any other art.

Baffled but "still curious" about Monk, Peck interviewed Teddy Hill, "the former bandleader, who is now part-owner of Minton's." Hill had some insightful things to say about the strange pianist:

"Monk is definitely a character," he said. "He's the type of fellow who thinks an awful lot but doesn't have much to say. Yeah, I've known a lot of musicians who were characters, but none just like him.'"

"Monk," Hill said, "is so absorbed in his music he appears to have lost touch with everything else. He just doesn't seem to be present unless he's actually talking to you and then sometimes all of a sudden in the middle of a conversation his mind is somewhere else. He may still be talking to you, but he's thinking about something else.

"Some nights I've seen him in here with a girl [probably Nellie Smith]. She's sitting back there and he'll get into a conversation with someone else, forget she's there, and the next thing you know he might get up, get his coat, and start walking out until somebody reminds him that his girl is there. She looks like a very nice girl but I wonder what the guy ever talks to her about. I've hardly ever seen him say two words to her."

Monk's preoccupation with his music, Hill said, makes him equally erratic when he is working.

"When I had him here, the band used to come to work at ten. He'd come in at nine, but at ten you couldn't find him. Maybe an hour later you'd find him sitting off by himself in the kitchen somewhere writing and the band playing didn't make any difference to him. He'd say, "I didn't hear it."

"I always used to be so disgusted with him and yet you never saw such a likeable guy. Plenty of times I'd have been happy to hire the guy as piano player in my band but I couldn't depend on him. Everybody liked the guy. Dizzy and Kenny Clarke once said they'd assume responsibility for getting him there on time if I'd hire him, they liked him so much. Everybody wanted him, but everybody was afraid of him. He was too undependable. He'd just rather mess around at home.'" . . .

Hill reached for a cigar and lit up. "Tell you something else peculiar about Monk," he said after he had cleared away some of the smoke. "I've never seen him have any emotion. I've never heard him in an argument seriously with anybody yet. He'd much rather take the worst of it than to argue too much about anything. I've never seen him excited except when he's playing. It only comes out in one place and that's when he sits down at a piano.

"He'll come in here anytime and play for hours with only dim light and the funny thing is he'll never play a complete tune. You never know what he's playing. Many times he's gone on so long I've had to come back and plead with him to quit playin' the piano so I could close up the place 'cause it was against the law to keep it open any longer."

I asked Hill about the roles of Monk and Gillespie in the creation of bebop.

Monk was actually "the guy who dug the stuff out," Hill said. "Gillespie had packaged the goods and delivered it to the consumers. Monk seemed more like the guy who manufactured the product rather than commercialized it. Dizzy has gotten all the exploitation because Dizzy branched out and got started. Monk stayed right in the same groove.

"Of course what Dizzy is playing today is not altogether what Monk had in mind. But the fundamentals are the same. Dizzy just twisted it a little bit. He decided instead of starting at the front to start at the back. But the stuff is essentially what Monk worked out."[6]

Monk, despite his ability, didn't get the credit, Hill said, because he was undependable. Virtually ignoring the picture he himself had just painted of Monk as a genius, the mastermind of modern swing music, whose mind was always on music, on creating music that he and others loved and on which they based their own careers and fortunes, Hill hypothesized that Monk was undependable because he was spoiled and overprotected. His rent was paid by his mother. He never had to worry about the landlord evicting him.

"I think Monk has possibilities of becoming outstanding in his field, provided he ever finds himself personally and makes a stand on his own instead of just being pushed and shoved all the time. He waits and sits until everybody does everything for him. I don't think Monk would ever get a job if other people didn't ask for him," Hill told Peck, talking from the vantage point of a businessman, an organizer adept at the politics—the toughness and practicalities—of the music world.

Hill also analyzed the position of bebop in the jazz and entertainment world from his experience as a traditional swing band leader. "It's difficult stuff to play. Right now you have good musicians trying to play it and they sound horrible. The stuff played improperly can be offensive—it hurts your ears. You never hear a big band except Dizzy play it. You hear a few guys take a riff or so but that's all. And who's gonna write it—all those chords clashin' and everything. A lot of guys don't think it's worthwhile to invest their time in it."[7]

Peck went back through the club from Hill's office and listened to a small band playing "hysterically fast" music, he wrote.

> Unlike most night clubs it was a bright, cheerful, gaily decorated place and the customers seemed to be enjoying themselves. Many of them were visibly stimulated by the music but only a few made any attempt to dance to it.
>
> I saw Monk, looking as withdrawn as he had earlier in the day, with a group of friends who were urging him to play for them. When the band took a break, Monk walked up to the piano and began testing it. Satisfied that it was in tune, he sat down and began playing. At first he played fairly conventional, recognizable tunes to which he gave his own twist but as he progressed, he played more and more of his own music.
>
> People shook their heads and marvelled at his playing. Most of them agreed that Monk has an original talent. "His chords, his way of thinking, his beat, they're absolutely unique," one listener said. "He's just enough off the norm to be a genius."
>
> I spoke to Monk again a little later and asked him whether he thought bebop would catch on.

"It has to," he said. "It's the modern music of today. It makes other musicians think—just like Picasso. It has to catch on."[8]

In February 1948, George T. Simon's article on Monk was also published in *Metronome*. Monk seemed more comfortable and candid when speaking to a music writer who also happened to be a jazz musician. Monk didn't seem to resent not having received the recognition that was due him, Simon said. Monk confided: "My time for fame will come." He talked about the patience, persistence, and dedication of his friend, Denzil Best, who began his career as a wonderful trumpet player—"he'd outblow everybody in the place." Best had been forced to give up playing the trumpet because of his health and, instead of quitting, switched to the drums. "He didn't blow his top because he was frustrated. To me, a true musician is a guy who never gives up, even though he feels like it sometimes," Monk said.[9]

Monk distanced himself from the rest of the bebop movement. Simon wrote, "Besides accusing some musicians of turning bop into something akin to dixieland, he also upbraided them with phrases like, 'they molest,' 'they magnify,' 'they exaggerate.' 'They don't pay any attention to swing, and that goes both for the horns and the rhythm sections. They don't know where to put those bops. When the horns say bloop, the drummer shouldn't say bloop, bloop, bloop with them. You should throw in your rhythmic bops when a guy's taking a breath.

"'Another thing is the chords. I can tell right off when a guy knows what he's doing. Diz and Bird, they know their chords. But too many horns use the flatted fifth where it sounds absurd, instead of where it should sound beautiful. They should try to keep their music melodious; when it becomes unmelodious, then it sounds like dixieland.'"

Of the big bands playing at the time, Monk liked Claude Thornhill's the best. Thornill's arranger, Gil Evans, like Monk, had loved and studied Duke Ellington's music thoroughly. Monk thought Stan Kenton tried too hard for effects—"though some of them are good"—and believed he would like Dizzy's band "if they played the music right."

Even with recordings out, it was very difficult for any musician, including Monk, to work steadily; it was hard to put a group together and keep it working. Furthermore, his style may have made it particularly difficult for him. Johnny Griffin was quoted by the authors of *Blue Monk* as saying that Monk was fired in the middle of a set in a Brooklyn club in 1948 by a club owner who told him he wasn't playing jazz. The owner would invite him to come back—ten years later, when he was a star at the Five Spot. Monk laughed at him. However, this tale contradicts Monk himself, who said he was never fired for playing his unusual music.

Monk's recordings didn't make him rich and famous in the 1940s. Though eventually they turned out to be of enormous historic and commercial worth for Blue Note, the sessions with Monk in 1947 and '48 and again those to come in 1951 and '52 were a luxury and a tribute to Alfred Lion's good taste.

The critical response to these recordings was mixed. Leonard Feather gave Monk short shrift in general. A critic for *Billboard* magazine acknowledged the release of Monk's records without raving about them, saying, for one thing, that the song "Thelonious" was "a controversial jazz disking worked out on a one note riff"—this for the melody of a spare, expressive, hypnotic blues that Monk wrote based on one note at a time when other modernists were using torrents of notes for their improvisations and new lines.

Few other critics understood or even paid attention to Monk's work in the 1940s. One who did was Orrin Keepnews, a writer for *Record Changer* magazine, who would later produce Monk's important Riverside label recordings. Keepnews praised Monk's Blue Note sides, which he called more interesting than recordings by other modern players because Monk's work was so disciplined and coherent. Keepnews understood that the style was original, even though it had similarities to the music of other beboppers. "Monk's strongly rhythmic style is pure piano," wrote Keepnews.[10]

Keepnews also recognized Monk's genuis as a bandleader. The performances of Monk's band reflected Monk's own ideas and direction, much as Duke Ellington's band reflected Duke's genius. Keepnews applauded the support of the bassists Eugene Ramey and Edmond Gregory and the "powerful, steady and complex drummer

Art Blakey." Keepnews thought that Ike Quebec's seventeen-year-old nephew, alto saxophonist Danny Quebec West, fit in well with Monk's music—possibly because the youngster had not yet become overexposed to the cliches emerging in the work of other progressive players.

Keepnews didn't know if he could predict greatness for Monk, but he perceived how talented and imaginative Monk was. Monk's band played with a warmth and close communion that Orrin hadn't found in the music played at frantic tempos by other modernists. "And— although this is a point that cannot be proved in writing but only heard in the music—he is capable of a sly, wry, satiric humor that has a rare maturity," wrote Keepnews. Monk's music reflected the growing complexity and edginess of the age he lived in without ever becoming arcane, narcissistic, or incomprehensible.

In Monk's individuality, Keepnews detected Monk's "probable genius," patently under the influence of Duke Ellington's harmonies, and he thought that Monk provided much needed optimism for the future of progressive music.

Monk appreciated this interview and article that Keepnews wrote at the early stage of his career; it led him to trust the producer when Monk was signed by Riverside later in the fifties, resulting in some of his best recorded work.

Based on the artistry of all his Blue Note recordings alone, which constituted nearly one-third of his known compositions, Monk's reputation as a composer undoubtedly would have gained sufficient strength to establish him as one of the most important jazz composers of the century. The figures he wrote were simple and couched in traditional forms—the blues, the American popular standard song—but all of them carried his distinctive, trademark harmonies and quirky rhythms, his runs, his suspenseful hesitations that sounded like "think" time and that reflect the nervousness of the post–World War II era, and his transcendent gift for sculpting hypnotic musical interludes from abstractions, swinging all the time. In the aggregate, his songs comprised an oeuvre, each a commentary on his unique universe of sound. They ran the gamut of emotions, some intensely moody, cerebral, or edgy and always lightened or at least tinged by wit, and others upbeat and optimistic.

The recordings Monk made for Blue Note range from tender, melodic ballads to what were for the time strangely dissonant, halting, emotional solos. The ballads "Ruby, My Dear" and "Ask Me Now," both lucid, romantic, and poignant, feature conversational, flowing melodies. "Well, You Needn't" has a tantalizing, exotic key change, while the baldly dissonant and moody "Off Minor" sounds so contemporary that it would be used as part of the soundtrack for a major movie, *Die Hard with a Vengeance,* in 1995. The happy, pretty, and swinging, though dissonant and driving, "Criss Cross" is its exact opposite in feeling, as is the whimsical, lilting, and flowing "Introspection."

Many Monk classics were recorded for the first time by the pianist in these sessions: the ineffably haunting "Round Midnight"; the mysterious, elusive, charming "Evidence" (based on the popular ballad "Just You, Just Me"); the especially aptly named "Misterioso"; and "Epistrophy," a rhythmic and melodic fantasy, which, Monk told George Simon, apropos the title, was a botanical term meaning "the reversion of the abnormal to the normal," and which Monk eventually used as his theme song. Monk also gave sterling performances of the ebullient and carefree "Four in One"; the modern "Eronel"; the taut, no-nonsense melody of "Straight, No Chaser"; the fleet "Skippy"; "Hornin' In," simultaneously taut and swinging; the confident and ebullient "Sixteen"; the exquisitely melodious "Let's Cool One" with a signature, dissonant ending; the lovely "I'll Follow You"; the pang and sweetness of "Reflections"; "Carolina Moon," as seen from a real New Yorker's vantage point; the mellow and whimsical "Monk's Mood"; and the frenetic "Who Knows?"

This treasure trove of hypnotic songs—each one, no matter what its message, anchored by an ineluctable, swinging beat—alerted people involved with the jazz world to a major new talent. One person who was impressed by them was a great recording engineer, Rudy Van Gelder, who would, after a few years, begin recording Monk for another label, Prestige. From listening to the Blue Note recordings, Rudy learned to respect Monk as a great jazz musician, though the public remained far behind.

Lorraine and Alfred Lion obviously recognized the importance of these early recordings:

> When Alfred came along, we got Monk at the peak of his inventiveness, of his compositions. I think those were the greatest recordings Thelonious ever made. I don't care how many other companies made records after that. This was fresh, the cream right off the top. It was so beautiful. When I think of them.

Village Voice jazz critic Gary Giddins would agree: "The Blue Note years capture Monk in the throes of youthful assertion . . ." In the early eighties, Giddins would find that immersing himself in reissues of Monk's Blue Note recordings was "both an exhilarating and dispiriting experience—the former because his music is eternally fresh, the latter because so much else seems tame and trite by comparison."'

More quickly than Monk became famous, Lorraine divorced Alfred Lion and married Max Gordon at the end of 1948. She and Alfred had worked very hard for Blue Note:

> We were very poor, you know, just struggling along. It was nothing. I was always in on the poor days. Alfred and I lived in Grove Street for $47.50 a month rent, and I got the landlord to make it less because Alfred was a veteran. So all right, pay $42.50, the landlord said. Everyday I was in the office doing all the bookkeeping and whatever I knew of public relations. I don't know what that meant. I just tried. I stuck labels on records. I did everything, went to the recording sessions. I was a kid, but I liked it. I was in step with my own feelings about where I'm comfortable, and I always have been. Oh, yeah, always. I was lucky in a way. I had that great interest in jazz. And for some strange reason it followed through my life in interesting ways that I didn't plan. It was just all I had to offer. And I married the right men. I certainly did.

Max ran the Vanguard and handled Monk's bookings there. "If Monk was committed to hospitals, it wasn't for his brain," Lorraine

Lorraine and Max Gordon at the Newport Jazz Festival in 1954. Courtesy of Lorraine Gordon.

would reflect many years later, after Monk's turbulent life had run its course. When she knew him, she never saw him use drugs —"maybe a stick of pot," she reflected. "I think he had a lot of respect for Alfred and myself. Here were these white kids coming into his life, and here was a man living with black musicians.

"We were the first, I believe," she said, "who came in to talk to him, to look, listen, and record him and befriend him. And I didn't think Monk was strange or eccentric at that time, certainly no stranger than Miles Davis or Sidney Bechet. Everyone had his different mode of behavior. I just accepted him the way he was. He wasn't a big conversationalist. But so what? Lots of guys weren't. We'd have fun, these silly conversations, challenging kinds of things. He would challenge your conceptions—maybe ready-made conceptions that he made a little different. It was like his music. It was always something a little different."

Notes

Personal interviews: Lorraine Gordon, Billy Taylor.

1. Some people would come to theorize that Monk played in his idiosyncratic way because his hands, especially his palms, were very small. In the October 30, 1958, issue of *Down Beat*, Frank London Brown wrote in his article "Thelonious Monk": "His small, smooth hands seemed out of place, connected to hairy, dockworker's arms." But Monk devised his style because he wanted a percussive sound, whether or not his hands were well suited to that approach.

2. Peck (1948).

3. Miles Davis wrote that he heard about Monk using Dexadrine in the 1940s, but Miles never personally observed Monk using it or showing the influence of the drug. See Davis with Troupe (1989).

4. Peck (1948).

5. Ibid.

6. Ibid.

7. Ibid.

8. Ibid.

9. Simon (1948).

10. Keepnews (1948).

11. *Rhythm-a-ning* by Gary Giddins (1985). This prize-winning book about modern jazz was named for Monk's swinging song that could be regarded as emblematic of the best and brightest accomplishments of the era.

Crepuscule with Nellie

By the time Monk was recording for Blue Note, the woman in his life was indisputably Nellie Smith, not Ruby Richardson. "They crisscrossed" in his life, his son explained. "He fell out with Ruby and in with Nellie" sometime in the 1940s, exactly when, Toot—as Thelonious Sphere Monk Jr was nicknamed as a little boy by his family—didn't know.

Nellie Smith was born on December 27, 1922, in Jacksonville, Florida, and moved to New York with her family when she was three years old. Eventually the Smiths rented an apartment on West 62nd Street between Amsterdam and West End Avenues. The first day her family moved into the neighborhood, her brother Sonny went to the basketball court in the playground and got into an argument with another kid. Thelonious, who happened to be there, jumped up and defended Sonny. After everyone calmed down, Thelonious said to Sonny, "Come home with me." Naturally, Thelonious played the piano for him.

"Sonny flipped out," Toot said, and went home to tell his sisters Nellie and Skippy, "I just met a guy on the block, the first guy I met, and this guy is going to be the greatest piano player who ever lived. And his name is—guess what?—Thelonious Monk."

"Sure, sure, sure, his name is Thelonious Monk," said the sisters.

Sonny kept raving about his buddy, Thelonious. Finally one day Nellie, who was about thirteen years old at the time, went out to the basketball court where Thelonious was playing ball with her brother. Thelonious, then about seventeen, was respectful and polite to his friend's sister, whom he regarded as just a little girl. At that time, he was involved with Ruby Richardson. He didn't really start talking to Nellie until he was about twenty and she was about sixteen and beginning to grow up into a slender, vivacious woman. For the next few years, until Nellie was eighteen, she and Monk talked occasionally. Toot believes that Nellie found Thelonious, a tall, well-built older man and very appealing. When Monk was in his early twenties, Ruby Richardson left town. And, as Thelonious's sister Marion recalled, Nellie "moved in to take her place." Nellie wasn't at all shy about expressing her affection for Monk.

"Thelonious and I were talkers," Nellie would later say. "This is how we became very, very close, because we talked all the time. And he never got tired of talking to me, and I never got tired of talking to him, 24–7, twenty-four hours a day, seven days a week, and it was always fun, and stimulating, and great." But those conversations were not for the general public, she added. She always refused to talk much about him to writers, believing that his personality had nothing to do with his music. "Beyond the music, what else is there?" she would ask. "I think it's a bit much to go into other people's lives."

Nellie was a likeable, friendly woman, who was easy to talk to, Monk's friends thought, as they came to know her in the late 1940s. Five-foot seven and 120 pounds, she looked delicate next to the bearishly big pianist. Nellie noticed that her brother, Sonny, became so worshipful of the pianist that he actually imitated the way Thelonious walked and talked. Nellie paid strict attention to Thelonious, and his friends thought she loved him devotedly. Most people with whom Monk had business dealings loved her; for one thing, they could depend upon her to keep his schedule straight.

Nellie described her family as "educators" and "strivers." Her father's brother worked his way through Harvard, she said, before World War

Thomas W. Monk, Jr., and his uncle, Thelonious, c. 1966. Courtesy of the family of Thelonious S. Monk, Jr.

I. One of his daughters became a lawyer, graduating from Yale; another became a psychiatrist who practiced in Los Angeles. Other relatives went to Morehouse and Spellman Colleges. Thelonious's family could claim no such credits or pretensions. Nellie's mother, who was also named Nellie, sang and loved music. All the children—Sonny, Skippy and two other sisters, and Nellie herself, who was next to youngest—developed an appreciation for music, including European classical music and gospel. "The whole nine yards," Nellie said, "and for people's abilities to perform."

The Smiths believed in supporting musicians—going to hear them play and providing them with an audience, so that the musicians would know people liked to listen to them. Nellie herself sang only in school, but she could not remember a time when she didn't love to listen to music. She felt that her family and Thelonious's had in common their "high morals, ethical standards, scrupulousness and sincerity," she said. Nellie spoke easily and fluently— seeming as educated and cultured as any college graduate though she never went to college herself. When she was a teenager, she recalled, her mother died, a momentous loss for Nellie, who thought she was "too young to be without a mother." Even in her old age, the memories of her mother's death were painful ones.

Through much of the 1940s, several of Monk's friends and some of his family, who spent time with him at his mother's apartment, didn't know much about Nellie; some didn't even know she existed. Monk's brother Thomas had children, who grew up in the 1940s either without seeing Nellie or without paying much attention to her. Their uncle Thelonious was simply their uncle, the family musician, who lived in his mother's apartment.

Thomas Jr., who was born in 1937, remembered a day when he was nine years old and stole a Fifth Avenue candy bar in a neighborhood shop owned by a Mr. Aisles.

> My father had given me a nickel to buy candy, but I put it in my pocket. The owner caught me. He was Jewish, beautiful the way he treated people. And he said, "I caught you, Monk." I got scared. He said, "I got to report you to your mother." My uncle

Thelonious happened to be passing by. Aisles called out to him, "Thelonious! Thelonious, I have to tell you something." He told my uncle that I stole the Fifth Avenue candy bar. I urinated in my pants. My uncle said to Aisles, "Let me talk to him."

"He took me with him. I said, "I didn't mean it, Uncle Bubba." He said, "Well, what did you do? You took a Fifth Avenue candy bar?" I said, "Yes." He said, "Well, why didn't you go to Fifth Avenue to steal it? A Monk never steals." He said that and walked right on and left me. My father didn't find out until twenty five years later. My uncle never snitched. So that tells you how he felt.

Another time, Thomas Sr., his wife Rita, and the kids were at home sitting at the dinner table. Rita liked to decorate the table with a dish filled with plastic fruit and vegetables. Thelonious opened the door, walked in, said hello to everyone, and picked up a plastic plum. He said, "Okay, I'll see you all later." He bit into the plum as he was walking out the door. Thelonious Theo, one of Thomas's sons, recalled, "We tried to keep straight faces. He came back and said, 'Rita, this plum is sour.' He always had that sense of humor. You couldn't get him."

These were the kinds of warm memories the nephews had of their uncle, who was relaxed and informal with his family. Their cousin, Alonzo Jr., Marion Monk White's only child, born in 1940, recalled, "When we were young, we were all part of one another." He and his mother and father lived a few doors away from Uncle Thelonious and Grandmother Barbara until Alonzo was ten; then his family moved to Queens. The kids weren't really impressed with Thelonious's growing reputation as a musician; they were more in tune with their family relationship.

The nephews felt close to Thelonious's first girlfriend, Ruby, whom they knew, and who became Alonzo's godmother. But "something tumultuous" happened in the relationship between Ruby and Thelonious, they recalled, without specifying exactly what it was. Ruby accepted the job down south, leaving Thelonious behind in New York. "Ruby was a beautiful person," recalled the nephews and Marion. One of the last times that some of the Monks went to visit her, in the 1960s, she was working as a dietitian in upstate New York.

"I don't think she ever married," recalled Thomas Jr. "I think she never wanted anyone else but Thelonious. Pride's a big thing . . . She had a grey streak in her hair and was a very attractive woman. She and Marion were like sisters, about the same height, the same complexion." Eventually Ruby moved to Washington, D.C., where she lived for the rest of her life. Thelonious, who outlived her by quite a few years, may have visited her there, Marion thought.

Marion had wanted Thelonious to marry Ruby. Though she left town, she apparently felt drawn back—and then discovered she had no one to go back to. "When Ruby came back from the job down south," Alonzo would recall, "everything had changed. Thelonious was with Nellie."

Even as late as 1947, when Monk was preparing to go into the studio for Blue Note and record for the first time, Monk was living the life of a bachelor, on the surface at least. Nellie wasn't obviously involved with Monk. Trumpeter Idrees Sulieman, who came to town with pianist Earl "Fatha" Hines's band, met Monk at Minton's, and became a close friend of the pianist in the 1940s. Idrees knew Monk as a lone musician at the time Monk was rehearsing for his first Blue Note sessions, and he was unaware of either Ruby or Nellie. At his first recording session, Monk included one piece, "Evonce," written by Idrees. A little later, Idrees would collaborate on another song, "Eronel," recorded by Monk for Blue Note in 1951.

"I wrote 'Eronel.' I had sixteen bars, but I didn't have a middle," Idrees recalled. Sadik Hakim, a pianist, composer, and another friend of Monk's, wrote the bridge. They took it to Miles Davis, but he didn't like the middle of the song.

"But we had it," recalled Idrees. "So we took it to Monk. And he played it. But the third note, he changed it. He played the wrong note. He played an F sharp, and it should have been an E natural. A tone higher. We said, 'No, no, it's the wrong note.' Three times he did it, and each time we said it was the wrong note. Finally we said, 'Leave it in. It sounds good anyway.' The note he added made 'Eronel' modern. He recorded it, and his name was on it."

Idrees had thought Monk was playing a wrong note, because Monk hadn't played the song through even once, and Idrees was under the impression that Monk wasn't an exceptionally good reader in those days. But Monk, who had to read music to notate it as well as he did, knew exactly what the opening would sound like with the note he chose, and it appealed to him more than what he saw written on the paper.

At that time, Idrees's name came first as the composer, then Sadik's, then Monk's because of his wonderful note. Eventually, "It became Monk's number," Idrees noticed. (After Thelonious died, Toot began to try to straighten out the proper rights for the song. The effort became complicated by the late Sadik Hakim's daughter, who couldn't be found in Canada, where she lived, and who had to agree to the copyright line.) Many times Idrees would say to Monk, "You let [the record companies] keep recording it, and you don't tell them to straighten out the rights." Monk would say, "They forgot it, ha ha." "Whatever happened, Monk could always smile about it," Idrees recalled. "I never saw him get angry about anything."

"We were going to name the song for Sadik's girlfriend, who was going with some gangsters," Idrees said. "We were working in a club the gangsters owned. Her name was Lenore, or Lenora. I said to Sadik, 'You can't name it Lenora, those gangsters will kill you.' So Sadik spelled it backward."

Idrees thought Monk was one of the best composers in the country and admired him also as a friend. "He was a very different person," Idrees said:

> He was quiet. But when he said something, it always made a lot of sense. There was a good vibration going on.
>
> Monk had friends in the Bronx, and he visited them a lot. They lived one block from my house. I was at 168th Street and Fulton Avenue; this friend lived at 167th Street and Fulton Avenue. We hung out there many times for many years. They admired Monk, and they had a piano. He came alone most of the time. We stayed in the house, played records and talked politics—the politics of the music business. But Monk was not into that too much. He didn't say much. When he talked, it was pretty straight. He laughed when we talked, but you never could pin him down too

much. It seemed to me that Monk was always thinking about compositions.

Randy Weston also became a devoted protégé and friend of Monk's in the late forties. Randy originally heard Monk playing with Coleman Hawkins in 1944 but didn't like the pianist's work. Sometime later, Randy heard Monk again. "The next time I heard him, I knew that was the direction I wanted to go in. That happened because [Ahmed] Abdul Malik played with Monk, and he would take me to Atlantic Avenue. His father was Sudanese. And I heard music with eighth tones and sixteenth tones—things in between. Malik and myself played for dances and marriages and little parties. And we got put out of the bands, playing something different from the Atlantic Avenue music." By the time Randy heard Monk again, Randy understood the beauty of dissonance—his music was not really atonal; there was always a tonal center in Monk's music. "That's the master," Randy believed.

"I introduced myself to him and asked, 'Can I visit you?' He said, 'Yes.' And he gave me his address. I went to his house and spent nine hours there."

Monk didn't speak to Randy at all, except to tell him, "Listen to all kinds of music." Randy finally left. "As I was going," he recalled, "Monk said to me, 'Come again.' I left, completely bewildered. I went back a month or two later. He played piano almost three hours for me. Then I spent the next three years with Monk. Later I found out that Sufi mystics didn't speak through words. Ancient wise people knew how to speak without words."[1]

In the forties, Randy was running Trio's, one of his father's little Brooklyn restaurants, and immersing himself in the jazz world. "Max Roach had a house in Brooklyn, and Monk had a house in New York. The cream of bebop musicians went to these two schools of high culture. I had my father's car, and I picked Monk up, and we'd just hang out. Once Monk, Duke Jordan, Sam Grady—all pianists—and myself hung out for three days, ringing people's bells. If you had a piano, we'd ring your bell and go in and play. Monk never gave me a lesson directly. Each day with him was a lesson."

Randy Weston. Courtesy of the Institute of Jazz Studies, Rutgers University.

Monk was all over town in those days. One night he rang Dizzy Gillespie's doorbell while traveling with Charlie Parker. Dizzy owned a piano, and they wanted to show Dizzy some music they were working on.

"After years in Africa, I came to believe that God sent prophets to bring us beauty in life," Randy said. "Monk was that for me. He shared music with me, Malik, Idrees Sulieman, and Frankie Dunlop [a drummer who would work with Monk eventually]. We shared and became inseparable."

Randy enumerated the pianists who influenced him the most: Basie, a master of space; Nat Cole for his beauty; Art Tatum for everything he played; and Monk and Ellington. When Randy went to Egypt and studied African history and music, he came to realize that Monk was "like the reincarnation of the ancient spirit of Africa." Randy didn't hear any of Europe in Monk's music. He heard the way an African hears. He heard spiritualism and mysticism. "Monk was from another dimension . . . . But most pianists in the 1940s didn't like Monk. They said he couldn't play. But I knew he was the most original pianist I ever heard," Randy said.

They went mostly to Brooklyn together, to Randy's restaurants, Max Roach's house, to Randy's parents, to parties, and to many clubs with young musicians who liked Monk. "And I could find the Modern Jazz Quartet guys in Brooklyn in the early 1950s, and Dizzy, too," Randy said. "We had the Putnam Central Club. Max Roach had a studio there. We had concerts there with Dizzy, Charlie Parker, and others, and Monk. We used to give concerts in Brooklyn and feature Thelonious. That's how much we loved him. Brooklyn musicians, pianists who admired him, Elmo Hope, Herbie Nichols, and myself. We were at the concerts. All of us were close to Monk."

And Randy, who is six feet seven inches tall, recalled that Monk, who was six feet two and weighed over two hundred pounds, had a towering presence, a special way of walking. As Nat Hentoff would describe Monk in 1960, "Monk is an imposing figure . . . physically impressive more by the forceful solidity with which he stands and moves and the intensity of his look than by his mass itself."[2] Some people thought Monk resembled Jomo Kenyatta. Randy Weston described Monk's bearing in the 1940s: "He walked like royalty." As for his music:

> Others were used to Bud Powell and not to Monk's way of playing. But I understood it . . . Monk's sound was African. I say this because everything we do is just an extension of our ancestors. Our music came out of thousands of years of development. We're taught to forget our ancestors. My father said "always look back."
>
> . . . America is young. . . . The music that black Americans created here didn't come out of the air but out of thousands of years of culture.

Monk never mentioned wanting to go to Africa. "No words," Randy laughed:

> He was not a jazz musician. He was someone sent from a higher plane to keep the culture. Monk played stride, and he made our music complete, for he was a traditionalist and a modernist. For me he made Louis Armstrong more important . . . .
>
> I loved Monk personally because he was a master, but not in the Western sense. In the West, to be a master, all you have to do is play well, and that's it. From my years with traditional Africans I learned that in the East you have to be respected in your community. And in Monk's neighborhood, when we walked together, people acknowledged him. [Monk stood on the sidewalk, and people gathered around him.] To be a master, you have to be clean of mind and spirit. And he was clean of mind and spirit. He did not speak it, didn't waste words; he lived it. In our tradition, our people didn't talk a lot. Parents with two words and a look could let you know what they meant. Monk was from that tradition. . . . When he said something, it was powerful. It was different. We're in a world where people have to blab all the time. Monk was on another level.

In the late 1940s, Monk went to live in the Bronx with Nellie Smith, sharing an apartment with some of her relatives. His brother Thomas knew all about Monk's relationship with Nellie, Thomas's sons recalled. But Marion didn't know the extent of it, and she didn't think her mother knew very much about it either. One day in 1949, Monk arrived at his mother's house holding an infant in his arms, and he told his mother, "This is my son, Thelonious." The child had been born in a hospital on Welfare Island at a time when the pianist was so poor that he didn't even have the money to visit Nellie there. Marion, who still lived in an apartment near her mother, came to see her new nephew. She was astonished because, in all his many visits to the apartment Monk had never told his mother that Nellie was pregnant. Marion was not jumping up and down with enthusiasm about her brother's relationship with Nellie, but Marion's motto was, "As long as he's happy, I'm happy." And Thelonious seemed happy, Marion thought.

Nellie, Thelonious, and their son moved into Barbara's apartment on West 63rd Street, where they usually lived throughout the next decade and a half. Once in a while they moved up to the Bronx again to Nellie's relatives.

Whenever Randy went to Monk's apartment to pick him up, beginning in 1949, Nellie opened the door. "She was friendly. We were really family. She knew I loved Thelonious. And she just loved that man. She was always with Thelonious," Randy recalled.

The close relationship between Nellie and Thelonious would become legendary in the jazz world. The couple was devoted to each other and their children, Thelonious Jr. and a daughter, Barbara, who would be born at the end of 1953. When Thelonious fell on particularly hard times in the early 1950s, Nellie went to work and helped support the family, keeping Monk's career buoyed up, through sickness and health, without complaint, and without a marriage certificate. Few people outside the family ever knew that Thelonious and Nellie were never legally married. Spiritually, they were conjoined. And both appeared to be married to Thelonious's music.

Thelonious, Nellie, Toot, and, later, the newborn daughter, nicknamed Boo Boo, lived primarily with Monk's mother through 1953. Marion recalled that the whole family showed Barbara Monk great respect, especially when they lived in her apartment. Marion hinted there might have been tension between Barbara and Nellie. And if Nellie was strong-willed, "she couldn't have differences of opinion with my mother, because it was my mother's house. We would have been up in arms," Marion said.

Whatever tension there may have been between Nellie and Monk's relatives—and a few musicians, over the years, sensed some tension for some unknown reason—Nellie was a thoroughly modern, alert, and articulate woman and an ideal comrade and helpmate for Monk. She loved her role, standing by the side of the musician whose work she idolized. Many of their friends and business associates believed without question that Monk would have been a lost soul without the exceptionally tolerant Nellie. There was something a little magical about her. If anything at all was amiss in their lives, it was that Nellie bore too much responsibility for Monk. He may have been too dependent on her. But it seemed to be second nature for him to be that way, and they had an agreement about their roles in their household. Nobody would ever know how Monk would have fared if he had been forced to take charge of all the practicalities of life.

Elsie Colomby, mother of a young schoolteacher who would become Monk's manager, met Nellie for lunch one day and feel very happy to be in Nellie's company. Elsie, a refugee from Hitler's Germany, and a woman with a very independent streak, felt immediate rapport and even kinship with Nellie. It seemed to Elsie that she had known Nellie for many years. Many people felt that Nellie was very easy to communicate with.

In 1953, not long before Christmas, Monk's mother Barbara died, probably of heart trouble and diabetes, Marion thought. Thelonious, Nellie, and their children kept the humble, little apartment for themselves.

NOTES

Personal interviews: T. S. Monk, Nellie Monk, Thomas Monk, Jr., Alonzo White, Jr., Marion Monk White, Idrees Sulieman, Randy Weston, Elsie Colomby.

1. A similar impression of Thelonious Monk was formed by Dr. Everett Dulit, a psychiatrist on the faculty of Albert Einstein College of Medicine and the head of child and adolescent psychiatry there. Although he had never met Monk, he spoke to one of the doctors who had treated the pianist and formed some opinions about him. Dulit believed that Monk "liked to be astonishing, surprising, unsettling, in a way that has to do with mysticism, a little like a Tibetan guru who unsettles [in order] to rise above it all to originality."

2. Hentoff (1960).

6 Life without a Cabaret Card

Monk might have lived his entire life in obscurity, in mundane comparison to the sublimity of his compositions, had it not been for several twists of fate. The brilliant and inventive Dizzy Gillespie drove himself as hard to promote bebop as he did to play his trumpet. Managing to insinuate himself and the modern musical revolution into American culture in the 1940s and '50s, he became one of the first and most important musicians to bring some of Monk's tunes to audiences around the world. Furthermore, the public was intrigued by the exotic, bohemian image of bebop, and Monk called attention to himself by dressing, as it were, in partial mufti, with various hats—some of them amusing, others quite elegant—and elaborate eyeglasses, such as bamboo-framed dark glasses. With his flare for an offbeat style, he cultivated an image of mysteriousness. And a small, devoted band of jazz business world insiders—the few recording company executives— made an intense effort to capitalize on any aspect of the bebop revolution that might tantalize the public. Alfred Lion christened Monk "the high priest of bebop," adding to his allure. Critics began to understand and support progressive jazz.

So a small ray of the light of public scrutiny shone on Monk. But he remained on the sidelines, regarded as a footnote to modern music.

His reputation as an eccentric experimenter in a jazz subculture hardly translated into high-profile gigs.

Jackie McLean met Monk in the 1940s and got to know him on a day-to-day, survival basis. Monk was playing at the Club 845 in the Bronx, a popular club with young beboppers. Helen Merrill sang there—when her name was still Helen Milcetic on the marquee—as did singers Betty Carter and Babs Gonzalez; and Miles Davis, Charlie Parker, Bud Powell, Al Haig, Oscar Pettiford, Roy Haynes, and Red Rodney played there, too. "Oh, it was marvelous," Helen Merrill recalled. "So much talent around. Something had to rub off on you." Helen had grown up hearing her mother sing twelve-tone folk songs from the Yugoslavian island of Krk, and so bebop sounded normal to her! Monk's group at the 845 included the alto saxophonist Ernie Henry, whose bluesy orientation Monk would always admire; when Henry wasn't available, Monk gave Jackie McLean a chance; also in the group were Art Blakey and Coleman Hawkins.[1]

One night, probably in 1949, Jackie worked with Monk at the Audubon Ballroom in Harlem. Jackie happened to mention that his mother had just baked a chocolate pie. Monk showed great interest in trying a piece, and he insisted on walking seventeen-year-old Jackie to his apartment after the gig to get a slice. Jackie was afraid of disturbing his mother at 4 A.M., but Monk said he would wait outside.

Jackie recalled, "So he walked all the way across Harlem, up to the top of the Hill, came up to the sixth floor, and stood in the hallway while I went inside and cut a piece of chocolate pie and put it in a piece of wax paper and passed it out to him. Then he thanked me and went downstairs. That's the way it was with Monk; if he wanted to do something, anything, he'd go on and do it."

In June 1950, Monk played in a session for the Clef label as a member of Charlie Parker's group, starring Bird and Dizzy Gillespie, with bassist Curley Russell and drummer Buddy Rich; although the music was beautiful, none of the songs the men recorded were written by Monk. Dizzy had done over thirty recording dates by then, while Monk had been a leader on only four sessions producing twenty-one songs. His only other recordings were made working with Coleman

Hawkins or Dizzy, in addition to the amateur, "live" recordings made at Minton's.

In 1950 Jackie McLean also had his own gig to lead. His drummer, Arthur Taylor, suggested Jackie hire Monk. "It was weird because I never thought of asking somebody that I admired as much as I admired Monk . . . He said he'd make it, and when I got to the gig that night he was already there in his suit and tie and everything and he worked all night and got his twelve dollars and left," Jackie recalled.[:])

"In those days Monk was playing just what he wanted to, more or less. But everyone was sleeping on [ignoring] him except for the active jazz musicians and a few jazz fans around them. That's why I get a little mad now [in the 1960s,] when I hear people expounding on Monk so much, because he has been playing close to the same thing since I can remember. Monk is one of the few musicians who you can go into the club every night and hear, and he'll play the same tunes, and you don't get tired of them or anything like that. I know I don't, he's always surprising me." Jackie didn't mention it, but people didn't often hire Monk as a sideman because they knew he was going to do exactly what Jackie said: play just what he wanted to. Most people wanted him to blend in with the group.

Jackie also felt that people mistakenly regarded Monk as "a talented nut." But Jackie, instinctively happy to accept a genius in his midst, found Monk "wise, lucid and informed," with wide-ranging interests. "He's very easy to know as long as you deal with him in a plain and friendly way. But if you try to be dishonest with him or play mental chess with him, then you might have trouble. His mind is something that should be respected at all times. People are too quick to think that a jazz musician knows jazz and that's it, you know."

In 1951, Monk had a brush with the criminal justice system one day when Bud Powell and a man and woman Monk had never met before visited him on West 63rd Street. A woman named Maely Dufty, a very good friend of Billie Holiday and a well-known figure in the jazz world, later wrote about the incident for the New York Citizen Call on July 2, 1960. Because Monk's mother was sick in bed in the tiny apartment, Monk suggested they sit outside in a car, possibly a car that

Bud Powell, c. 1940s. Courtesy Frank Driggs Collection.

was going to take Bud Powell to the airport so he could fly to work in Europe. Two narcotics cops came to the car and flashed their badges. Monk felt no fear; he had nothing to hide, because he didn't use heroin—at least not at that time.[1] For one thing, it would have been far too costly for him. But a glassine envelope fell to the floor and landed between his feet. The police arrested everyone in the car.

At the police station, Monk remained silent and refused to blame Bud for the presence of the drugs. Maely related that Bud shouted, "Monk, why did you make me do it?" Monk just shook his head in disbelief. That night Bud became so distraught that he was transferred out of the Tombs, the downtown jail where he and Monk were held, to a psychiatric institution. Bud's male friend was a drug pusher out on bail; the woman was the pusher's friend. They were released on bail, but Monk was unable to raise $1,500 for his. Nellie went to Maely the next day for help in raising bail and hiring a lawyer. According to Maely, Nellie had just undergone abdominal surgery a few months earlier; she was working at the time as a seamstress for forty-five dollars a week plus carfare.

Maely tried to reason with the police, asking them to put Monk in isolation for three days; that way, they could see that Monk had no withdrawal symptoms and couldn't be guilty of using heroin. Furthermore, the amount of heroin in the envelope was so small; it didn't amount to enough to make Monk seem like a pusher. But the police didn't listen to Maely. When she approached the N.A.A.C.P. for help, she discovered that it didn't handle drug-related matters; instead, she was referred to a lawyer, Andrew Weinberger. He took on the case, but there was still the matter of bail money. A disk jockey and a jazz club owner turned Monk down. Maely said they laughed at the idea. "My dear friend and fellow European Alfred Lion from Blue Note Records . . . paid the attorney's fee," Maely wrote, at a time when Lion had very little money. And Monk—the only innocent in the case—languished in a deep depression in jail for sixty days. The judge accepted the time Monk had already served as full payment for the minor narcotics violation.

A few years later Monk would confide in Harry Colomby, his manager, that at the time of his arrest, he wasn't guilty of anything. But he "took the weight," as jazz musicians said. Monk could have given the police information about Bud's heroin habit, but Monk told Nellie that he wasn't going to volunteer whatever he knew because, once he got out of jail, he had to live in the jazz world.

When he was released, Monk walked right into another kind of prison. The New York City Police Department required anyone working in clubs to have a cabaret card, and no one could get or keep one if he or she was convicted of a crime such as drug possession. When Monk lost his cabaret card, he lost his right to work in New York. More than ever, people called him "weird" behind his back, and he knew about it and felt hurt—a lonesome, very unhappy man.

Monk often brought up the word "weird" in some interviews and disdained it. Even in his interview with Ira Peck, who had used the word, Monk had tried to squelch it, explaining that once people were ready for something, they didn't think it was weird anymore.

There were jazz scenes in the boroughs—Brooklyn, the Bronx, and Queens—and of course there were out-of-town jobs. But, Monk hated to travel. Many of his gigs from 1951 until the summer of 1957 took place in the boroughs, at low-profile clubs with audiences drawn from the neighborhoods. A struggling young trumpeter, Johnny Parker, found himself a gig at a Queens club called Big George's on Northern Boulevard in Corona and hired Monk. The pay was $12 a night per man. Johnny was thrilled not only to have Monk play with him, but to witness Monk's grace and dignity under difficult circumstances. Monk showed up well-dressed in a suit, just as he had done for Jackie McLean, played his own "Round Midnight" as well as many standards—"I Should Care" was one, a tune Monk had recorded in 1948—and didn't complain at all about having to travel to Queens and receive so little money.

It was probably in this period that Monk went to work at a club in Detroit, where "a clubowner, terrified by Monk's glowering intensity, asked the police to throw him out . . . Other [club] owners refused to serve Monk liquor or told him that their three-year-old sons could play better piano. Monk endured the abuse without losing his sense of humor. Once he was hired with tenor saxophonist Sonny Rollins for a one-night stand at a club in New York, but Rollins never arrived. When Monk tried to collect Rollins's pay as well as his own, the owner refused. 'Man, you're twelve drags,' Monk said. 'Ain't you got no ears? I was playing twice as fast.'"[4]

Monk played at rent parties at Randy Weston's apartment, and he managed to work in Manhattan clubs in a furtive, clandestine way; that is, without an advertisement that he was on the bill. On September 14, 1953, he played at the little Open Door, a club in Greenwich Village near Washington Square South, in a group with drummer Roy Haynes, bassist Charles Mingus, and the leader Charlie Parker. A well-known jazz photographer, Bob Parent, took a picture of that rare

Charles Mingus, Roy Haynes, Monk, and Charlie Parker at the Open Door, 1953.
Photo: Robert W. Parent.

group that night. Monk didn't often play with Parker, who was banned
from Birdland, the club that was named for him, also because of his
drug use. Parker used to play at the Open Door frequently and passed
out flyers to friends, telling them where he was playing. The club
featured jazz from spring, 1953 to early 1954. If the police knew Monk
was playing there, they looked the other way and didn't bother him.

Lou Donaldson also recalled playing with Monk often at the Open
Door in the mid-1950s, along with Max Roach, Oscar Pettiford or
occasionally Charles Mingus, and Kenny Dorham. Monk probably
played at Minton's in this period, too, since clarinetist Tony Scott,
during a long stint at Minton's, played with Monk there. The Baroness

Pannonica de Koenigswarter recalled that Monk was playing at Minton's when she moved with her husband from Europe to New York. Birdland was open by that time, she said.[5] The baroness would become a very close friend of Monk's.

Probably around this time Monk had a gig with Sarah Vaughan at the Paramount. When Monk started playing his chords, she said, "No, no, I can't make it like that." "They had to get another piano player. Everyone who played with Monk had to be an instrumentalist," trumpeter Idrees Sulieman said. "Monk never wanted to play conservatively. He could do it, but he didn't want to. He was not a good person to accompany a singer."

Yet Billy Taylor had heard Monk playing in a little, after-hours club on 135th Street in Harlem for a cabaret singer who knew him. She coaxed him to play, saying, "C'mon, remember this?" He did, and he sounded very good, playing an offbeat song, perhaps "Lover Man," not a pop song. And Monk accompanied an obscure singer, Frankie Passions, on a record for the Washington label in the 1950s. Furthermore, on two of his first Blue Note recordings, Monk comped admirably for singer Pancho Hagood, supporting the singer and never overshadowing him. Even so, gigs as a singer's accompanist were rarities for Monk.

Nellie kept working to support Monk, herself and their children—*Us*, as she called the family. Whatever she did, she did for *us*, she emphasized. Nat Hentoff, who met Nellie when he wrote an article for *Esquire* (April 1960), observed, "Nellie is tall, thin, nervous, and singularly attractive in the way that many people with oversize strength of spirit often are." He quoted her:

> Thelonious had trouble getting work even before he lost the card. Therefore, it wasn't a sudden total calamity. People had told so many stories about his being unreliable and eccentric that it had always been hard. But during the worst years we didn't feel the struggle as much as other people might have because we were very close, we felt each of us was doing the best he could, and we didn't suffer for things we couldn't have. In fact, nobody talked about

them. If it was a matter of clothes, for instance, I felt it more important that he have them since he's before the public. During those
long stretches when he wasn't working, it was torture for him not
to be able to play. But you'd never know it from looking at him,
and he didn't get bitter. Anybody with less strength would have
snapped. And he was continually omitted from things—records,
concerts, and the like. We'd listen to the all-night Birdland radio
show, and maybe once in two months they'd play a record of his.
There was no money; no place to go. A complete blank. He wasn't
even included in benefits. He even had to pay to get into Birdland.

Dizzy, Miles, Charles Mingus, Basie, Lester Young, and hundreds
more played in Birdland and had their recordings broadcast often on
the influential "Symphony Sid" show—but not Monk. Monk's
nephews would remember the names of the relatively few people who
hired Monk in those days. Without a cabaret card, Monk was of no
value to Birdland. One musician, who knew Monk well later in life,
recalled him saying he had been banned from Birdland for a while. For
Monk, it was tantamount to being banned from Birdland if he had to
pay to get in, because he had no money. Harry Colomby also remembered Monk saying he had been banned from Birdland for a while,
probably in the very early 1950s, because of some kind of argument
with the club manager, Oscar Goodstein.

Randy Weston admired Monk enormously for the way he behaved
even when he had very little work: "He never compromised or
complained or begged for a cabaret card." Monk said of those days, "I
didn't get raggedy. They thought I'd become a bum, but I fooled 'em.
I stayed on the scene."⁵ Without a cabaret card, "he was not a happy
guy," observed Lou Donaldson, who arrived in New York the year after
Monk lost his card. Billy Taylor, too, noticed Monk wasn't working
much. A cabaret card was crucial for musicians, and Monk was not the
only one who lost his. Billy, among many others, thought the requirement was unconscionable because it kept a man from earning a decent
living, or any kind of living. The police used the cabaret-card ruling in
"a mean-spirited way," said many musicians. It was generally believed

that it was a way of harassing African American jazz musicians in particular. Eventually prominent white entertainers helped get rid of the cabaret-card restrictions by refusing to work in New York until musicians were no longer punished by the requirement of having one in order to work. For Monk, the relief came too late.

In 1952 Monk signed a contract to record with Prestige Records—like Blue Note, a small, specialty label focusing on jazz—but he had little opportunity to play in public and publicize his recordings. His career reached a nadir. Undoubtedly, it was the worst time in his life, and yet, in stark contrast to his situation, his music sounded as if he were the happiest man in the world. If misery didn't agree with him, he knew exactly how to vanquish it at the keyboard.

Monk's first recording for his new label included "Little Rootie Tootie," a charming, bright melody introduced and accented by disso-nant chords sounding exactly like the whistle of a tugboat, or a train. Regarded by some people as one of his best songs, "Little Rootie Tootie" was inspired by a happy celebration. Monk wrote it for his son, Thelonious Jr., who could whistle before he could speak. Monk's nephews had gone to see a Walt Disney cartoon feature about Little Toot, the Tugboat, which had a whistle on it. When they got home, they began calling their whistling cousin "Toot." For his Prestige debut, Monk also reworked the standard "Sweet and Lovely" and played a happy, swinging composition, "Bye-Ya," and "Monk's Dream," one of the few songs he dedicated to himself. He had his dear friend and musical compadre Art Blakey in his trio for these first recordings made on October 15, 1952.

Three days later, Max Roach replaced Blakey in the trio for Monk's recording of "Trinkle Tinkle," another of his well-loved compositions. Three other tunes were recorded on that date, including Monk's collaboration with Denzil Best, a driving, upbeat "Bemsha Swing"; "Reflections," one of many among his best compositions; plus the standard "These Foolish Things."

Monk didn't record again for Prestige until November 13, 1953, when he played his songs "Let's Call This," "Think of One," and "Friday the 13th." The last tune was named for the day on which it was recorded. "Let's Call This" was Monk's response to the question, "What shall we call this?"; "Think of One" was his response to that same question. Many of Monk's tunes ended up having their odd titles because he answered such things as "Worry Later" when people asked him for titles in recording studios. ("Worry Later" turned out to be the name of a song that would also be known as "San Francisco Holiday.") For the "Friday the 13th" date, Monk recorded with Julius Watkins on French horn, Percy Heath on bass, Willie Jones as the drummer, and most notably Sonny Rollins, whose work Monk loved, on tenor saxophone. This was Sonny's first recording date with Monk, and artistically it was a very successful one.

Midway through 1954, Monk recorded "We See," "Smoke Gets in Your Eyes," "Locomotive," and "Hackensack," the last tune, derived from the chord progression of "Lady, Be Good," whimsically named by Monk when he heard he was going to be recording in Rudy Van Gelder's studio in that city. These cuts were made with Art Blakey as the drummer, and Frank Foster, normally in the Count Basie band, doing a great job on tenor saxophone. Magically, all of this varied music continued to sound as if it were being played by a happy, confident man.

One day that year, French pianist Henri Renaud, visiting New York, took a walk with Monk along the Hudson River, and Monk remarked that he would like to see what was going on across the ocean. Though Monk didn't really like to travel, he had to think of ways to escape the frustrations and constraints—the straitjacket of loss of the cabaret card—in New York. Renaud called Charles Delaunay, an influential French jazz producer, who was then organizing the second Festival du Jazz de Paris. Delaunay, an admirer of Monk from his recordings, hired him to join other Americans—Gerry Mulligan, Lalo Schiffrin, Mary Lou Williams, and Jonah Jones—for the festival. But the festival couldn't afford to bring Monk's rhythm section to Paris. So he went alone, truly alone. Nellie stayed at home to take care of Thelonious Jr., then almost five years old—he had been born on December 27, 1949 (coincidentally Nellie's birthday)—and Barbara, born on September 5, 1953.

For the festival at the Salle Pleyel, Monk was assigned a French rhythm section of young players, including bassist Jean-Marie Ingrand, who didn't know his music at all. There was only a short rehearsal. Monk followed a popular French pianist, Claude Lutter, for the concert. The audience was, at best, puzzled by Monk's music. Monk said to the rhythm section, "It's all right," but actually it was not all right. Monk announced in French to the audience that he would play "Well, You Needn't," then reflected for a moment, changed his mind, and played "Off Minor"—no easy tune for the musicians, either. Burdened by the rhythm section, which was far over its head at that time, Monk walked offstage, drank some Scotch (though he preferred bourbon, which has always been scarce in Europe), and went back onstage briefly. Then the concert ended. Some French people at that time thought it probably was impossible for anyone to follow Lutter successfully. But it was also true that French jazz musicians would have to spend years playing jazz before they could equal the Americans who brought the art to their country and taught talented musicians there. And Monk's music was especially difficult. No musician could simply look at it and interpret it well. Reflecting on this situation in 1956, Monk told Nat Hentoff, of *Down Beat*, "I enjoyed that visit very much. The only drag was I didn't have my own band with me . . . I'd like to go back over with my own group."

During that visit to Paris in June 1954, Monk recorded solo in a studio for *Radiodiffusion français*, where he was delighted with the good piano and his freedom to play whatever he pleased. The recording was eventually released on the Swing label, then under the aegis of Vogue, an important European jazz label. Monk was so cheered by the session that he went to buy a supply of berets to take home to friends in New York.

Monk stayed eight days in France; the bassist Jean-Marie Ingrand, who could speak English, became his companion. Charles Delaunay had rented Monk a room at a hotel on the Champs Élysées, not far from the Blue Note jazz club. Monk secured a phonograph so that Ingrand could listen to Monk's recording of "Friday the 13th." They listened to it a thousand times until Ingrand finally learned to play it.[*]

Ingrand observed that Monk had only a couple of shirts and suits and ties packed all in one suitcase and not much money. Furthermore, Monk didn't know how to handle the day-to-day business of survival in Paris. Ingrand even had to knot Monk's ties for him. Monk seemed as awkward as a teenager, perhaps a little strange and incomprehensible at times, yet gentle, warm, and likeable. But at the piano Monk took command. "He lived only for his music," Ingrand concluded.

At the Salle Pleyel, Monk seemed[[Au/?-sense-OK?]] to play solely for his own pleasure, and the musicians who showed up to hear him loved him. One of his most loyal and enthusiastic admirers, Mary Lou Williams, who was living in Paris then, went to Salle Pleyel and introduced Baroness Pannonica de Koenigswarter to Monk backstage; after that the baroness tried to stay close to Monk, according to both Ingrand and the baroness. However, Harry Colomby was under the impression that Monk barely noticed the baroness in Paris; she did not really make an impression on him until he returned home. Pannonica, known as Nica, renewed her acquaintance with Thelonious in New York three months later while she was staying at the Stanhope Hotel. Many musicians visited Nica's suite, and a friendship developed between Nica and Monk.

After his return to New York in September, Monk went to Rudy Van Gelder's studio in Hackensack, where since the mid-1950s he had made all of his recordings for Prestige. Monk recorded "Work," "Nutty," and the lovely, flowing, slowly swinging "Blue Monk," his first recording of this song, which he would sometimes call his favorite. He was accompanied by Blakey and bassist Percy Heath; it was one of his best trio recordings ever. He also played solo in his hestitatingly pensive, stabbed-chords style for the standard "Just a Gigolo," infusing it with the feeling of airiness and the forlorn, insecure, but whimsical outlook of the title character. He had never recorded these tunes before. "Blue Monk," one of his masterpieces, would become very familiar to audiences, even though people wouldn't always know its name. Monk was composing with freshness and brilliance; yet almost no one knew about his work. Prestige gave him very little support and focused on its other artists—Miles Davis, for one, and the Modern Jazz Quartet—who had higher profiles and cabaret cards.

Monk did his last two albums as a sideman for Prestige—first with the Sonny Rollins Quartet, with Tommy Potter on bass and Art Taylor on drums on October 25, 1954, and then with Miles Davis. Monk did a brilliant job of comping for Rollins and sounded especially relaxed as a sideman on such tunes as "The Way You Look Tonight."

Out of Monk's recording session with Miles Davis on December 24, 1954, came a rumor that Monk and Miles had a fight. But people who had been in the studio knew better. From the first moment he had met Monk, Rudy Van Gelder had been impressed with Monk's height, stature, and quiet dignity. With his intense expression, Monk always seemed to be in control of himself. Miles Davis, leading his group in a rehearsal of "Bag's Groove," told Monk, "During my solo, lay out." He didn't want to hear Monk's "funny" chords, as Davis described them in his autobiography; they might divert attention from the solo. Miles, a very small man, was sitting down, pointing the bell of his trumpet at the floor, as he always did when he played. When it came time for Miles to play his solo, Monk got up from the piano bench and stood there, towering over Miles. After his solo, Miles said to Monk, "Why did you do that?" Monk said with mild irritation, "I don't have to sit down to lay out." Years later, the memory still made Rudy laugh.

Percy Heath, the bassist on the date with Miles and Monk, remembered the same incident. Miles told Monk to "stroll"—"lay out" or not play for a song. Monk knew that Miles didn't want to hear harmonies from a pianist who might steal his thunder or interfere with the trumpet's lines. Miles often told a pianist to lay out, Percy Heath recalled. Percy remembered that was all there was to the incident.

The story would become magnified until it portrayed Monk and Miles battling in the studio—big, intense, athletic Monk and well-built, wiry, but little Miles Davis, unlikely sparring partners. Percy denied that the men fought at all. Eager to dispel any rumors to the contrary and protect his friend Monk to the nth degree, Percy jokingly hypothesized that the recording date may have been the first time Monk literally took a stroll during a gig. A few years later Monk became a champion "stroller"; famous for his charismatic, eye-catching strolling, he danced around on stage, or in recording studios, during gigs, while his sidemen played. (But Monk never missed a cue to come in on a tune; ending his strolls, he always got to the piano to join his groups on the exact note needed to enhance the performance—unless he decided not to play at all.)

Heath regarded Monk as a great player. In New York for only about six years at that time of Miles's and Monk's recording date, Heath was thrilled to be "with all those great cats." He recalled, "My mother used to call [Thelonious]; The onliest.' She got mixed up with his name Thelonious. I told her he sure was 'the onliest'!"

Rudy Van Gelder noticed that Monk talked only about what he wanted for his sessions. "He knew exactly what he wanted to do, to make a good album," Rudy observed. He was always dressed well, not eccentric or especially striking in his appearance—except for a very intense expression on his face. Once he brought his son, Toot, to a session. Rudy coached Toot to speak on a recording. In his little baby voice, Toot said, "This is Thelonious Monk, Jr. You are tuned to the call letters of the stars, and this is take one."[7]

Although he welcomed any work and played as if he were intensely happy to be composing and performing, Monk felt unhappy during his days with the Prestige label. In the early 1950s, when Randy Weston was recording regularly for Riverside Records, that fledgling little label's owners began asking Randy to talk to Monk about recording for them. Riverside wanted to become associated with modern music. When Monk's contract with Prestige was ending in 1955, Nat Hentoff tried to help Thelonious by calling Orrin Keepnews and Bill Grauer, who ran the Riverside label, and asking if they would be interested in recording Monk. Nat would see if he could convince Monk to change labels. The Riverside men decided to sign Monk. They wanted to signal to the world that they were going to become deeply involved in recording progressive jazz.

Monk still had not earned back all his advances from Prestige, and Orrin Keepnews lent him the $108.27 outstanding on Monk's Prestige account so he could leave the label. Thus ended Monk's interlude there that produced a small, exquisite, overlooked body of work.

Monk felt pleased about signing with Riverside, where he would work with Keepnews as the producer in the studio; for one thing, he remembered Orrin's very flattering article in the *Record Changer* in 1948, one of the few articles or reviews that paid tribute to Monk's debut as a recording leader. And Monk had "very little to lose," as Keepnews appraised the situation, by taking a chance with a fledgling label.[8] Monk's son, Toot, and Harry Colomby, who became Monk's manager at around this time, recalled that although Keepnews gave Monk $108.27 to buy out his contract, Riverside later deducted that money from his royalty check. Futhermore, Harry would never be convinced that Monk knew how many pressings were made of his records for Riverside, or how much royalties were owed to him. Colomby blamed Riverside's accountants, not Keepnews, for poor bookkeeping.

But the good news is that there *were* royalty checks and more artistic successes. Though Monk had no way of knowing it when he signed with Riverside, the hard times were about to end for him—in the reality of his everyday life, if not often in his memory, and perhaps never in his bones. As he said about his situation to the distinguished pianist and arranger Jimmy Jones in a club one night, "It takes a long time."

There was still one monumental problem that Monk had to contend with: his image as a drug user. Some people believed that Monk began using drugs when he was playing at Minton's.[9] It's unlikely he did anything much, and certainly not regularly, but smoke marijuana in the 1940s, or the army would never have found him eligible for limited service. Possibly his limitation at that time was the vestiges of a lung problem—perhaps childhood asthma or even a mild case of tuberculosis. Many people recovered from both those illnesses without treatment.

Billy Taylor never saw Monk do anything but drink, and he didn't even drink much with Billy, who neither drank nor smoked at all. Whether Monk used any other drugs except for alcohol and marijuana during his Minton's days, certainly drugs were available to him and many other musicians there. A great number of musicians began using heroin in the early bebop era. Some became addicts and died; others recovered. It became fashionable, or anyway commonplace, for musicians to use drugs at that time—those that weren't afraid of needles and their repercussions—and it would later become the accepted idea that Charlie Parker's drug addiction had inspired many younger musicians to use heroin. They felt that if they imitated Parker's habit, they would be able to play the way he did. He tried to discourage them, but to little avail.

And some musicians began using drugs simply because life was so difficult. Drugs eased the stress for a while and gave them the illusion that they could relax. Not only musicians in those days, but many other people used drugs without knowing how dangerous the side effects were and how likely they were to become addicted. Amphetamines—"speed"—were popular with undergraduates who wanted to stay awake to cram for exams, and medical students, interns, and medical residents, who had to study around the clock and do marathon shifts in hospitals. Musicians used speed, too, at times.

Monk, a few years older than Bird, was notoriously proud of being influenced most of all by himself. He was, to put it mildly, high on music much of the time. Monk loved to smoke cigarettes—tobacco and marijuana—and he loved to drink. He did begin using drugs, but exactly what he used and when is open for speculation mostly because he mixed things together, "whatever showed up," said one musician who worked with Monk closely. "Drugs were no big thing," tenor saxophonist Johnny Griffin recalled about those days. But it was the rare musician who would ever discuss Monk's drug use except by alluding to it. No one surviving in 1996—and among the survivors were a few of Monk's close friends—would admit to witnessing him use heroin at all and certainly not intravenously. Perhaps they never saw it happen, bur even Johnny Griffin, who loved to drink alcohol and who met Monk first in New York in the 1940s, said definitely and excitedly, "He was no drug addict, you know!"

Griffin knew Monk as a drinker; almost everyone knew Monk as a drinker. Some people thought he favored cognac—he did drink cognac, but most often friends drank bourbon with him. He was always ready to have a drink. Musicians met each other and socialized at the bar. The musicians that worked on 52nd Street had a favorite hangout, the White Rose, where they could get cheap drinks. Bars were the focus of a musician's social life. Other people played golf, went to museums, art galleries, and clubhouses, but musicians met at the bar. Griffin met Monk at a bar; Johnny Carisi socialized with Monk at the bar. And in Johnny Griffin's estimation, "The social drug that destroys you is alcohol, alcohol, baby; there are more people in hospitals from alcohol, from the nut houses to everything, and the government permits it because they want people stupid. So it's legal."

Nevertheless, it is true that Monk used a variety of drugs throughout his life, some of them obtained by prescription, some by illegal sources, and some as gifts. One musician, who knew Monk well in the 1940s and claims he never saw Monk use heroin, said, "Monk never refused anything." (That would not always be absolutely true, because, by 1970, he drank fruit juice instead of alcohol one night in a club, and by then he didn't go out of his way to drink anything.) It's most likely that Monk started a broader involvement with drug use of all types in the 1950s, after he lost his cabaret card. But most musicians instinctively closed ranks and said they knew nothing about the specifics of Monk's drug use. For the most part, they really didn't.

Max Roach later admitted to using heroin and going home to his family's house down south to get himself free of the addiction before returning to the playing scene. Miles Davis had the same experience, repairing to his father's farm in the midwest. Countless other famous musicians, some of whom worked or associated closely with Monk over the years, used heroin and other drugs. Monk never discussed his drug use with reporters for publication. Even so, rumors circulated. And it's no secret that whatever Monk's drug use was, it certainly did his image and mental health no good; drugs didn't seem to help him cope with his existence and career at all, as he undoubtedly hoped they would, and some of them damaged the sensitive man permanently.

Beginning in the mid-1950s, Monk began to behave at times as if he was using amphetamines and even LSD. He did have periods when he completely withdrew from his surroundings and then hallucinated beginning in the 1950s. Most likely he began using various drugs to try to fit into the modernists' culture, to become one of the guys—a status he had never achieved, because he was so completely a creator, a genius, in a sea of great interpretive artists. Monk was a man who disappeared from the scene altogether for weeks at a time, Lou Donaldson recalled, and sat home alone and wrote music.

Monk's manager, Harry Colomby, thought it was possible that Monk used drugs at least in part to help himself break out of a shell, to ameliorate the strictures of his very formal background. Colomby thought Monk "had a stuffy mom." (She had definitely brought up the children to live in a straight, conservative style.) "He was shy and unable to be social," Colomby thought. "People wound up talking and he listening. He had a reputation for being the hippest, weirdest man because of the sound of his music and his lifestyle"—working at night, sleeping by day.

Monk's life was very hard, as an African American, a jazz musician, and an introspective, dreamy composer. He was a poor man who, by inclination and upbringing, sat back and let others manage his business affairs and all other aspects of his career while he kept his own counsel, studied what he wanted, and wrote music for which he got precious little credit. At forty, without a cabaret card in the Big Apple, he was a shadowy figure behind the scenes in the jazz world. Randy Weston came to view Monk's behavior as his way of reacting to and handling racism and his disappointments in the music business. Monk held his ground, seeking solace at his beloved piano; in the early days of his relationship with Nellie, she would tell Harry Colomby, she could not pry him loose from the piano.

Eventually doctors, other musicians, and friends gave Monk a variety of drugs to help him feel better, to lift his mood. Even though he could walk out into the street near his house, where a crowd of admirers gravitated toward him and rallied around him, there remained about him an aura of apartness and social awkwardness. One musician who sometimes walked with Monk perceived him as acutely lonely. Walking with friends lifted his spirits, and so Monk loved to walk.

Into this miasma of commercial failure and aristocratic creativity that constituted Monk's early career and image and which shaped his personal feelings and guided the conduct of his life, a young schoolteacher, Harry Colomby, stumbled in 1954. It was shortly before

Monk's mother died. Monk had already signed with the Riverside label, as Colomby recalled, and was about to prepare his first recording for Keepnews and Grauer. They were planning that he record an album of Duke Ellington standards, not his own music. The Ellington album was intended to bring Monk into the mainstream, to make him seem familiar, and to secure at least a slice of the pie for him.

Almost intuitively, Monk gravitated to Harry Colomby to better his own lot.

NOTES

Personal interviews: Herlen Merrill, Harry Colomby, Nellie Smith Monk, Johnny Parker, Randy Weston, Lou Donaldson, Tony Scott, Idrees Sulieman, Billy Taylor, Thomas Monk Jr., Rudy van Gelder, Percy Heath, Joe Williams speaking about Jimmy Jones, Johnny Griffin.

1. Portion on Jackie McLean from Spellman (1985).
2. Ibid.
3. Monk wasn't guilty at that time, he later told his manager Harry Colomby.
4. From Lapham (1964).
5. From the chapter "Jazz Didn't Do My Marriage Any Good," in Gordon (1980).
6. From Ponzio and Postif (1995).
7. Years later Toot's message would be used for a recording called *Take One* that Toot, a drummer, led on the Blue Note label.
8. From Keepnews (1986).
9. From Ponzio and Postif (1995).

7 The Colomby Connection Begins in Earnest

Harry Colomby, considerably younger than Thelonious Monk, taught English and history in the New York City public schools when he first encountered the great jazz pianist. His elder brother, Jules, who played the trumpet and hung out in Greenwich Village clubs, had told him about the pianist's work. Jules knew many jazz musicians as intimate friends and introduced both Harry and an even younger brother, Bobby, who would become a drummer, to some of them.

The son of a handyman for the building where the Colomby family lived in Manhattan's Washington Heights gave the Colombys an old 78 recording of the Coleman Hawkins quartet with Monk as a sideman playing "Drifting on a Reed." Jazz was always being played in the Colomby house. Harry loved the recording, particularly Monk's unusual piano playing, and became an instant fan. "The way he attacked the piano was so interesting." Harry said.

Harry recalled the first time he saw Monk; he was playing with bassist Charles Mingus at the Open Door in the Village. "A drunk in the audience started dancing, waving his arms like wings. The manager or someone in the club was going to put the drunk out, but Thelonious said, 'It's okay.'" When Harry saw how lenient and comfortable Monk was with the drunk at the Open Door, Harry thought Monk

Harry Colomby.
Courtesy of Harry Colomby

might be especially sensitive to people who acted in a strange way. Then, Harry heard Monk's recordings for Blue Note. "I had never heard piano played like that before—the timing and space and harmonies," he recalled about his attraction to Monk.

In the early fifties, Jules Colomby was still living with his mother, while trying to organize a jazz label. He was preparing a recording session, featuring Gigi Gryce as the leader, with Monk as a sideman.' Harry, already teaching, was living in Cedarhurst, was visiting the family apartment when the musicians gathered; that's where he met Monk. "At the time, he was a cult figure, a strange man. I had heard about him as that." But it was Monk's music and not his reputation that intrigued Harry, who was not interested in strange people.

In 1954, when Harry was teaching at Far Rockaway High School, his students knew he liked jazz and asked him to invite a group to play for a school event. Harry arranged for Art Blakey and the Jazz Messengers to go to Far Rockaway. But Harry was worried about the show going smoothly, and particularly about Blakey keeping the date. So Harry went to Cafe Bohemia on Barrow Street in Greenwich Village to speak to Blakey. Cafe Bohemia, which drew fans away from the uptown clubs, Birdland and Basin Street East, was a small but important place, a favorite jazz club with musicians, with a long bar just inside the entrance. The tables were past the bar, and the bandstand stood against the back wall.

Monk walked into Cafe Bohemia and went up to Harry. "You're Jules Colomby's brother," Monk said, remembering Harry from their meeting in the Colomby apartment.

Harry said, "Yes." Quickly the conversation turned to cars, which Monk loved.

Then Monk said, "You got your short?" That was a slang word in the jazz world for a car. Harry didn't understand at first, but when he caught on, he said, "Yes."

Monk said, "You can give me a ride to the Bronx." At the time, Monk and Nellie were living with her brother Sonny in "a shitty little apartment," Harry recalled.

Harry said, "Sure," thinking: "I would go to Tacoma with him, if he asked me to." Harry knew Monk was an original, and Harry identified with this "underdog genius." They hung out for a while at Cafe Bohemia.

Then Monk said, "You ready to quit it?"

Harry thought Monk was asking if Harry was ready to quit teaching, but Monk explained he was asking if Harry was ready to leave the club. Driving Monk home, Harry encouraged Monk to continue playing and composing, and keep his spirits up. Harry really put his heart and soul into his speech.

Monk said, "You want to be my manager?"

Immediately Harry said, "Yes"; he later wrote for the liner notes of Monk's album *Misterioso* that he agreed quickly before either of them changed their minds. At that moment Harry said to himself, "My life is going to be different! Here is this great genius whom I look up to as a demigod—a maligned, weird guy. I'm going to be in a position to help this guy. I suddenly feel totally responsible for him." Harry was twenty-three years old; Monk thought it was "cool" were he learned during the conversation that Harry was a teacher.

"He didn't want a run-of-the-mill manager. And no one wanted him, because he was odd, unreliable. People were afraid of him. I think that his appearance had something to do with it. He was actually of regal stature. When he entered a room and just stood there, people 'defended' themselves." There was something "scary" about Monk— something indefinable about his expression, Harry surmised. Nellie would also reflect later that Monk seemed to frighten some people; she had no idea why. Monk was a tall, hefty man—"bearish," many writers called him. Monk did smile, and even cracked jokes and giggled or chortled, or occasionally laughed heartily, but his moments of mirth didn't ameliorate the overall effect of his size and stolidity—a rugged, very tall, quiet black man simply standing there, usually with a very intense expression on his face even when he smiled. "I had such respect for him," Harry recalled.

Harry used to fool around on the piano, but he never had the nerve to speak up and ask Monk to explain the chord progressions in Monk's song, "Off Minor," for example. Harry was too much in awe of Monk to ask him anything like that. In any case, Harry envisioned his role in life as a mandate to get work for Monk, not to ask him for piano lessons.

"Cool," Monk said when Harry told him he felt he had a mission. "It's different. I want you to get rich, get ten percent, then I'll get rich."

Harry recalled saying to him, "I don't know how rich we're going to get, but I'll guarantee you this: that you'll be recognized and appreciated in your lifetime."

All Harry really knew was that Monk was important. The colors of his music expressed a subterranean passion. Harry didn't simply want to get jobs for Monk but to have critics, scholars, and audiences realize how important Monk was. His music was a profound expression and interpretation of contemporary life. At that time Harry didn't think there was much money in jazz, and he thought the most he could hope to earn was a few dollars.

"I was so proud to be involved with him. The next morning when I woke up, I thought, 'I'm the manager of this great player. What's in the future for us now? I want to cultivate a friendship, hang out with him.' I called and asked him if he wanted to go to a museum. He said, 'Uh, no, maybe some other time.'" Harry didn't know yet that museum outings were not for Monk—at least not in Harry's experience, though other people later in Monk's life, after Monk became accustomed to earning a good income, would find him not only intelligent and well-informed but culturally curious and even occasionally adventurous. At the time Harry entered his life, Monk never had a spare dollar for movies, plays, or museum entrance fees. It was a mystery how he paid for all the cigarettes he smoked.

Not too much later, Harry began to cultivate a friendship with Monk. At the end of 1954, Harry was invited to a New Year's Eve party in Greenwich Village and invited Monk to go along. "Wow, wouldn't this be cool?" Harry reasoned. "He doesn't seem to have too much of a social life. I would like to walk into this party with Monk."

Monk said, "Okay, I'll meet you."

The people at the party were actors, artists, and Village types in dark turtleneck sweaters. Monk came in, wearing sunglasses, a coat, and a cap; he looked like an interesting, mysterious man and behaved in a very shy way, speaking very little. From there Harry and Monk went to a second party, where they sat on the floor. "There was music and candles—a beatnik scene," Harry recalled, "and people dancing. A very pretty girl came over to us; she was probably from India, because she had an accent, and maybe she was dressed in a sari." She looked at Monk, then Harry, and said, "Is he blind?" Harry said, "No, those are just sunglasses."

But Harry learned it was not usually that simple to hang out with Monk. Monk used to tell Harry by telephone, "Come over," Harry recalled, "and I would go, and he wouldn't be there. It wasn't the normal kind of responsiblity people have to time or schedule. I don't know if he ever got to know me. He knew I would work for him and stand up for him." Harry learned quickly that Monk had no regular schedule. "It was never: 'It's time to lie down, to rest before work.'

Sometimes he was up for three days and then asleep for three days. He didn't have a schedule for eating. He ate when he felt like eating." He needed so much attention and coddling, living according to his own laws and whims, that Harry began to perceive that Nellie really had three children—not only "Junior," as Harry called Toot, and Barbara, "but Monk himself."

Sometimes in the middle of a telephone conversation with Harry, Monk asked him to come to the apartment so they could discuss the topic in person. Harry thought Monk wanted company; Harry rarely saw people in the Monk apartment. Monk probably did want company, Harry suspected, but sometimes Monk would forget about inviting Harry to the apartment before he arrived. Harry would go to the house, ring and knock, and sometimes Nellie answered the door and said Monk was sleeping. Or there would be no answer. So, Harry stopped going to Monk's apartment every time Monk called. "But if I said I was coming over with a contract, Monk would be there," Harry recalled.

Harry believed Monk was a dedicated family man who related well to his children, despite the image of his being somewhat aloof. When Toot was about five or six years old, Harry saw Thelonious eating a candy bar. He asked Toot, "You want some?" And he broke off a piece and gave Toot the smaller piece. "So that will tell you something about him," Harry recalled. "He was a loyal husband—and traditional." He was so well-mannered that he took off his hat in elevators at that time. Johnny Griffin never heard Monk talk about women. Many other musicians were womanizers, but not Monk; he never even said a woman was "fine." He talked about Nellie, saying "Nellie wants me to do this," or he had an errand to do for her. As a man, he was really quite square. One explanation might have been, as Harry observed: "He was shy and overwhelmed by stuff going on in his mind." And he didn't waste time or add more complications to his life by chasing after women, when he had a family at home and music to pursue.

In 1954 Harry started working with Monk on a handshake basis and remained Monk's manager until 1967. In many ways, Harry became a protector for Monk, as Nellie was.

Harry quickly found out he couldn't work any overnight miracles. In addition to Monk's unreliablity and the loss of his cabaret card, he didn't have the critics on his side. Many simply ignored him. And Monk made no effort to cultivate any of them as friends. Although Harry didn't remember the exact date, he recalled one review by Leonard Feather that said Monk must have been looking at a racing form when he wrote one song. Monk was incensed.

Otherwise, Harry, like most people, almost never saw Monk angry at all. Monk usually walked away from fights; he never was inclined to start one. The last thing he wanted to do was injure his hands. With all the strikes against him, Monk, the gentlest of men to people who knew him, had a scary, dangerous public image.

Harry personally had good experiences with Monk from the beginning of their relationship. Once, Harry got Monk an advance of $100 for a $300 weekend gig in Baltimore. As they were traveling together to the train station, Harry asked for a few dollars because he was stone broke at the moment. Monk went to get change and gave Harry three twenty-dollar bills. Harry knew that Monk didn't have a dime, and he never asked Harry for money. Harry said to himself, "I will make sure he makes it." Harry knew that Art Blakey used to ask people if they wanted to be his manager, and when they agreed, he would immediately ask them for "a taste"—advance money; Thelonious never did that. Once Harry, who was earning $6,000 a year as a teacher, left five dollars under an ashtray in the Monk apartment, sneaking it to the Monks. "For him, a manager was about someone believing in him," Harry said, who had to keep working as a schoolteacher to support himself while he managed Monk.

At that time, only Milt and Billy Shaw, the Associated Booking Corporation, and the Moe Gale agencies dealt with jazz artists. No one wanted Monk. But when Colomby went to the Shaw agency and saw booker Jack Whitaker, Whitaker said, "If you have the nerve to manage Monk, I guess I could book him."

In the early 1950s, a prominent bebop-era drummer had a group with a starring front-line horn player. And the leader was supposedly a friend of Monk's. "They were hot," Colomby recalled. He called the leader to get the names of clubs and club owners, "so I can help Thelonious," he said. The leader said, "You can find all that in *Down Beat* magazine," and hung up without saying goodbye. Colomby thought that rising star, who would always try to present himself as Monk's friend, was a selfish guy.

On June 10, 1955, Monk was booked to become a guest on Steve Allen's television show at the Hudson Theater in the Broadway theater district. Exactly who brought about the booking isn't clear—possibly the Shaw agency or Associated Booking, though the latter firm may not have done any bookings for Monk until the 1960s. On the program, Allen did an excellent job of explaining Monk's background and artistry in capsule form, calling him:

> a musician's musician. He has never particularly courted fame in the usual sense. He doesn't have a publicity man or wear funny hats or bother to travel around much. He just sort of sits where he is and plays the kind of music he likes, and he's got a large number of rabid fans, and many of them are musicians. He's particularly loved by fellows like Dizzy Gillespie and . . . the late Charlie Parker, and they kind of worked out jazz abstractions, which, as Dizzy used to put it, were designed to scare away no talent guys. Originally there might have been something too exclusive about it, but it's gotten pretty organized since then, and now it's a pretty profound effect on jazz. It seems to be the direction it's going in. You can't stop progress . . . Thelonious stands out because he's inconspicuous. He's the kind of a guy who thinks a lot. He doesn't say much. He just plays, and . . . here he is, I think you might like to meet him.

The audience applauded. Allen then engaged Monk in a discussion of his musical abilities.

Steve: "Monk, you're from New York, aren't you?"
Monk: "That's right."
Steve: " . . . did you just pick it up yourself or did you study?"

Monk: "I took lessons."

Steve: "Do you read well?"

Eddie Bert, who was playing trombone with Monk on this appearance, was aghast at the question. Monk was far from being an illiterate musician!

Monk: "Of course, sure." (He laughed, suggesting the question was embarrassing, silly, or both.)

Steve: "Some people say: 'Well, I don't.'"

Allen demonstrated some simple chord progressions on a piano to show the audience what it was *not* going to hear, and then he asked Monk if the modernists worked on harmonies? Monk hesitated.

Steve: "That's what I thought you'd say ... I wouldn't have phrased it quite that way ... Why don't you show them what the harmonic structure of the first tune will be so we'll get a little road map of what's to follow. What key are you working in?"

Monk: "D minor." Monk played the chord, said it again, followed it with D flat, then an F-sharp seven for the first chords of the song.

Steve: "And that's more or less it."

Monk: "That's it."

Steve: (to the audience) "That's the basic idea, those three chords. I hope you can keep track of them. Some of you aren't going to be able to make it. But don't feel bad. What's the name of this tune, Monk?"

Monk: "Off Minor."

He played it with the group, then followed it with a sparkling, effervescent "Well, You Needn't" at a fast tempo. Told the name of the song, Steve Allen quipped, "I'm sorry I did," getting a laugh from the audience, and introduced the group without saying what instruments they played; Monk was accompanied by Charlie Mingus on bass, Art Farmer on trumpet, Willie Jones on drums, Teo Macero on tenor saxophone, and Eddie Bert on trombone. "A good show," Eddie Bert recalled about the music played by the interracial group. Afterward, Eddie overheard Monk talking to someone about payment. Monk said, "What do you mean, scale?" referring to union scale; apparently, he expected better payment for his work. Eddie said, "I didn't wait to hear more. I split."

And so Monk had that precious bit of exposure on national TV and was given some attention by the mainstream entertainment world, enough to be able to afford to buy a black-and-white, 1955, Buick Riviera car. He was delighted and told Harry: "I got a car."

Harry said, "Oh!"

In his deep, flat, gruff voice, Monk said, "It's a prize-winning model."

Harry hated to think of Monk driving a car. He was already having some unusual spells, when he disconnected and stopped communicating with people altogether. Nellie told Harry that by the time he met Monk, Monk was already "mad as a hatter," Colomby recalled. The car turned out to be nothing but "trouble" in Harry's estimation. "There were plenty of tickets—tickets, tickets, tickets, parking tickets," Harry recalled. Once Monk hit a little girl. He felt so terrible that he grabbed her and took her to a hospital. She wasn't really hurt, but Monk was rattled. Harry hated that car. "Once I saw it in front of the Village Vanguard. The car had a broken lamp in front. It bothered me to see that. It attracted the police. It attracted trouble. I didn't want him to have that. [But Monk] loved that car. To him, it was like a house, a home," Harry said.

Early in 1956, Thelonious was driving record producer Orrin Keepnews home from Hackensack, New Jersey, where they had just completed one of Monk's recording sessions for the Riverside label. It had snowed during the sessions, and the roads were icy. Monk was following a car carrying bassist Oscar Pettiford and drummer Art Blakey, sidemen on the session. Another car came out of a side road and separated the sidemen from Monk. "Thelonious, alarmed at the thought of losing the others, swerved to pass the newcomer," Keepnews wrote years later, "and skidded sharply across the highway, stopping mere inches short of smashing into a telephone pole, and then calmly informed me: 'It's a good thing I was driving. If it had been someone else, we might be dead now.'" Keepnews had never been Monk's passenger before and afterward tried to forgo that pleasure as much as possible. Monk used to joke that he had taught Harry Colomby to drive, possibly because he knew that Colomby didn't think he was much of a driver.

One day, around this time, Thelonious was driving Nellie through Central Park, heading west to the Hotel Bolivar where his friend Nica, the Baroness Pannonica de Koenigswarter, lived. Monk stopped in the middle of the park, looked at Nellie, and asked, "Who are you?" Nellie knew there was trouble. They went to Nica's hotel, from which Nellie called Harry and told him the story. She said, "I don't think he should be alone."

Harry went there to find Dr. Robert Freymann attending to Monk. Nica had called the doctor, a general practitioner who at the time was well known for injecting his patients with special "vitamin shots" that, many years later, were revealed to contain large doses of amphetamines.[1]

"Thelonious was just off," Harry recalled, "laughing without reason, and Nellie was very disturbed. It was the first evidence of a mental episode. Before that day, it was just Thelonious Monk being a little eccentric or odd. She had not been disturbed enough by his behavior before to call me. But the day he didn't know her was a shock for her."

A day or two later, Monk was driving home in the rain when he had a collision with another driver just off the West Side Highway. Monk came sliding off the highway. Harry didn't know whose fault the accident was, but the other driver noticed something unusual about Monk and called the police. They arrived, tried to speak to Thelonious, who wouldn't talk to them, and took him to Bellevue. Nellie called Harry; distraught, they went to a police station on Amsterdam Avenue on the Upper West Side to find the car; on it there was a tag stating, "Psycho taken to Bellevue." Harry realized that his mission was becoming extremely complicated. Now he had to promote the career of a man who was becoming mentally ill.

It's likely that Monk's reaction had something to do with amphetamines. These drugs could have made him react with terror to the police interrogation, imagine he was being threatened, and render him unable to talk to the police when they approached him. Harry knew that

Monk standing with the Baroness Koenigswarter in the 5 Spot Club's kitchen/
dressing area, New York, March 21, 1967. Photo: Raymond Ross.

Monk was already a client or "patient" of Dr. Freymann, who obviously was "treating" his customers to something stronger than aspirin. Harry occasionally drove Monk with Nica to Freymann's office at 3 East 78th Street near the Stanhope Hotel on Fifth Avenue, across the street from the Metropolitan Museum of Art. Harry saw musicians nodding in the waiting room there, sitting next to socialite dowagers.

Nica herself was a socialite, a member of the powerful Rothschild banking family in Europe, a daughter of the English banker, Lord Nathaniel Charles Rothschild, and the sister of a jazz fan, the third Baron de Rothschild. She had driven ambulances for the French Resistance during World War II and married a hero of the Resistance, Jules de Koenigswarter. She had fallen in love with jazz and with jazz musicians themselves. A wealthy woman, she not only appreciated their music and enjoyed their company, but she also gave them money by drawing on her annual income from a trust fund—estimated by some people to be $200,000 a year. In any case, whatever the amount, it was a considerable sum in those years.

Nica had befriended Charlie Parker and probably fallen in love with him, though it was not the most opportune time in his life for him to have a romantic involvement with anyone because of his dependency on drugs and alcohol. But she had taken him into her suite at the Stanhope Hotel on Fifth Avenue when he was terribly sick in 1955. He died in her suite, as he was listening to music on the radio, she later told Max Gordon, owner of the Village Vanguard. The publicity did Nica's reputation absolutely no good. She would later say that her estranged husband—a stickler for details, punctuality, and orderliness—read a newpaper headline about Bird dying in her suite; the scandal prompted the baron to divorce her. They had had five children together, but she had not been able to stand her husband for years; she had not even wanted to marry him in the first place, because his values reminded her too much of the excessively orderly household she had grown up in as a privileged upper-class European. Her life style among jazz musicians was the antithesis of her upbringing.

From the vantage point of the jazz world, where she was very well-liked, she had saved the great Charlie Parker from an ignominious death in the street. The owners of the Stanhope Hotel didn't feel as grateful to her or as sanguine about the publicity and asked her to leave. Bird, too, had visited Dr. Freymann and may even have introduced Nica to him—or vice versa. She brought Monk to the office for the doctor's famous "vitamin" shots to help lift his mood.

Monk's erratic behavior at this time led to his hospitalization for "treatment." While Monk was undergoing his first hospitalization— "the most dramatic hospitalization for him, because it was his first," Harry said—Harry had to get someone to perform at Far Rockaway High School. Harry had booked Monk for a performance there, but he was in the hospital and couldn't keep the date. Harry went to visit Monk in the hospital. Monk said: "You've got to get me out of here." Harry saw that "Monk's head was clear; he put sentences together clearly, and he was actually normal. He had a slight lisp, and his bottom jaw wasn't lined up with his top precisely. He was a very shy person. And that probably affected his behavior."

When Monk was eventually released, he took a taxi home from the hospital and arrived with his coat over his shoulders. Harry and Jules Colomby were waiting for him. Monk hugged them and said, "Nothing should break us up." Harry found it very moving and thought Monk meant: "This is the kind of normal life that I want to have." It had been very frightening for him to be in a mental hospital. "He never talked about his daily experiences there, but he made it clear that it was a major relief for him to be out." He did say that there was a man who worked there, "Helpful Harry," Monk called him, for whom Monk was going to write a tune. But Monk brought home no diagnosis with him. Harry was very disappointed: "I had hoped they would keep him there longer and come up with a diagnosis."

During the years when Harry managed his career—and subsequently through the rest of his life—Monk would be hospitalized several times in a state of withdrawal, altogether at about half a dozen hospitals. One time Monk checked himself into a hospital; Harry thought that was a good sign. Curiously, the doctors always kept him under observation until he felt well again after a few days; but doctors came to no conclusion. Harry's private opinion of Monk's problems was: "It had to do with what he was taking." Nellie would eventually say the same thing to her son. She, too was perplexed by the doctors who never seemed to come to conclusions.

Monk's medical records were never made public.[4] However, the medical reports themselves made throughout Monk's life could only reflect what the doctors thought and what Monk had allowed them to glean from him. It's hard to imagine that Monk would have unburdened himself to doctors—undoubtedly white ones for the most part—when he talked about himself so little even to his best friends.

One psychiatrist compiled a lengthy report on Monk for Beth Israel Hospital where he worked on staff in the early 1970s when he treated Monk.[5] This doctor took into consideration reports from other hospitals where Monk had been a patient, which showed, in his opinion, that Monk had been misdiagnosed and incorrectly treated by previous doctors. The report states that Monk was neither schizophrenic nor manic depressive.

Many people who knew Monk and traveled with him on tours had no idea that the pianist had ever been hospitalized or had taken medicines. Monk didn't talk about it. But, from the mid-1950s on, many observers knew that Monk was by turns sometimes completely disconnected from his surroundings, or only partially in touch with them. Harry could recall a day when Nellie asked him to drive with Monk to the Bronx, because she didn't want Monk to go alone. The night before, there had been a fire in their apartment, and some of his music had burned, including a song that he had been preparing for a recording date. That date was postponed. His upright piano was either destroyed or damaged by the fire, too. On that trip, Monk drove like a madman, Harry recalled, but Monk was undoubtedly upset because of the fire.

On another day, Harry drove to the Bronx with Monk when, for no particular reason that Harry could see, Monk looked upset, or anyway had a very intense look on his face—an expression that Harry feared could attract attention from the police. Harry's worst fear was always the police, because they were so prone to pick on jazz musicians in those days. And Thelonious's size and expression were magnetic,

Harry believed. He actually feared a policeman might shoot Monk just because of his demeanor.

Harry began to watch Monk carefully for signs of his mental state. "It would usually take him a couple of days to come back to normal. I was always aware of a mental problem and looking for it. Sometimes a stress situation, someone dying, triggered it, but sometimes nothing that I could see upset him. Usually a spell was preceded by three days of no sleep," Harry recalled.

Monk's son Toot would recall for the documentary *Straight, No Chaser*, that it was frightening sometimes to look at his father and realize that he didn't have a clue about who his son was. Nellie didn't shield the children from the truth about their father when his behavior became bizarre. She made them face facts, telling them that their father took care of them when he could and that they must, in essence, treat him with respect.

Toot felt his father was odd for another reason. Although renowned musicians frequently came to the apartment, Thelonious was definitely not well known himself. He was playing in a different style from his friends. Toot was embarrassed by his father's difference; it took Toot many years to understand that his father was truly a genius and had followed the right course. Eventually, Toot could articulate his mature view: "Thelonious was far better focused than even Charlie Parker and Dizzy and those guys. He had struck the motherlode early in life. He had found a sound that was so unique and that everyone was looking for. And it was such a natural thing for him."

But Toot as a child also felt proud, because his father took Nellie and their children to gigs, even on the road occasionally. Toot didn't see any other musicians doing that with their families. At home, there were good times, too. Thelonious and Nellie played games with their kids, especially card games, all the time. "He and my mother spent thousands of dollars [in play money] playing hearts and spit [card games], and he was crazy about Yahtzee," a commercial Parchesi-type board game made by Parker Brothers that is played with dice. Toot thought his father, on balance, was actually "a very personable guy and a very good father."

Harry never saw Monk use anything stronger than pot. But he knew that Monk took all kinds of "stuff." When Monk reached a point where he felt sick from taking too much, he went to sleep. That was how Monk cured himself—at least temporarily. People gave Monk "stuff," Harry said, even heroin perhaps, beginning in the days before Harry met Monk. Nica might have given Monk pills, too, of some kind. Both she and Nellie were interested in herbal and natural medicines for healing and health maintenance, and they shared some doubts about traditional medicines.

Nellie did go along with traditional medicines in an attempt to help Thelonious. At some point during the years Harry managed Thelonious, from 1954 to 1967, Nellie even administered doctor-prescribed Thorazine, Harry thought, to Monk. "She had to get it into him before he had progressed into one of his spells. Otherwise he wouldn't take it, claiming that it was no good for him," Harry recalled.

Toot would remember his mother blaming Thelonious's troubles—his disconnection and, as time went by, hallucinations and odd remarks—on all the drugs he took. "Nothing good ever came out of whatever he took. It made him worse," Harry Colomby summed up. Nellie also recalled Monk taking a test that prompted a doctor, or doctors, to suggest he take "megadoses of vitamins." She didn't know if they worked because she didn't know what they were supposed to do for him, she said.

If Monk had begun taking various drugs to try to make himself feel that he belonged to the community and was one of the fellows, and to lift his spirits and try to allay the extremely depressing hardships in his career—and those were likely motives, in addition to his urge to experiment and have a good time—the drugs had the opposite effect on him; he was too sensitive, intellectually preoccupied, and withdrawn into his musical creations to withstand the stress of taking drugs. Amphetamines alone would have made it difficult, even impossible at times, for him to maintain his somewhat tenuous connection to the everyday world.

Harry Colomby didn't really think Monk took drugs primarily to be one of the guys. Instead, Harry thought Monk was "just a curious guy who saw himself on the cutting edge of things. He didn't really want to belong to the group; he said he was taking so much to show that he could take more than other people." Harry's perception fit in with other people's assessment of Monk's personality, from his sister Marion, who knew how competitive Monk felt, to Steve Lacy, a saxophonist, who would play with Monk later and observe that Monk dabbled in everything just to try it out. But their perceptions don't preclude the possibility that Monk used drugs in the hope they would help him overcome his shyness; he showed off to the group to become a part of it, even if the part he wanted to belong to was at the head of the vanguard.

And there were times when Monk seemed to handle drugs very well. Harry recalled that Monk came back from playing in Boston one time and told the story of having met a Harvard professor of psychology. "Monk always was proud of having some kind of academic recognition and connection. It turned out the guy he was talking about was Timothy Leary," Harry said. "Leary invited Monk to his house after the show. Monk said, 'He gave me some mushrooms to take and see what happened. He took a couple and got stoned. I took the whole jar, and it didn't do shit to me.'" This happened at a time just before Leary began using LSD. Harry thought: "It was a strange, racist thing that went on. Someone said to himself: 'Here's an interesting black musician; let's give him drugs and see what [they do].'"

In 1956, Nellie developed a thyroid disorder—a hyperactive thyroid, as she would recall—that required surgery. (A person may be genetically predisposed to the disease, but it is frequently brought on by a shock.) She had to go to Roosevelt Hospital. Her brother Sonny visited Monk on West 63rd Street. Monk was very upset when he returned from a visit to the hospital, Harry noticed. He was sweating and pacing, emotionally overwrought, and he kept his hat and coat on in the house. He kept working on his song, "Crepuscule [Twilight] with Nellie," spending a long time on the bridge, the "inside," until he got it the way he wanted it. At one point he said to Harry, "I'm drunk and dangerous." Monk hated the thought of Nellie being in the hospital. He was afraid she would die and leave him alone. He got her out of there as quickly as he could. Harry was under the impression that Monk insisted she come home a little earlier than her doctor might have liked.

Notes

Personal interviews: Harry Colomby, Nellie Smith Monk, Johnny Griffin, Eddie Bert, Dr. Everett Dulit, Marion Monk White, Steve Lacy, Thelonious Sphere Monk Jr.

1. The label was supposed to be Signal, and the tunes were "Brake's Sake," "Gallop's Gallop," "Shuffle Boil," and "Nica's Tempo," Harry recalled; the recordings eventually came out on Savoy in 1955.

2. Keepnews (1986).

3. In 1972, *New York Times* reporter Boyce Rensberger wrote an exposé about Dr. Max Jacobson, stating: "For many years Dr. Max Jacobson, a seventy-two-year-old general practitioner in New York, has been injecting amphetamine—the powerful stimulant the drug culture calls speed—into tens of dozens of the country's most celebrated artists, writers, politicians and jet setters." Following this article, reports flowed into the *Times* about a number of other doctors, one of them Dr. Freymann, Monk's doctor, who were also giving amphetamine-laced vitamin shots to their patients. A second story appeared in March 1973, stating "According to former patients, [Freymann has] provided amphetamine injections routinely to a large number of patients, many of them prominent in artistic and social circles and some of them heavily dependent on the drug." The side effects of regular use of amphetamine seem remarkably like the strange symptoms that Monk began exhibiting at this time. Rensberger noted, " Longterm use can lead to heavy dependence and such toxic side effects as behavioral changes resembling paranoid schizophrenia. Attempts to quit the drug can produce such a profound depression that a number of users have committed suicide." At first, amphetamine users felt euphoria, but when they crashed, they suffered from nausea, chills, sweating, headaches, anxiety, total despair, and physical exhaustion. Amphetamines were not illegal, but state and federal restrictions were tightening at that time. Other doctors had been convicted and lost their licenses for selling speed at ten to twenty-five dollars a prescription. Medical associations could expel doctors but could not stop them from practicing. Born in Leipzig, Germany, Freymann, sixty-seven at the time of the news release, had been in trouble with authorities as early as 1963 for procuring and performing abortions and for such unprofessional conduct as administering narcotic drugs to people who were known narcotics users. Freymann "denied wrongdoing" and said he used amphetamines to treat obesity, depression, and "just a tired, generally rundown feeling." He said he would give Desoxyn to any addict who said he was tired.

4. Monk could have waived his right to privacy while he was alive, but he died without waiving that right. Under New York State law, according to a lawyer for New York State Surrogate Court in Manhattan, only Monk's heirs have the right to make the information public. Monk's son and legal heir doesn't want to make the family matter public even though his father was a public figure.

5. The doctor was constrained by law from releasing the contents of his report to the author. However, another doctor who knew about Monk's case discussed the subject with Dr. Everett Dulit, who discussed some of these findings with the author.

At the Five Spot

In 1956, following his debut album of jazz standards for Riverside, Monk recorded an album, *Brilliant Corners*, a breakthrough performance for him, of extremely complex, original music. He was accompanied by Sonny Rollins on tenor saxophone, Ernie Henry on alto saxophone, Max Roach on drums, and Oscar Pettiford on bass. In his liner notes, Orrin Keepnews wrote that the *Brilliant Corners* album was "the real beginning" of his work with Monk.

The album featured many new original compositions by Monk, written in his characteristic spiky style. "Blues Bolivar Ba-lues-are" is a blues named for the Hotel Bolivar, where Nica rented a suite, after she left the Stanhope and then the Algonquin hotels. The Algonquin had objected to Monk's wandering around the lobby in a bright red shirt, Nica said. Monk's appearance had frightened some guests, who packed and left. (One can't help but imagine that there was an element of racial prejudice in the attitude of the guests, though Monk's singular appearance surely didn't help him blend in with the conservative ambience.) There was another blues on the album, "Bemsha Swing" composed by Monk with his friend, drummer Denzil Best, and Monk's ballad, "Pannonica," written for the baroness.

"I had no way of foreseeing how incredibly more difficult this would be for me," wrote Keepnews about producing his first album of Monk's original music. Monk's first recordings for the label had been of Ellington's music and standard popular songs, with which the label, and Monk, too, hoped to take the edge off Monk's image as an exotic in the jazz world. "Basically, dealing with Monk in full-scale action meant that it was my job to supervise and control the creative flow of recording sessions that involved a perfectionist leader driving a group of sensitive and highly talented artists beyond their limits," Keepnews wrote. At the time, Monk couldn't understand that his music could stymie players.

Keepnews described the session for the song "Brilliant Corners," which the group attempted at least 25 times during four hours in the studio:

> The composition is incredibly tricky; it has an off-center rhythmic pattern; and every second chorus is played at doubled tempo. The mere fact that such thorough professionals as Roach and Rollins and Pettiford were unable to satisfy Thelonious says all that need be said about the immensity of their task .... Late in the evening, Pettiford and the leader exchanged harsh words, leading to an amazing situation that perhaps could only have happened on this night. During one take, we in the control room were sure the bass mike was malfunctioning; Oscar was obviously playing, but not a sound could be heard. The unpleasant truth was that the bassist actually was not playing; he was merely pantomiming quite convincingly. [Not surprisingly, this was the last time Monk and Pettiford ever worked together.]
> When we finally quit, I was aware that several portions had been very excitingly executed; I could only hope that the pieces could be welded together—in particular, that one abruptly concluded opening chorus could be used as an ending ... it all succeeded far beyond expectations. The finished product still sounds quite miraculous to me.

After he left school on the day of that session, Harry Colomby went to the studio. Colomby overheard Oscar Pettiford make some remarks

Sonny Rollins, c. mid-'50s. Courtesy of the Institute of Jazz Studies, Rutgers University.

about "Brilliant Corners"—there were not enough bars, and the music was wrong, Pettiford said. As time went on, Monk became upset and said to Harry, "Why is this happening to me?" Ernie Henry also had a big problem with the music. Thelonious got more and more tense. "I think he was embarrassed," Harry recalled, "not mad at the guys, but embarrassed that his date was turning into [a frustrating scene], and he wondered, 'Is there something unplayable here?' Oscar turned into a

Art Blakey. Photo: Raymond Ross.

rebel. Max Roach was laughing at the conflict. Sonny was more
helpful. I don't know what the musical problem was, a difficult passage
to play. They stopped, started, stopped. I really felt awful and left. 'Brilliant Corners,' that tune was a killer."

Preparing for *Brilliant Corners*, Monk had carefully considered which
musicians he would like to play on the album. He remembered Ernie
Henry, with his traditional blues-based approach. In a rare burst of

enthusiasm and determination, Monk commandeered Harry Colomby and said, "Let's find Ernie Henry. I used to play with him." Harry had never heard of Henry, but Monk insisted. Usually Monk didn't undertake a great search for a sideman for a group. This time he directed Colomby to drive and drive on a rainy day, until they located Ernie at his father's basement apartment in Brooklyn. Ernie was not playing much professionally at that time because he had been ill from his heroin addiction. Monk brought him back onto the scene. (Ernie Henry would later be found dead from an overdose in Bickford's cafeteria.)

Henry made an ideal contrast for the modernist Sonny Rollins, another inspired choice by Monk. Rollins was not only a great player leading his own groups, but he could perform Monk's music, interpreting it correctly as part of a team, without sublimating his own, enormous strengths. He was considered to be the most important young tenor saxophonist in jazz at the time, and he would not be overshadowed as an innovator by John Coltrane for several more years. Monk loved Sonny Rollins's playing most of all, a style directly connected to and blending the jazz traditions of Coleman Hawkins, Lester Young, Dexter Gordon, Charlie Parker, and Gene Ammons.

Brilliant Corners—a fully realized, self-sufficient project—called attention to Monk as a composer, as his interpretations of Duke Ellington and popular standards had not done. The album was released in 1957 and received critical acclaim. Nat Hentoff, reviewing the music for *Down Beat*, gave it five stars. In 1959, Monk would record similar additional music for an album which, together with *Brilliant Corners*, would be named *Brilliance*.

Soon after recording the song "Brilliant Corners," Monk went to Birdland to see Clark Terry, the trumpeter and fluegelhornist, who was playing there in Dizzy's group. Monk said to Clark, "Man, I want you to be on my record date." Clark said "Cool." After the show ended at Birdland that night, Monk took Clark to the baroness's apartment to discuss recording together. A fire was burning in the fireplace; Monk started throwing things on the flames to make them change colors from blue to yellow, without speaking. "We sat there for hours and literally said nothing to each other," Clark recalled. When he looked out the window and saw that it was bright daylight at about 8 A.M., Clark said, "It's getting past eight, I have to drive to Queens." Monk said, "Okay, "I'll see you on the date." And they played together on the songs "Bemsha Swing" and "I Surrender Dear" on December 7, 1956. Clark later realized that Monk hadn't really wanted to talk about the music; he had just wanted to see if Clark really wanted to do the date. Clark very much wanted to do it.

Without telling Harry Colomby, Monk decided to play as a sideman for an Atlantic recording session for his old friend, Art Blakey, with the Jazz Messengers in 1957. Monk and Art played so well together that Monk wouldn't have dreamed of refusing to do that date. And the music turned out to be superb. Critics said that Blakey was the best drummer ever to play with Monk. Blakey kept framed photographs of Monk, and only Monk, on a wall in his apartment. Even though Monk appeared on the album cover with Art, Harry Colomby was furious with Monk for working and receiving only union scale pay for a sideman. Harry knew that Art had talked Monk into doing the date out of friendship. Nevertheless, Harry called Nesuhi Ertegun at Atlantic, and "I called him an exploiter," Harry recalled, though it hadn't been Ertegun's fault. "He felt bad."

Clark Terry may have already invited Monk to play for his album, which would be called, *In Orbit*, for Riverside, to be done in May 1958. Orrin Keepnews suggested that Clark use Monk, and Clark was glad to agree. Harry Colomby wasn't so angry about Monk playing as a sideman that time, because at least the date was for the Riverside label, to which Monk was signed as an artist. Keepnews, producer of the sessions, recalled that Monk had received no more than twice union scale for working with Terry. Because Monk didn't shoulder the responsibilities of a group leader, the recordings turned out to be "the most relaxed, happiest and funkiest Monk performances I ever witnessed," Orrin wrote in his fascinating, historic liner notes, an intimate view of Monk, for the collection *Thelonious Monk: The Complete Riverside Recordings*.

When Monk was not playing or composing at home, working in little clubs on weekends for small fees, or hanging out in clubs, listening to his friends play, he frequently visited the baroness in her suite at the Hotel Bolivar. Sometimes he fell asleep there with his clothes on. Nica told Harry Colomby that Monk exuded strength. "It's true he had almost a royal appearance," Colomby recalled. "Part of it might have been his mental condition, because he looked impenetrable. Nica claimed she stopped drinking because of her friendship with Monk. He had that charisma. So did Miles."

British-born Marian McPartland, the jazz pianist, recalled meeting Nica in the 1960s, when Marian was playing at the Hickory House in midtown Manhattan. Actually Nica still liked to drink. One night, Marian saw Nica sitting in her Rolls Royce outside Birdland. Nica called, "Marian, I want to talk to you." Marian got into the front seat. Nica said, "I have something to show you," and she produced a beautifully bound leather book, which she opened. In a niche was a bottle of good whiskey. She and Marian shared a few drinks during Marian's intermission. "Nica had long, black hair hanging down her back and a very upper-class British accent. And she would swear away. I used to get so amused by her," Marian said.

Marian also thought, "Nica liked black men." Harry Colomby believed that Nica, like many Europeans, put black American jazz musicians on pedestals and glamorized them. She was drawn to them, in part, because they symbolized rebellion. She was a rebel, "an eccentric, interesting lady," he said. The Hotel Bolivar, on Central Park West, came to take a dim view of the parties she gave. Idrees Sulieman remembered one happy party at which he saw Monk but not Nellie. The police came at the request of the neighbors, probably because of the noise. Nica gave the cops photographs of Louis Armstrong and they went away happy. But Nica decided she wanted to move. She soon ensconced herself in a house in Weehawken, New Jersey, with a panoramic view of the Hudson River and the Manhattan skyline. There her friends could come and go, and nobody could tell her what to do. Monk was one of her frequent visitors.

Harry and most of Monk's friends, unlike Monk's sister Marion, thought there was nothing but friendship—no romance at all—between Monk and Nica. Monk was clearly enthralled by Nica's wealthy and powerful family background. The wealth of the Rothchilds had changed the balance of power between European countries; a person with any other name would not have been as fascinating to him. And Nica idolized Monk, catered to him, and supported his career; she was always looking for little ways to please him. Monk was not the only musician on whom she lavished affection and gifts; Art Blakey, as only one example, received at least two cars as presents from Nica.' But Monk appreciated Nica's generosity and support of his career, and he came to trust Nica with his welfare.

At this time, Harry also observed that Monk was depressed and behaving strangely in his family's small apartment on 63rd Street— though not because of the apartment. "He was just depressed in general in that period. He felt connected to the apartment and the neighborhood; he felt good about both of them," Harry Colomby remembered. Monk's malaise came from within, not from his living quarters or family connections. "Nellie did the best she could," Harry said.

Nica was becoming, with Nellie's approval, a member of the Monk family's inner circle. Harry thought that Nellie actually felt grateful for some of the help and attention that Nica gave Monk. The women didn't plan it, Harry thought; their cooperation just happened. Otherwise, Nellie had a full-time vocation nurturing Monk through their lean years and his increasing instability and depression over, for one thing, his inability to make as big an impression as some of his less-talented contemporaries had done.

Paul Jeffrey, the tenor saxophonist who would play in Monk's group in the 1970s, gave a brilliant explanation of the everyday realities that bothered Monk:

> There's a whole litany of things germane to a black person who is a genius living in this society. There's the inequity of the sociological status of black people here. . . . An ordinary person can more or less . . . get along, but it's really hard for someone with [Monk's] amount of ability. A couple of times, from things he said, I got that feeling—that things the average person would feel

uncomfortable with but pass over really affected him. Because he knew the worth of his contribution; he knew he was contributing something; he always knew. If he hadn't known, he would have given up, with all the adverse conditions ... He said something one time to me: "You know, if I hadn't made it playing music, I would have been the biggest bum in the world." That meant to me that nothing else really mattered to him; he was going to play music.

In short, because Monk was a genius—and a black genius of awesome dimensions physically and artistically—he had a far harder time convincing people, both African American and white—but especially white people in positions of influence and power—to let him emerge and find his place in the sun.

All the while, Harry was thinking about how he could get Monk's cabaret card back. He and Monk knew it was the *sine qua non* to further Monk's career. "He needed to have a place to open in New York to get a card," Harry recalled. "In those days you had to have an urgent need to get a card in time for a gig coming up. I was driving by the Five Spot one day, a tiny place on Cooper Square, and I heard music coming from the place. I stopped and went in and saw David Amram playing an upright piano. The place seated fifty people. The Termini brothers, Iggy and Joe, had inherited the place from their father."

It was a bar where Greenwich Village painters went in the afternoons to socialize with their friends. The African American poet, Imamu Amiri Baraka, who then called himself Leroi Jones, hung out there. Many intellectuals and artists who lived in the neighborhood liked to go to the Five Spot—just a little, unpretentious saloon, not really a jazz club. But Harry envisioned lines forming outside the place for Thelonious Monk. "People would say, 'Monk is working there,' and they would show up. It would be perfect for Monk, who needed a card and would be happy to play at the Five Spot for months at a time. Monk didn't like traveling. It was scary for him," Colomby recalled, in part because of the antipathy Monk encountered as an African American man and a jazz musician in some cities.

L to r: Iggy Termini, "Sonny" Canterino, and Joe Termini photographed on January 5, 1976. Joe and Iggy owned the 5 Spot; "Sonny" with his father Frank and his younger brother Mike owned the Half Note club. Photo: Raymond Ross.

Harry had to lie to get Monk's cabaret card from the police department, so Monk could work in clubs again. Harry swore up and down that Monk was clean. Harry was a teacher; if he had been involved with any drugs, he would have lost his living, his reputation, his teaching license—everything. Harry took the risk of lying, because he was convinced that Thelonious was "a unique presence in the fight for the future. He symbolized a regal presence; he stood up for things and did things his way. He was a man. He stood up straight. He was a role model, a black man to look up to. Whites were the jazz fans. I would see Blakey [and other musicians] in the audience for Monk. There was something about the way people regarded Monk. His inarticulateness symbolized something for them."

To get the cabaret card back, Colomby went to the State Liquor Authority, got an application, filled it out, and stated why the card was lost in the first place. In need of a couple of letters to accompany the application, Harry put in a letter saying that he was a teacher and vouching that Thelonious didn't take drugs. Joe Termini went to Carmine de Sapio, the Democratic boss in the Village at that time. A little money—a few dollars, as Harry recalled—was paid, and Monk had his card back. It has usually been reported that the baroness helped Monk get it back, but she didn't have the necessary political connections. "She would have been an obstacle, if anything—a rich white woman looking for a cabaret card for Monk," Harry believed.

The word got around about his opening on July 19th at the Five Spot at Five Cooper Square; as Colomby predicted, there were lines outside. Suddenly in 1957, Monk became successful, winning space and flattering attention in the press. The Termini brothers expanded the room, so that it could seat 75 people, and replaced the old upright with a grand piano. Later they got another, lighter colored, better piano for the club; Harry thought it was a Baldwin, and that company also gave Monk a grand piano for his apartment.[2] Monk was soon being paid $600 or $650 a week; out of that came taxes, sidemen salaries of about $200 altogether, and Colomby's percentage. By the time Monk got his cut, it was a little more than $250. "He wasn't making much," Harry recalled. (It wasn't until the 1960s, when Monk would play in a new Five Spot club opened near the original bar that he got a percentage of the gate. Once the Termini brothers made their nut, they gave Monk 50 percent. Then Monk came away with about $1,500 for himself.) "It was a tiny, friendly place," Harry recalled about the Five Spot—both the first and the second club. But most of all, for Monk, it was an important engagement; the place became world-renowned among jazz fans, recording executives, and jazz fans in general.

The New Yorker magazine, a Baedeker for hip urbanites, soon added the Five Spot to its list of "Goings On About Town," under "Mostly For Music," describing the club as epitomizing "Greenwich Village of 'The Iceman Cometh' period and decor, but full of questing youth.

The accompanying jazz, which is over the hills and far away, comes from the quintet of Thelonious Monk [actually a quartet], whose office hours are rarely the same on two consecutive evenings. Mondays are assigned to Mal Waldron's band . . ."

Monk's group included bassist Wilbur Ware to start, but he didn't last for the entire engagement. Colomby recalled that one night, after the first set, Ware's bass was simply left lying on the bandstand; he was strung out on drugs at the time. Bassist Ahmed Abdul-Malik was his replacement. The first drummer was Shadow Wilson.[3]

Tenor saxophonist John Coltrane was a key member of Monk's first group. Monk wanted Sonny Rollins to play with the group, but he wasn't available at that time. Coltrane was free to play with Monk, because he hadn't been invited to play, as he had the year before, with Miles Davis's group. Sonny played with Miles in the summer of 1957, and then he kept himself busy with his own groups and studio recording dates. Coltrane, a relative newcomer, was about to establish himself, and he learned a great deal working with Monk's group.

At the Five Spot, Monk quickly affirmed his position as a fascinating musician and eccentric personality, arriving late for the gig most nights and dancing around on stage, while his sidemen took solos. Other musicians quickly realized that Monk was crazy like a fox. He knew exactly what he was doing; in his own way, he had come to understand exactly how to put on a mesmerizing show. Other people thought that Monk was simply extremely eccentric, even nutty, but the musicians trusted their instincts about Monk's antics.

Coltrane became well loved in Monk's group. One night, Coltrane didn't show up for Monk's gig. People shouted to find out what had happened: "We want to hear Coltrane!" Finally Monk answered from the stage: "Coltrane bust up his horn." The people called out, "What does that mean?" Monk replied, "What does that mean? Mr. Coltrane plays a wind instrument. The sound is produced by blowing in it and opening different holes to let air out. Over some of these holes is a felt pad. One of these felt pads has fallen off, and in order for him to get the sound he wants, so that we can make better music for you, he is in back making a new one. You dig?"[4]

John Coltrane at the Half Note. Photo: Raymond Ross.

Eventually Coltrane discussed the techniques and artistic elements he had learned from Monk—how to play two notes on his saxophone at one time, and how to use space for drama and suspense. Coltrane was quoted in *Down Beat*:

> Working with Monk brought me close to a musical architect of the highest order. I felt I learned from him in every way— through the senses, theoretically, technically. I would talk to Monk about musical problems, and he would sit at the piano and show me the answers just by playing them. I could watch him play and found out the things I wanted to know. Also, I could see a lot of things that I didn't know about at all.
>
> Monk was one of the first to show me [in 1957] how to make two or three notes at a time on tenor. . . . It's done by false fingering and adjusting your lip. If everything goes right, you can get triads. Monk just looked at my horn and "felt" the mechanics of what had to be done to get this effect.[1]

Monk at the Five Spot wore wonderful clothes: fur or silk hats, sunglasses with bamboo rims; he had learned to look and act the part of a celebrity, as he had acquired the ability to take charge of his destiny as a masterful musician onstage with the canniness to communicate, in his own labyrinthian way, with audiences. No matter what the critics would write about him from then on, Monk had arrived; the unique sound of his music held people in thrall, and he commanded attention at the helm of his group. The first Five Spot gig that year lasted until October.

In the studio, Riverside had already recorded "Monk's Mood" with Coltrane in Monk's group in mid-April, 1957, "Ruby, My Dear," with Wilbur Ware and Art Blakey in the group, and then "Ruby, My Dear" (again), "Trinkle Tinkle," and "Nutty," with Coltrane, Monk, Ware, and drummer Shadow Wilson, probably in July 1957. The sessions with Coltrane were so good that it may have inspired Monk to invite the saxophonist to join the group for the Five Spot job later that month. Both drummers Philly Joe Jones and Shadow Wilson played with

Monk in the club that year. The group with Philly Joe never made a recording live from the Five Spot. And Coltrane never recorded for a record label with Monk live from the Five Spot—probably because Coltrane was signed by that time with the Prestige label, and Monk was with Riverside. The legend is that Prestige's owner, Bob Weinstock, would allow Coltrane to record as Monk's sideman at the Five Spot only if Monk would play as a sideman for a Coltrane record date; Monk refused.

But years after Monk and Coltrane died, a tape of one of their performances at the club surfaced. Naima Coltrane, the saxophonist's first wife, had taped the legendary group in the summer of 1957 A CD culled from this tape called *Discovery!*, with Monk, Coltrane, bassist Ahmed Abdul-Malik, and drummer Roy Haynes was released on the Blue Note label in 1993. Without the emotional constraints and technical smoothness of a formal studio recording, the moodiness, exoticism, and adventurousness of the music—and indeed of the era itself—transcended Naima's simple equipment. The group probed Monk's music unselfconsciously, with palpable freedom. Among the pieces they played that night were "I Mean You," a whimsical figure that, with Coltrane's relentless tenor work, had its level of intensity upped a millionfold; "Trinkle Tinkle," which was transmuted into a relentless, edgy piece; and the grave and stately ballad "Crepuscule with Nellie."

There was one frenzied incident involving Monk and Philly Joe Jones at that time. The Five Spot gig was really supposed to be Shadow Wilson's, but Philly Joe took his place for a while. On his first night, he was surprised when he collected his fee; Philly Joe thought it was too little money. Shadow Wilson had arranged the fee, but Philly Joe, always a volatile character, blamed Monk and got so angry about it that he hit Monk. Protective of his hands, Monk fended off Philly Joe by picking up a chair. Joe Termini may have been hit with the chair when he got in the middle and tried to try to break up the fight—that was the story Monk later told Paul Jeffrey—or Termini may simply have witnessed the fight from across the club. Harry Colomby recalled thinking that Philly Joe had been playing too loudly for Monk's music, and the fight might have sprung from that. There was some shoving, with Monk holding a chair aloft. "It was a quick fight in the back somewhere, nothing really," Harry recalled. Nobody was hurt. Termini didn't get in the middle. He spent most of his time "in the front, breathing heavily, looking at his watch, and worrying about them getting on the stage," Harry recalled. Monk and Philly Joe's friendship survived in the long run, too, and, great admirers of each others as musicians, they played together again years later.

In June 1957, shortly before the Five Spot triumph, Coleman Hawkins recorded "Ruby, My Dear," with Monk as the leader, accompanied by Ware and Art Blakey. Monk loved his mentor and never forgot the early support that Hawkins had given him. It is probably testimony to Monk's love and respect for Hawk that, more than twenty years later, when Monk was in a hospital suffering from a very bad spell of withdrawal, he played this recording of "Ruby, My Dear" that he had made with Hawk—and only this version—over and over again.

Monk's success at the Five Spot led him to be included in all kinds of things he had been left out of during the first forty years of his life. He played for the CBS production "The Sound of Jazz," aired on December 7, 1957, as part of the acclaimed "Seven Lively Arts" series. On the program, Count Basie and a group of other musicians gathered around Monk, who was playing solo piano on "Blue Monk." Basie looked mesmerized, and the others swayed their bodies and heads to Monk's rhythms, while Monk kept shuffling his big, right foot as if it were a coxswain's paddle propelling the rhythm under the vessel of the piano.

Harry Colomby later recalled how nervous he had been as the day of the show's taping approached. Would Monk do well? Harry wasn't even certain Monk would show up; he had missed a rehearsal date for the show, and the producers, one of whom was Nat Hentoff, used pianist Mal Waldron instead. But for the live show on Sunday, Monk made sure to be on the scene. Nellie told Hentoff that Monk had stayed up the entire previous Saturday night to be sure to get to the job. Hentoff would later ruminate that Monk's periods of withdrawal may have been "a low energy thing" that alternated with his bursts of creativity.

Harry Colomby was delighted to see Monk sitting at the piano, turning in a wonderful performance; everything was going smoothly. "What's there to worry about?" he asked himself. Afterward, Monk told Harry he was annoyed that Basie had pulled up a seat close to the piano and looked at him throughout the performance. "The next time he plays someplace, I'm going to look at him," Monk said. What Monk didn't understand, Colomby thought, was that the CBS crew might have positioned Basie next to him to add some drama and activity to the solo piano performances. Furthermore, Basie was better known than Monk, and his appearance might have made Thelonious seem more acceptable and glamorous to the public.

The next year, Monk led his group at the Newport Jazz Festival for the first time. That year, a film was made of the festival called *Jazz on a Summer's Day*. Louis Armstrong, Anita O'Day, and Mahalia Jackson, among others, introduced audiences to the charm of the festival and the glories of jazz. Monk, however, was not featured on screen; his music served as a mood-setting soundtrack for shots of Newport and people at play there. John S. Wilson, critic for *The New York Times*, reviewed the festival's tribute to Duke Ellington and the Mahalia Jackson concert at length, reserving only a few words of praise for Monk as one of the best modernists at the festival: "The most successful individualists and groups were those whose playing has been honed and molded with a definite, strongly projected style. The strikingly original pianist Thelonious Monk (and two other groups) made their points quickly and most effectively." At last the *Times* had given the nod to Monk, heralding him as a brilliant *arriviste*.

Both the 1958 Newport festival film and "The Sound of Jazz" became classic jazz movies watched by many people who may never have seen another jazz documentary—or even a jazz performance—in their lives.

In 1958, when Coltrane returned to work with Miles, Monk needed another tenor saxophonist for his return engagement at the Five Spot. Monk again approached Sonny Rollins, whom he admired for his transcendent vitality and naturalness, but Rollins was still not available. However Johnny Griffin had just come back to town.

Griffin had first met Monk in the 1940s in New York. Then, in late 1955 or early 1956, they had played together in Chicago, where Monk had needed a tenor man for a group. Wilbur Ware, already in the group, called Griffin to play at Chicago's popular Bee Hive club with Monk. Monk would later tell Nat Hentoff how much he had enjoyed working with Ware and Griffin there.

Griffin quickly learned that Monk's enunciation of words wasn't very clear at times; his speech made it difficult for Griffin to understand any directions Monk might toss out. But Monk communicated brilliantly through his music; he was one of the musicians Griffin admired most, and he had been delighted and excited about playing with Monk. Griffin never thought that Monk was at all crazy, "not ever, not ever. He was well aware of what was going on, very intelligent, learned, and coherent when he wanted to do something. He had a way of putting people off, because he couldn't support idiots. He had that mask; he walked around looking like Jomo Kenyatta." Monk wasn't very verbal, Griffin allowed. When Griffin didn't want to say something too revelatory in an interview about Monk, the saxophonist answered with a laugh, "It's beyond words."

There were times that musicians played Monk's songs for him, and Monk told them they were playing the wrong chords; that was often the end of his contact with musicians who were too intimidated to try again. But that didn't occur in Johnny's relationship with Monk.

Griffin was playing with Art Blakey's Jazz Messengers in 1957 and knew what close friends Art and Monk were, always asking each other to play with their groups. When the Jazz Messengers returned to New York from California, Johnny stayed at Art Blakey's house on Central Park West and 110th Street. He went to Birdland one night, where he saw Nica. She had bought a Bentley convertible "to race Art Blakey in his Cadillac," Johnny remembered, "because her Rolls Royce was not as fast as Blakey's Cadillac." (For a brief time Nica, like many others, tried managing Blakey's group, but she had not been good at the job. She and Blakey may even have had a public row, possibly about a matter related to the management situation.)

Monk and Johnny Griffin (background). Courtesy of the Institute of Jazz Studies, Rutgers University.

Nica told Johnny, "Come with me. I want to go down to the Five Spot. I want to show you my new car, and I want to catch Monk's last set." Johnny said "Okay." They got in her car at 52nd Street and Broadway, and she went flying straight down Broadway at 2 A.M.; Johnny didn't think she stopped at one red light. "She scared me to death," he said. "By the time we got to the Five Spot, the band was coming off the bandstand. The people were applauding. Monk saw Nica, then me, and he said, 'Hmmm, Johnny Griffin ain't afraid of John Coltrane.' I said, 'Ooooooh.' He was always like that, like a devil, like a kid—mischievous, oh definitely, with a twinkle in his eye to see what reaction he was going to get out of people."

Griffin was not surprised when he learned Monk once said to a journalist that he loved good actors: "Monk was an actor, always acting. He had no pretensions. He was natural, but he was acting, always on stage. And Monk was always making his gestures, getting up, dancing around in circles, patting his foot, stomping his heels. He was always like that. He didn't do anything without reason. He didn't play an extra note on the piano. He used space like a genius, and he taught a lot of musicians—Miles Davis and others—about space." (Miles Davis confirmed Griffin's opinion in several interviews.)

Leaving Art Blakey in 1957, Griffin went to Chicago to play with Gene Ammons and Lester Young, spending the winter there, then returned to New York in the spring. Monk heard that Griffin was back in town and called him at Art Blakey's house. "He asked would I come play in his band at the Five Spot," Griffin recalled. "I said I'll be down there." Dizzy then called and asked Griffin to play in his band, but Griffin said it was too late; he was going to work with Thelonious.

When he hired Griffin, Monk used his classic method of teaching other musicians his tunes. He had sculpted his songs in all their three-dimensional glory, and he didn't want them merely read in a two-dimensional form on paper. He wanted the musicians to have depth perception. "Monk never rehearsed with me," Griffin recalled:

> He would play a tune, and I was supposed to repeat what he had played in that first chorus. Now, can you imagine Monk's music? Maybe I had never heard the tune. So I made mistakes. And he played and stopped when I made mistakes, and he'd play the music again. And maybe I'd make another mistake. And he'd stop it again. Now, the joint is loaded. And at the same time, he has the written music in his portfolio on the piano. I told him, "Hey, T-bone, give me the music. I can read it."
>
> He said, "No no no no no, it's better if you hear it."
>
> Now, the people are sitting there. The Five Spot is loaded. And a couple of the tunes could last a whole set. I'm still playing some-

thing wrong, whether it's the melody, the rhythm, or maybe I'd
soloed wrong, because it could be I had the melody right but the
harmony changed, and the melody's the same, 'cause there's a
couple of tricky tunes he's got like that. Not once was I ever embarrassed. The people loved it. It was the same mess. I'm messing up.
But I never felt embarrassed. I felt "what the hell," 'til I got it right.

Critics and fans admired Johnny Griffin as a dazzling, flashy, exciting
player, and he definitely brightened Monk's music—but perhaps he
wasn't the team player that Sonny Rollins was. Griffin's explanation
made clear why he sometimes seemed, to some critical ears, to be
playing his own ideas, solos that had, perhaps, less to do with Monk's
tunes than they could have. Griffin would have been helped immea-
surably in his improvisation, he thought, if he had been allowed to read
the music. Some musicians proved to be better at learning Monk's
music by ear, some by eye. However, Monk never criticized Griffin's
work, and he must have been satisfied with his performances.

Griffin enjoyed the gig for the music and the company. After work,
he, Monk, and Art Blakey went to Blakey's house and "argued" all
night, Griffin said; they got steamed up when they talked about the
difficulties they had encountered with the people who ran the clubs,
record executives, managers, and other businesspeople, and they
compared notes about how they were being treated unfairly. "That's
when Monk talked, when he was around people he liked," Griffin
recalled. Monk might not say a word in a room filled with musicians
talking, but instead pace the floor up and down and stroke his little
beard. However, when a lull would come in the conversation, "Monk
would say two or three words and break everything up, making people
laugh or filling them with awe. His remarks would be offbeat yet perti-
nent to what the musicians were talking about. They could have just
been joking and lying and acting crazy," Griffin said, "and Monk could
throw in some remark and turn around to look you in the face. And
he would keep walking the floor. Mischievious, that's what it was."

Johnny Griffin has a blend of sweet and sour memories of the
season with Monk at the Five Spot. He recalled how Monk once drove

him to the gig and bragged about his car. Griffin could imitate the gutteral way Monk spoke lovingly of his Buick, "the greatest car in the world," a good car that ran well, Griffin recalled, but "so dirty, it looked as if had been sitting under the [elevated subway] train tracks." In the 1940s, Griffin recalled, none of the musicians had owned cars, so Thelonious was very proud to own one in the 1950s.

Griffin remembered that Monk arrived at work late every night, "and he would rush to the piano with his hat and coat on and start to play 'Just a Gigolo' forty minutes late." This memory was so hilarious that Griffin laughed for a while. Monk undoubtedly liked the song for its musical value, but it may also have appealed to his sense of irony about his situation during the days when Nellie, not he, was earning a living for their family.

"People he worked for were afraid of him," Griffin recalled. "The Termini brothers would come to me to ask him to please play the second set. They were afraid to ask him themselves, because they were afraid he might quit. They knew how sensitive he was. And by that time everyone was glad he was a big star. They had people lined up on the sidewalk trying to get in. They were terrified. They made so much money off him, and they weren't paying any money. They weren't paying me anything. I don't know what they were paying him." Johnny's impression was that nobody was making any money to speak of. "I was working six nights a week, on Tuesdays to Sundays at the Five Spot, and on Monday nights at Birdland with Philly Joe Jones, and Wynton Kelly [the pianist], and Wilbur Ware or Paul Chambers [the bassists]."

Harry Colomby handled payments for Monk's group, withholding taxes from the paychecks and giving tax payments to the accountant. Harry recalled the musicians' surprise at seeing the taxes deducted from their paychecks:

> Every week I gave the paychecks to the musicians. I gave them envelopes with deductions listed. They always looked at it and said, "WHAT!" It was always like a surprise to them. The taxes were withheld because, in those days, musicians would have to pay taxes. But they didn't think about it, there was no idea of

providing for the future. It was very NOW, the cash now. "We'll do that later, pay taxes later." No one would ever organize that aspect of his business at the moment. Probably jazz musicians thought of themselves as artistic outsiders in those days. And the way they collected payment wasn't conducive to their having another approach. Joe Termini picked wet dollar bills out of wads from all his pockets to give me as the pay. It was unprofessional to say the least. There was no crisp check. It was as if he was paying for a round-trip bus ticket. It was that kind of existence.

Joe Termini, who was about six feet three inches tall and weighed about 250 pounds, was a bar owner who suddenly had turned into a world-renowned club owner who had to deal with editors and other prominent people. He wasn't used to running a formal "business"; in Harry Colomby's words:

> He breathed hard and scratched his head, with a worried, sad look on his face when he paid me. So really the attitude of the musicians was to take the money and run. And there was a basic lack of trust. So, on the other hand, they would go so far as to say that, if they weren't playing one night, the club owner was still making money off them, because "my name was still up there; they made millions of dollars off me." They didn't envision themselves playing a role in society.

Thelonious continued to keep his own schedule during the Five Spot gig, as Harry recalled:

> Technically Thelonious was supposed to begin at 9:30, but it went to 10:10, 10:20, close to 11. Monk said ten o'clock was too early for jazz. It should begin at midnight; that was the best time. "'Round midnight." I told him that people wanted to hear it earlier. They couldn't stay up all night. But he never disappeared. He was there.
> That club was so small, and 9:30 was an early hour for Thelonious Monk. He'd go to sleep at 6 P.M. in the evening. Termini

would say, "How is he going to get up if he just went to bed?" But he got up. The Terminis were terrified that he wasn't going to get there, and they had a club full of people."

As Monk would be heading out the door of his apartment sometimes, he would look at his socks and say, "Damn, they don't go together. I have to change them," Harry recalled. And then, "Where's that other cufflink?"

"So it was a production to get him out the door," Harry said. Driving Monk regularly from West 63rd Street down to the Five Spot, Harry began to learn every little way to save a second. "A helicopter should have filmed me weaving in and out [of traffic] to get there," he would muse years later. "Then Monk would coach me, 'You can get past that, you can get through there.' If someone was in front of us, Monk would say, 'Damn, he's keeping me from getting to work!' and 'You can get past that, shit. I'll have to teach you to drive, shit.'"

Harry would say, "Have you ever thought of going to work ten minutes early?" But Monk's existence had its own routine.

Occasionally Joe Termini drove Monk to the gig, or Monk even drove himself. Sometimes Monk fell behind schedule because he busied himself talking with Harry—or rather *at* Harry—about how the clubowners were making a pile of money by selling liquor to people who showed up because of Monk's name. At times Monk liked to hold forth about the music business, the scene, or even current affairs. Harry noticed that Monk usually had a good grasp of the overall details of current events, even though he might have huge gaps of knowledge or missing key details. Monk often inserted some racially pat ideas, zany ideas, into his opinions, such as "Kennedy was killed because he liked jazz," or "Rockefeller would never be President because he loved jazz." Harry heard Monk saying things in that vein to people, and they would say, "Yeah, Monk." Art Blakey would always agree with Monk. (Monk didn't invite discussion of his ideas; either he held forth, or he listened to the degree that people talked at him and got no response.) When Monk preached in this way, before heading to the Five Spot, Harry was sure he did it simply to procrastinate about leaving the house. But for the most part, Harry noticed, Monk showed up and did the job. And though at the Five Spot he might be late, in other places he rarely was. Despite the many myths surrounding Monk's ability to stay on schedule, Harry placed Monk's reliability for punctuality in the ninetieth percentile.

Harry also noticed that Nellie and Nica influenced Monk's sense of conspiracy with their beliefs that club owners and other businessmen were working against his best interests, seeking to keep all the money for themselves and giving Thelonious short shrift. Compounding that tension, Harry observed, other musicians became envious of Monk for having a steady gig in New York City—an unusual and very desirable situation. Other musicians had to endure the stresses of constant traveling to enhance their glamour and marketability.

All in all, in Harry's opinion, Monk bore the tensions remarkably well. Harry recalled how the audience included many Village characters, most of whom Monk tolerated. "One time Brendan Behan, the playwright of *The Hostage*, which was playing off Broadway [in 1958], staged at a Second Avenue theater, came into the crowded Five Spot, completely drunk, with a florid face," Harry remembered. "He was weaving around, and he sat on the piano bench next to Monk. Monk just smiled and kept going. Monk was really a nice man."

Johnny Griffin left the group in 1958 because he could not make enough money to provide for himself in New York and his wife and three kids in their apartment in Chicago. "What saved me was that I was making a lot of recordings for Riverside, with Nat Adderley, and Donald Byrd, the trumpeters, and my own dates—plenty of record dates. That's what kept me going."

On the more positive side, Griffin recalled, "The records we made live from the Five Spot [in August 1958, with bassist Ahmed Abdul-Malik and drummer Roy Haynes on twenty songs recorded by Riverside, with Art Blakey replacing Roy for "Bye-ya/Epistrophy"] made me famous in Europe and all over the world. They were very well received." For the records, Monk still didn't give him any instructions, "no instructions about nothing, just play, that's all, and have another drink. He didn't say that exactly; he just said nothing, he just started

Monk hurriedly eats between sets at the Five Spot. Photo: Raymond Ross.

playing, and that's what happened. I never even knew the names of the tunes most of the time, and I still don't know the names. I knew 'Blue Monk,'" Griffin said. (Curiously, many musicians, diehard jazz fans, and Monk devotees and aficionados often had trouble—and always would have—matching up the sound of Monk's tunes with their proper names. People recognized instantly that a tune was written by Monk, but they had a very difficult time remembering its name.)

Above all, Johnny Griffin would always remember that the job was uplifting, exhilarating. "The whole atmosphere was thrilling. Playing in that club every night, we had such a rapport with the public. All the musicians came down to visit, from Max Roach to Coleman Hawkins to Benny Goodman. You name it. Benny Goodman tried to get me to play with his band. I told him, 'I'm going to stay with Thelonious.'"

In May 1963, Griffin left the country and went to live in France for the rest of his life, returning to the United States only for concerts and tours. He saw Monk only when Monk and Nellie traveled in Europe

FPO

Monk and Charlie Rouse performing in 1966. Photo: Raymond Ross.

on tours. For one of them, Griffin played with Monk again. Griffin saw more of Nellie in Europe than he did in New York because he had never seen her at the Five Spot, only at Monk's apartment. Rarely did the wives of jazz musicians regularly attend their gigs.

Griffin, like everyone else around the Monks, noticed that Nellie took care of Monk on tour. Griffin would go to their hotel room, have a few drinks, and laugh: "She had his clothes ready for him, whatever he needed. She kept the machine running well. Monk was no baby like Bud Powell. Bud might really need help. He was sick, but not Thelonious. He was out driving his car, taking care of his music and his business. This man was brilliant."

Griffin thought that people had always known how important Monk was. They might not have admitted it, but they knew it. Griffin thought that wider recognition of Thelonious was delayed because, he said, "Americans are so commercial-minded and stuck in their ways that they couldn't see the forest for the trees, or the trees for the forest, I don't know which way to put that."

Replacing Griffin, Sonny Rollins played for a couple of weeks with Monk at the Five Spot in the summer of 1959. Then Sonny, believed to be unnerved by John Coltrane's growing, surpassing fame, left the playing scene for two years to work on his own powerful style and fine compositions. Before he left, he told tenor saxophonist Charlie Rouse, "Thelonious is looking for you to join the band." Rouse had met Monk in the 1940s at the jam sessions at Minton's, and they had even played a few gigs together.

Born in 1924 and raised in Washington, D.C., Rouse had years of experience playing in bands led by Billy Eckstine, Dizzy Gillespie, and even Duke Ellington; and he had co-led his own struggling group, Les Jazz Modes, with French horn player Julius Watkins. That group, which had recorded for the Atlantic label, received a good review from John S. Wilson at the Newport Jazz Festival in 1958, along with Monk. In 1959, at the Five Spot, Rouse began a long-term commitment to the interpretation of Monk's music. It was probably for that reason that Rouse, an instinctive team player, didn't earn sufficient respect from the critics, and he sometimes received mixed notices. A consummate, perfect sideman for Monk, a virtual rudder for Monk at times, Rouse would play in Monk's groups for the next thirteen years.

Rouse did his share of dabbling in the party refreshments of nightlife and the quirkiness of employment in nighttown. Nothing about Monk's lifestyle upset Rouse—at least not on the surface. He later said that Monk had been easy to work for and had some leadership qualities in common with Duke Ellington: "If you played the music, that was all that was required. Anything else was your business."[4]

To rehearse, the men would sometimes go to Monk's apartment, or more often to Nica's house in Weehawken, where she had a baby grand in a huge, second-floor room overlooking the New York skyline. She had bought that piano when she had lived at the Bolivar, and Monk sometimes had composed on it there. The musicians began rehearsals at midnight or 1 A.M. at Nica's house and worked until late the next morning. "We never did anything the normal way," Rouse reminisced. "We rehearsed when Thelonious felt like rehearsing."

Thelonious taught Rouse one or two tunes a night—usually just one. Monk played the tune for Rouse, then got up and walked around the house while Rouse practiced it. Rouse thought Monk wasn't listening, "but he was, and when I got the melody down and started to turn it around, he'd come upstairs and say, 'Okay, let's play it.'"

Monk wrote out some of the "'harder tunes'—'Trinkle Tinkle,' 'Played Twice,' 'Four in One'—the tunes you can't just hear. But tunes like, 'Well, You Needn't' and 'Jackie-ing,' he would just play on the piano." He preferred that his musicians simply listen to the chord changes. But when they couldn't learn them by ear, he wrote them out—unless there was a tune he felt the musicians should absolutely be able to hear. Then he insisted on just playing it, sculpting it for them.

Monk did not want his men to practice the chord changes themselves, because then, Rouse said, "You'd play the chords as such and he didn't want to hear that. He wanted you to experiment. He wanted you to be as free as possible and not be boxed in by playing from the chords." He wanted the musicians to fly, or to dig deep, and not let their playing become dense, plodding, or turgid by focusing on the chords. Many times he told musicians to listen to the melodies he had written, and not simply the chords; if the musicians did that, they would be able to play better solos, Monk thought. And, of course, he loved his melodies and hired people to play them.

"He didn't instruct you on how to improvise, but he did want his melodies played the way he heard them," Rouse said. "For example, when we recorded 'Criss Cross,' I wanted to play it an octave lower and he didn't want me to, he wanted it higher. I said, 'Man, it's going out of the range of my horn,' and he said, 'No, it's on your horn,' so I had to play it that way. He wanted to hear it high, but he wanted a tenor sound, because he could have had Steve Lacy, who was playing with us at the Five Spot, do it on soprano. What I'm saying is that he wanted you to play the melody the way he felt it, but after that, you were on your own."

Other musicians would recall struggling to play music Thelonious had written, complaining that it was too difficult and couldn't be played. To one musician having a problem, Monk said, "You have a union card. Play the music." Some musicians marvelled at Monk's use of dissonance—for example, he would play two notes simultaneously to suggest the sound of a higher note in a chord, or overtone, and two more notes that did the same thing, and on and on, sometimes augmented by Monk's use of the pedals. Monk made seemingly simple changes in chords to achieve his signature sound; for example, a C7 chord with a flat 9 would normally be played as C–B flat with the left hand, and E–G–D flat with the right hand. But Monk played C–D flat with his left hand, with the two dissonant notes eight-and-a-half notes apart, fighting with each other, dominating the chord and creating his signature sound.

Rouse improvised differently for Monk's music than for anyone else's because so many of the tunes had such strong melodies, and Rouse, as required by Monk, referred to the melody frequently. Furthermore, "Thelonious had such a rhythmic pulse!" he said. "I can remember playing 'Rhythm-a-ning' [Monk's classic, powerful song inspired by the chords of "I Got Rhythm"] at three different tempos and thinking differently on it at each tempo."

In concert, Rouse was never sure what the group was going to play until he heard Monk start a song. When Rouse recognized it, he would come in. Sometimes Monk taught Rouse a song, then didn't play it for three weeks and sprang it on him during a performance. At recording sessions, Monk sometimes came into the studio, played a new song at the piano until he got the music to sound the way he wanted it, and then he yelled: "'Hey Rouse! Come here! Play this.' And he would teach it to me. Then we would record it. Even so, you don't find many tunes with third and fourth takes. If you didn't get it after the second take, that was it." Rouse said that if the musicians didn't get the song right by the second take, then they would have to listen to what they did for the rest of their lives.[7]

Monk didn't like to lose the spontaneity and spirit of the songs by overworking them. Rouse felt challenged when he had to learn a tune fast. He once found a blackmarket record called "Sphere," which the group had recorded in Italy, though the album's liner notes said it had been taped in Spain. "On that particular concert Thelonious was in great form. There were some nights that were unbelievable, especially when he felt strong and energetic. He could play chorus after chorus without repeating himself. The more he played, the more magic he performed." Rouse thought Monk's ability harked back to his apprenticeship days in the 1940s, when, Monk had reminisced for Rouse, great jazz pianists used to get together and play for each other, developing their stamina and imagination.

In every possible way, for better or worse, working in Monk's group was a master class in spontaneity, and not only in the music. Protective about Thelonious, Rouse eventually fended off questions about certain curiosities of Monk's behavior that Rouse had to deal with over the years by simply saying, "Monk did a lot of things."

NOTES

Personal interviews: Harry Colomby; Clark Terry; Marian McPartland; Idrees Sulieman; Marian Monk White; Paul Jeffrey; Johnny Griffin.

1. According to Russ Musto, who is working on a book about Blakey.

2. Later some journalists reported that it was a Steinway.

3. In later years, bassists Butch Warren and John Ore played regularly in Monk's groups, and there were many others eventually—Larry Gales and Larry Ridley, to name two of the best-known. Drummers Roy Haynes, Art Taylor, Frankie Dunlop, and Ben Riley, among others, played in Monk's groups, and in the 1970s, Monk's son, Toot.

4. This incident is recounted by both Goldberg (1965) and Wakefield (1995).

5. Coltrane, with DeMichael (1960).

6. Franklin (1987).

7. From an interview with Charlie Rouse in *Straight, No Chaser*, a documentary film about Monk's life, Warner Brothers, Inc.

9   Monk—Misterioso

The telephone had begun ringing with offers for Monk as soon as he scored a success at the Five Spot. In 1958, he won first place in the *Down Beat* magazine critics poll, outstripping Duke Ellington, Erroll Garner, Oscar Peterson, and Dave Brubeck. Monk mused to Nellie and Colomby, "I wonder if it will last." Harry Colomby was overjoyed. He had the luxury of telling people that Monk wasn't traveling at that moment. Before the Five Spot, Harry said, chuckling, "We would have considered . . . anything."[1]

If Harry Colomby had to pick one moment when Monk's career seemed to turn a corner, it was the appearance of critic Martin Williams's laudatory appraisals of Monk beginning in the 1950s. Williams called Monk "a major composer—the first . . . since Ellington—and one whose work drastically extends the concept of composition in the idiom." In fact, in the late 1950s, all the critics began to do a complete about-face in their regard for Monk's music. They even realized that Monk's technique was ideal for his music, that he had devised his technique to achieve his sound, and his sculpted, swinging creations were inimitable. Nobody played the harmonies or solos, made the arrangements, created phrasing and percussiveness, or drove the rhythms in quite the same way. No one made suspenseful pauses and hestitations flow, sounding so clean and correct, or communicated the edginess of the modern age so artfully. The reviews made a big difference for Monk's career. With hindsight, Williams, in his collection *The Jazz Tradition* published in the mid-1960s, wrote about Monk and his recordings for Blue Note: they "seem among the most significant and original in modern jazz."

After Monk became celebrated at the Five Spot, a debate began about who modernized jazz: Monk, Charlie Parker, or Dizzy Gillespie. Monk himself dismissed the controversy, saying that many people had contributed to modern jazz over many years, and he himself had not even realized it was developing. He was just playing what he wanted to.

And then Monk had a mishap that had major ramifications on his career. In October 1958, about a week after his forty-first birthday, he was booked to play a gig in Baltimore. The night before he was supposed to leave New York, Harry Colomby recalled, Monk began to "act strange"; by "strange," Colomby meant that Monk first began making twitching motions with his arms, and then said odd things that had no connection to the conversation, both signs of a spell of oddness, disconnection, or exhaustion. Usually these spells didn't happen when he was working. When Monk began to show signs of a spell as he prepared to go to Baltimore, Colomby said to himself, "Oh, no, not now."

The spells were different from Monk's ability to withdraw, talking to no one (not even Nellie), while he concentrated on his music. Once Harry had slept overnight at Monk's apartment and awoke to find him composing a song at the piano, while the radio was blaring a country and western song. Harry asked, "Shall I shut that off?" Monk said, "No." As Harry recalled, a Bing Crosby tune was broadcast next. Monk kept working, astounding Harry. Monk could concentrate so deeply that he blocked out extraneous noises—the sounds he wasn't hearing in his head. But that sort of withdrawal from his surroundings—the conscious withdrawal of the driven genius—differed from his spells. In his spells, Monk seemed to lose touch with reality, both losing control of his body and his speech.

Nellie didn't feel well enough to make the trip to Baltimore, so Nica drove her Bentley convertible—nicknamed the "silver pigeon" for its eye-catching, light, paint color—to take Monk and saxophonist Charlie Rouse south. Nica would later tell several people of their misadventure. As they were passing through New Castle, Delaware, in blistering hot weather, Thelonious was very uncomfortable: "silent, sweating, and miserable," Nica told Max Gordon, owner of the Village Vanguard.[2] Finally Monk spoke up: "Could we stop somewhere for a cold drink, a beer, a glass of water, anything?"

Nica saw a sign, "Motel and Bar," and stopped for Thelonious to go in for a drink. Rouse—almost no one in jazz ever called him Charlie—was sleeping in the back seat and didn't see Monk go into the motel. Later Rouse reflected that, if he had only been awake, he would have stopped Thelonious. Nica began to get very nervous when Monk didn't come out quickly. She didn't realize that Monk had walked into a segregated motel. A Jeep quickly drove up, and two policeman ran into the motel, exiting with Thelonious held between them. The police demanded to know who the baroness was—a white woman traveling in an attention-getting Bentley with two black men. The police were very angry at Thelonious because he wouldn't talk to them.

Nica explained their trip. One of the policeman searched Charlie Rouse. Finding nothing incriminating, he searched Nica and found a little bit of marijuana in her purse—"enough for one stick," she said.

> Now the cops were sure they had the evidence for an arrest. We were addicts, criminals, and I was the pusher. They ordered Thelonious into their jeep.
>
> But Thelonious was so mad he wouldn't move. He took hold of the car door, darling, and couldn't be budged, until one cop started beating on his hands with a billy club, his pianist's hands. I screamed as a crowd gathered.
>
> Well, they finally got us to police headquarters several miles down the road. Charlie and Thelonious were dismissed, but I had to stand trial. I was a dangerous criminal because of that bit of marijuana in my purse. I was found guilty and sentenced,

mind you, to three years. Three years! . . . And my Bentley was
to be confiscated.

Rouse later told the writer Lewis Lapham what happened to Monk
and himself in police custody: "It was awful. Cops jumping out of
squad cars all over the place and beating up on Monk. They handcuffed
him and took us to jail. But Monk didn't back down. If he thinks he's
right, he sticks by what he thinks. We stood there and defied the judge.
If they told him to sit down, he stood up. If they told him to say something, he said nothing. Finally they let us go, and I said, 'Monk, you're
sure some stubborn black man.'"[1]

Monk was fined $123.50 for charges of disorderly conduct and
assault, according to a newspaper report. He arrived at a hearing on
November 25 to be fined, bringing a doctor with him and sitting
through the proceedings silently—in "a daze," said Magistrate Samuel
Hatton in New Castle. It took Nica a couple of years of appeals, with
letters of support from various influential people, before the case
against her was dismissed. "Needless to say Thelonious never made that
gig in Baltimore," she reflected.

Reporting for *Esquire* about what happened in the motel, Nat
Hentoff, one of the people who eventually vouched for Nica in the
state of Delaware, discovered that the motel owner had been shocked
by Monk's request for a glass of water and told him to leave. Monk,
perceiving the motel owner as rude, fell silent and was slow to leave.
Perhaps frightened by the big, silent man, the owner called the police.
Monk later told soprano saxophonist Steve Lacy: "The next thing I
knew I was in a strait jacket."

Lacy felt horror at Monk's story: "It was a hell of an experience, like
a test of him. That's what you call being uptight literally. I say that,"
Steve said. "He couldn't joke about that. But he had a tremendous
willpower. He could take a lot of punishment without flinching. He
was tough." Other people would learn that about Thelonious, too. He
once told Steve about how a German shepherd had bitten him,
"and he stared the dog down until it dropped him and ran away,"
Steve recalled.

Because of the incident in Delaware, Monk again lost his cabaret card and couldn't work in New York clubs until June 1960; Charlie Rouse also lost his card.

It was at this time that Monk began preparing for a much-touted concert, billed as "Thelonious Monk at Town Hall," to be held on February 28, 1959, with arrangements of his music by himself and Hall Overton. For Monk, it was a virtual extravaganza, including nine musicians under his leadership. It was conceived of by Harry Colomby and his brother Jules, in part to keep Monk's career going at full blast before the public in his beloved Manhattan while his cabaret card was suspended.

Hall Overton and Harry Colomby lived in the same apartment building between 1952 and 1954. A classical composer, Hall liked jazz. Harry began taking piano lessons with him, and as they became better acquainted, Harry brought Hall a recording by Monk of "April in Paris" with "Nice Work If You Can Get It" on the other side. Not only Harry, but his elder brother Jules Colomby was friends with Overton, to whom the brothers introduced Monk. Several years passed. Jules nurtured the idea of putting together a big band led by Monk, with Overton doing the transcriptions of Monk's solos. Monk liked the idea and respected Overton.

Harry had seen music very neatly written in pencil by Monk and stacked in a box in Monk's apartment. Among these manuscripts was a piece titled "Grand Finale" which Harry recognized as an early version of "'Round Midnight." When the big-band project got underway, Harry gave the music to a copyist hired by Hall. "I want to get all Monk's music nicely copied," Harry decided. By that time, Hall, a distinguished looking man a few inches taller than Monk and with a Midwestern look, had moved to "a creaky old loft," Harry recalled. That's where Monk went for rehearsals of the big band.

Jules Colomby later told Paul Jeffrey an amusing tale about the rehearsals. A copyist had made a mistake on the baritone saxophone part for Pepper Adams, and Pepper kept playing what was on the sheet: an E natural, where there should have been an E flat. Monk waited quite a while before saying to Pepper, in his typical, elliptical fashion,

"I see you like E natural." Pepper was a bit unnerved. He thought Monk didn't like him. Then he realized what note he should have been playing.

Jules Colomby presented Monk at Town Hall, with trumpeter Donald Byrd, trombonist Eddie Bert, French-horn player Robert Northern, tubist Jay McAllister, Phil Woods on alto saxophone, Charlie Rouse on tenor, Pepper Adams on baritone sax, Sam Jones on bass, and Art Taylor on drums.

Two of the leading jazz critics of the day, Whitney Balliett, who wrote for the *New Yorker*, and John S. Wilson, of the *New York Times*, covered the concert. In his review, Wilson acknowledged that Monk was one of the few jazz musicians who had written music that could sustain a full concert: "Mr. Monk is an extremely melodic composer, although he couches his melodies in angularities and dissonances that give them a rough and unfamiliar surface on first meeting. But they wear unusually well and when he ponders them on the piano (he has carried apparent uncertainty to a high and refined art) he makes each performance a fresh and provocative experience."

"This sense of constant surprise and discovery enlivened his performances with his quartet. [Monk played part of the concert with his small group, the rest with the bigger band]." Wilson divined that Monk's personality had a very important effect on the musicians playing with him: "Monk has made recordings of his works . . . and while these recordings have often been rough and occasionally chaotic, Mr. Monk's determination to impose his musical personality on his musicians and the surging, sweaty efforts of the musicians to wrestle with Mr. Monk's music gave the disks a raw excitement."

Unfortunately, Wilson thought this quality was lost in the performances of the big band at Town Hall: "But none of this could be found in the bland, workaday performances of the large group with which Mr. Monk played Saturday evening. The arrangements smoothed out the characteristically Monkian humps and bumps, diluted his tartness and robbed the works of their zest. It was a pipe-and-slippers version of a music that is naturally querulous," Wilson ended.

Balliett's review was a longer, more painstaking attempt to define Monk's accomplishments at Town Hall and in general: "Monk's works are basically straightforward, often charming melodies, which, in the process of composition, he appears to stretch, compress, twist, and bully, so that by the time they are on paper, they have already become industrious improvisations of what first popped into his head. But that is only the halfway mark. When Monk plays one of his pieces, he takes a single aspect of it—a certain phrase or rhythmic pattern—and goes to work on it again to see how much more pressure it can bear and still retain its fundamental qualities. When he is finished, one has the impression of having viewed the restless, exciting, surprising aerie that only a handful of jazz musicians have inhabited."

Balliett shared Wilson's view that the band was not up to performing Monk's material: "Unfortunately, 'An Evening with Thelonious Monk' ... only suggested this height ... The trouble was not with Monk, a remarkably consistent pianist, who was always close to his best, but with his accompanists, whom he was forced to tow like barges."

As soloists, Charlie Rouse was called "dull" and Art Taylor "monotonous"—"almost forcing one's attention to Monk's accompaniment, which is invariably exhilarating." It's true that Monk's music was relatively new to Rouse, while Taylor's drumming style at that time wasn't up to Monk's requirements.

Balliett, however, found something to praise among the large-band numbers:

> The exception [to Balliett's criticism of the scoring and the sidemen's performances] occurred in the last couple of choruses of "Little Rootie Tootie," when the whole group admirably executed a stunningly worked out transcription of Monk's solo part in his first recording of the tune. The number revelled in Monk. In the opening chorus, the ensemble played an unadorned version of the melody; then Monk presented a spontaneous distillation of it; and finally, the whole group magnified his earlier effort (while he himself gloriously banged his pots and pans in the background) into a wonderful, jarring, dissonant contrapuntal form that sounded like a dozen Monks all playing at once and

that explained what the rest of the evening had failed to do . . .
Monk had survived.

Quibbles about the concert notwithstanding—and critics in other
cities would find faults with the recording of it, while some would
even reveal they hadn't gotten used to Monk's style and music—Monk
had risen above it all and enjoyed his greatest personal success to date.
Among the audience, including many noted jazz performers, the
concert solidified Monk's reputation as a true pioneer. Trumpeter
Maynard Ferguson and his wife, who had gone to the concert, thought
Monk was splendid. Maynard was fascinated by Indian music, and
Monk was into that "beauty dissonance," as Maynard called it. Maynard
even thought Monk's stagecraft was a "knockout."

Ferguson recalled that Monk was playing a ballad and perspiring a
great deal. While continuing to play with his left hand, he reached into
his right pocket and took out a handkerchief. But it wasn't a neatly
folded white handkekrchief like Oscar Peterson used to mop his brow.
Instead, Monk pulled out "this outrageous Chinese red silk handkerchief." The crowd tittered slightly. Monk held onto it for a while, still
playing, and then put it on top of the piano. "Most of us were into the
music, of course, but the red handkerchief did get a laugh. And that was
part of the character of Monk that I really loved," Maynard recalled.
Monk often went through that attention-getting routine during
performances, wiping his face, crumpling his handkerchief in one hand,
and continuing to play before stowing the cloth on top of the piano.

More critics were coming to understand the quality of Monk's
work. In the October 1959 issue of *Esquire*, Nat Hentoff published a
review of Monk's 1956 album for Riverside, *The Unique Thelonious
Monk*, which had been repackaged in 1959. Hentoff wrote several articles about Thelonious between 1959 and 1961 for *Esquire*, helping to
make up for the critics' lost time in calling the public's attention to
Monk. Hentoff enthused:

> This is one of [Monk's] sunniest and most immediately beguiling
> set of performances. It contains his tartly unpredictable treatment

of seven standards, among them "Liza," "Honeysuckle Rose," and "Darn that Dream." In creating them, Monk indicates several of the sources of his buoyantly dissonant, vigorously asymmetrical language. There is, for example, some stride piano . . . in "Honeysuckle Rose" and "Tea for Two" that is uniquely Monk in that he projects respect for that older tradition of men like James P. Johnson and Fats Waller and at the same time has affectionate fun with it.

To Orrin Keepnews, Monk had remarked, in April 1957, how pleased he was at sounding like James P. Johnson on a solo recording of his own blues composition, "Functional."

Hentoff continued:

> The album is also particularly valuable in that with Monk are two of the four or five musicians in all of jazz who are most qualified by temperament and musicianship to play with him. Drummer Art Blakey and bassist Oscar Pettiford have never been intimidated by Monk's precipitously careening turns of phrase and they've also been able to fuse their own highly assertive personalities into a team that puts Monk into deeper and freer relief. The presence in contemporary jazz of Monk, Bill Evans and Ray Bryant—in addition to the still not wholly formed but brilliantly explosive pianist Cecil Taylor—underlines this listener's conviction that jazz is at the start of the most absorbing and enliveningly variegated decade in its history.

Though the best critics had caught on and caught up, their praise didn't seem to add anything to Monk's personal equilibrium. He still ceased relating well to the world at times, as if he were simply too exhausted by his bruising experiences, boiling creativity, and drug dalliances to continue. One of his few public displays of dire mental distress took place in Boston in 1959, during the spring after his Town Hall concert. He was booked for a week at George Wein's Storyville club. Nat Hentoff reported that Monk had gone for three nights without sleep before arriving in Boston. There he went to the desk of the Copley Square Hotel, in which the club was located. He had a glass of whiskey in his hand in the lobby, where he apparently spent some time examining the walls. The hotel wouldn't rent him a room. He refused to go to the Hotel Bostonian, where his sidemen were staying. He showed up on the bandstand at 10 o'clock and played two songs, left the bandstand, went back on at 11:30 to play the same two songs, and then for a long time sat still at the piano. Bewildered, his sidemen left the bandstand.

Monk began wandering around the club—George Wein recalled that Monk had gone around inspecting the walls in the club and in the men's room—left it, registered at the Bostonian, disliked the room he saw, and left there, too. He tried the Statler, was refused a room, and took a taxi to the airport. Hentoff wrote that Monk planned to go to New York, get Nellie, and take her back to Boston with him for the rest of the gig. But the last plane had left for the night. A state trooper approached him and, unable to get him to talk, took him to Grafton State Hospital near Worcester, Massachusetts for observation.'

George Wein recalled the crisis without excitement many years later. "A good few people showed up at 8 P.M. and sat around, waiting for him to play. There was nobody saying, 'When's this guy going to play?' They were very respectful of him. I never saw anything like that before." When Monk cut the evening short, it amazed George that nobody asked for money back.

Harry Colomby remembered that he and Nellie received a phone call from the club from Wein, who said that he didn't know what to do: Thelonious was sitting at the piano, and he wasn't playing; he was just staring into space. Furthermore, Monk had thrown a woman's purse across the room. The scene seemed violent and scary to Harry, who asked George, "Can you get him to the phone?" George said he didn't know.

After Monk disappeared—probably the next morning—George Wein called Nellie and Harry again to ask if Monk was in New York, and, if so, was he going to return to Boston? That was how they learned Monk had disappeared; no one knew what had happened to him. Nellie and Harry Colomby were frantic and hired a private detective to try to find Monk. "I found [the detective] in the phone book," Harry recalled. He imagined all kinds of disasters—even that Monk had drowned. The Boston police were questioned, but not the state police. The private detective, "an ex-cop with connections," Harry recalled, eventually found Monk at Grafton State Hospital—but not before the detective suggested that Monk may have simply disappeared. In the month of May, a lot of husbands did that, the detective explained. Harry and Nellie knew that was a ridiculous idea about Thelonious. They were particularly terrified because he had never acted in such an extreme manner in pubic before. When he was found, Nellie hurried to the hospital.

By that time, Monk had recovered from whatever had ailed him. The spell evaporated; the hospital had no reason to hold him, and the doctors let Nellie take him home. Many times in the future, Monk would refer to his hospital stays, saying. "I can't be crazy, because they had me in one of those places and they let me go."

Harry developed a scenario based on what he had seen happen to Monk before: Monk must have withdrawn, become uncommunicative, perhaps made jerky movements with his arms. The state trooper must have become alarmed, confronting a big, powerful-looking black man who made strange gestures and wouldn't talk, so he took him to the state hospital. Hentoff reported that it was decided to have someone travel with Monk all the time after that incident. Despite these periods of unusual behavior, Monk was able to continue playing, writing, and performing. Without a hint of any problem, he played brilliantly in both the Boston and the Newport Jazz Festivals in summer, 1959.

However, Monk was gaining a reputation for elusiveness and idiosyncratic behavior that attracted the notice of the New York press. New York's *Amsterdam News* reported one such anecdote. Peter Long, producer of the Randall's Island Jazz Festival, told the paper that the previous summer Monk had raced from a rehearsal for a concert in Manhattan to get to Randall's Island for a performance. He had trouble getting through traffic to the island—at that time Monk still had his

The famous "Great Day in Harlem" photo taken in 1959. Photo (c) Art Kane.
Inset photo shows Monk at far right; Mary Lou Williams is to his right.

driver's license and drove his own car. He was warming up backstage
when he realized that he had forgotten all the music. "Without telling
anyone, he rushed off to get his car and go back to Manhattan to pick
it up. His wife saw him leave and started after him, immediately
followed by Peter Long," said the *Amsterdam News*. Some festival
workers joined in the chase, and they were followed by several
policeman who worked at the festival. Monk was already on the bridge
going back to Manhattan when "the police car with sirens blaring"
overtook him. When the police found out what had happened, they
escorted Monk to his apartment, picked up his music, and got him
back to the concert "just in time for him to go on."[5]

This story seems apocryphal, perhaps simply a bold bid for publicity
for the upcoming 1960 festival. It's unlikely that Monk would forget

the music or run for it himself if he did, and in mid-1959 he wasn't rehearsing for a concert in New York. Whether the story was true or not, Monk's movements on the surface lent themselves to "good copy," as the journalistic phrase goes. There was always some kind of commotion going on around him, or one could be invented. Musicians thought he was a sly publicity genius; he knew exactly how to call attention to himself. And if he did nothing, other people had the feeling that he was fair game and did the publicity job for him.

Still lacking a cabaret permit, Monk was forced to travel outside New York to earn a living. In October 1959, while traveling from a gig in Chicago to one in San Francisco, Nellie became sick on an airplane. They were planning to make a stopover to visit Nellie's cousin in Los Angeles because they had a week's vacation between engagements. By the time she arrived at her cousin's house, she had to be rushed to the hospital for emergency surgery for an obstruction in her lower intestine. Nellie began to believe, with all her illnesses, that she would die before Thelonious.

"That's how the album *Thelonious Alone in San Francisco* got its name. He had to go to San Francisco alone to make the money to pay for the operation," she recalled. "When he had to leave, he said to me, 'Now you make sure you don't kick the bucket, and you're here when I get back, because I don't want to pay for an operation if you're gone.' I almost died. I don't know where I was, but I said to myself, 'Oh, I can stay here, it's so beautiful here. Oh, no, Thelonious is waiting.' I fought my way back. It saved my life when he made that joke."

To get around the cabaret-card requirement in New York, Monk performed with his quartet at the off-Broadway theater Circle in the Square, technically not a club. The *New York Times* jazz critic John S. Wilson heard him there and, according him full acceptance, wrote that the "angular, crab-gaited melodies of Thelonious Monk have seeped into the bloodstream of jazz . . . in the brief span of ten years [Monk's compositions] have lost their original, jarring, eccentric sound to take on the comfortable familiarity of a pair of old shoes. During this same time Mr. Monk has become an increasingly adroit technician and a polished and disciplined performer. Both he and members of his quartet gave impressively clean-lined, full-bodied performances . . . highlighted by the strong empathy that has developed between Mr. Monk and his tenor saxophonist, Charlie Rouse."[4]

In April 1960, in San Francisco again, Thelonious recorded for Riverside, this time with Shelly Manne on drums. The session wasn't as successful as Orrin Keepnews's partner, Bill Grauer, had hoped it would be. But when Manne was replaced by Billy Higgins for the group's live performances recorded at the Blackhawk jazz club, the results were much better. Thelonious liked Higgins's work and wanted to keep him as part of the regular quartet. Unfortunately, that didn't happen.

Russ Wilson of California's *Oakland Tribune* wrote about the gig's shaky start. Higgins's drums didn't arrive from the airport until midnight on opening night, and Monk didn't show up on time either. His group had to start without him, and Higgins had to use borrowed drums. When Monk showed up the next day, he told the tale that he was driving on the Triborough Bridge on his way to La Guardia Airport when his sainted Buick blew a tire. The AAA man came to change the tire; by the time he finished, the Monks—Nellie, Toot, and Barbara—had missed their plane. "We couldn't get another one until today," Monk said. "It sure bugged me, you know." His hotel reservation in San Francisco had been cancelled, and he had to find rooms in another hotel.

In May 1960, Monk was supposed to play on an ABC television series. He went to the first rehearsal of the show, "Music for a Spring Night," then flew to Detroit to play in a club for a week. Because he didn't have his regular drummer with him, he had to find a local drummer. That drummer arrived late for the opening, and so the clubowner docked Monk $500 pay. Disgusted, and sick with a cold, he headed back to New York by train and missed the second rehearsal of the ABC show. On the phone with Harry Colomby, the show's producer said, "I'm not excited, but I'm having a nervous breakdown." He substituted another jazz pianist, Phineas Newborn. Harry tried to reach Monk by telephone, but Nellie later said nobody had tried to call, and Thelonious was sick. Harry reportedly said, "Oh, well, he probably would have lost all his jazz fans" had he appeared on the mainstream program. Although this story appeared in *Down Beat*, it had a hokey feeling, along with the title, "Same Old Unusual Story." Read from the point of view from which it was not written, it expressed the chaos of the jazz musician's life.

Traveling itself still distressed Thelonious. Though he inspired an owner of the Blackhawk in San Francisco once to praise him for his punctuality and agreeableness, another club owner in Detroit became incensed and unburdened himself to a writer when Monk played a great deal of a set one night with his elbows; Monk had been very shaken by a rough plane ride on the way to the gig, and he had simply expressed his outlook on life that night—the exhilaration and terror that a stressful life on the road could inspire. Another clubowner in Toronto worried so much about whether Thelonious would make it to his gigs that Harry Colomby took less money in payment "in order to have peace of mind," he recalled. Some club owners proved greedy. Writers had their own motives for heightening the impression that Monk was unreliable. It was not surprising that Monk simply closed the door on 63rd Street and blocked out the world sometimes. To further protect himself from the world—or perhaps to keep the neighbors from complaining—the ceiling of the Monk apartment was soundproofed, and the front door was reinforced with thick wood.

In January 1960, Monk and Rouse had been cleared of the charges in Delaware. By June, Monk got a cabaret card again—actually a temporary permit—that allowed him to go to work at the Jazz Gallery, a new club opened by the Termini brothers, at 80 St. Mark's Place, close to the old Five Spot. Leaning against a wall of the Jazz Gallery, Monk smiled and answered a stranger, "Yes, I like, you know, to be back. Yes, it's nice." That night, Monk was only an hour late to start the first set. He rubbed his chin with its fringe of beard and with an abstracted manner sat at the piano, striking the keys in his flat-fingered style and keeping time with his flapping foot, wrote a reporter for the *New York Post*.

Nica had brought Monk to the Five Spot to hear Steve Lacy, a young, white soprano saxophonist, who played with Jimmy Giuffre's group. A few months later, Monk hired Steve for the Jazz Gallery quintet including Rouse and drummer Roy Haynes. Lacy knew that Monk was doing well with his quartet and didn't need to add him. "It was a very generous step for him to take," Lacy recalled. "I had been on his case for years. I was working on his music since the mid-1950s. I recorded the first records of his music that anyone had ever done. He couldn't not be aware of me. I used to hang around where he was playing and speak to him. I gave him my record."

Steve was sure that some people probably asked Monk what he was doing, hiring a young white musician.

Monk favored tenor players and liked trumpets, Steve knew, but:

> Monk had no preconceptions, really. He told me once that whatever you think cannot be done, someone will come along and do it. So he liked something exceptional, something different. He also liked errors. He loved and collected mistakes, to study them, to get ideas and inspiration from them. He was an inventor above all. He did a lot of research. Part of his research was in musical mistakes. He would hear someone play his tunes wrong and experiment with them and do them wrong also to see what they were like. Sometimes he adapted mistakes into his songs. He was very, very open.

As usual, there were no rehearsals to speak of. Monk let Lacy play what he wanted to and then began to give him some direction—not about the notes but about his improvisations. Monk wanted him to listen carefully to the melodies and make his improvisations fit the intention of each piece, and he wanted Lacy to make sure he kept swinging. That group rehearsed only a few times, usually in the club after everyone else had left, or at Nica's house where the musicians spent most of their time playing ping-pong. Even so, the group coalesced. A camaraderie—a sense of cabal between the acolytes and the master—developed in part during the ping-pong games, at which Monk excelled, and carried over to the music, which Monk taught slowly, one song and sometimes only one note at a time.

Steve Lacy. Courtesy of the Institute of Jazz Studies, Rutgers University.

Monk's teaching methods paralleled his way of approaching a song written by someone else. Lacy heard the way Monk took a popular standard, "Body and Soul," into his repertoire and developed it— enveloped it, really—to express it with his own vocabulary and sculpt it into a work of art. Lacy recalled: "He started playing that around the middle of the summer, as a solo piece. I remember the first time he played it. It was kind of fumbly, and he played it every night after that. Each night it would get a little more complex and a little surer, and harmonies would change into his own harmonies, until by the end of the summer he had quite a good piece, but it was Monk." It evolved into "something multi-colored and wondrous to behold. He changed all the harmonies, and it worked out to be beautiful."[7] He had already done the same thing with "Tea for Two" and "Remember," among

other standards that were metamorphosed into symbols of his individ-
ualism and artistry. Pianist Barry Harris, a close friend of Nica's, heard
Monk concentrate on another song, "Lulu's Back In Town," rehearsing
it in tempo for two hours—an amazing example of Monk's capacity
for unswerving concentration and devotion to his craft.

During the sixteen weeks that Steve, then twenty-six, worked in
Monk's group, he went to Monk's apartment every day.

> I took walks with him. He was beautiful, glad of the company,
> too. And I was genuinely interested in his music. He was very
> generous, glad, human and humorous. He liked to take a walk
> around the neighborhood. One thing about Monk was very
> important. He was very oriented, and part of his orientation was
> New York. He loved Manhattan. He knew that place, and he felt
> at home there. He loved the traffic and the river and the build-
> ings and people and family and friends. He was really a happy
> New Yorker, and he loved to play with New York.

Monk himself would try to tell interviewers that the sounds of New
York inspired his music. In his prize-winning book, *Rhythm-a-ning*, critic
Gary Giddins, extolling the virtues of *The Complete Blue Note Recordings
of Thelonious Monk*, honed in on Monk's relationship to the Big Apple:

> The Blue Note years . . . remind us, as indeed all of Monk's work
> does, that he was the quintessential New York jazzman. A proudly
> chauvinistic resident of West 63rd Street—where a circle is now
> named in his honor—for most of his life . . . Monk lived and
> breathed the sounds of the city as surely as Louis Armstrong was
> nurtured by New Orleans. It's there in everything he wrote and
> played—the clangor and ambition; the nostalgia and irreverence;
> the influences of the church, big bands, Tin Pan Alley, Harlem
> stride, modernism. He embraced it all.

"When we worked at the Jazz Gallery," Lacy recalled, "we walked
out between sets. And he would play with the traffic. He would dance

with the traffic. He was like a matador, with the red lights and green lights and the cars coming. He would be dancing with all that. He loved that kind of rhythm. All his music is based on New York sights and sounds and the members of his family and his friends, very descriptive music really."

Monk never mentioned Ruby to Steve, but Nellie did. Eventually he couldn't remember what Nellie said, but he thought that Nellie was mindful of Monk's earlier romance. Yet "Nellie appreciated Monk for himself and understood him. Her role was very important. In the years when he couldn't work, she believed in him, supported him and allowed and encouraged him to stay with his research at the piano and to just write. She took care of him. That was very important to his development. He had the luxury of continuing his research without having to go out and take a day job." Steve thought Nellie and Monk were more "married"—much closer—than most legally married couples.

Unlike many jazz musicians, Monk was never tempted to "fool around"; he was true to Nellie. Harry Colomby recalled a night at one of the Five Spots, when a beautiful, pale, blonde woman wearing a light-colored dress approached Monk. Instead of flirting with her, he said, "How do I know you're not a ghost?" Harry never saw Monk making any overtures toward women; they never telephoned him. Monk's attitude toward female fans supported Harry's thought that "nothing, zero," was going on between Monk and Nica. "It was almost asexual, the way he acted, never saying anyone was fine looking, and yet he had a sexual charisma," Harry said. Celebrities like Lauren Bacall and Jason Robards came to the Vanguard during the early 1960s to see Monk, while Elizabeth Taylor went with Eddie Fisher in the 1950s to the Five Spot. "There was something fascinating about [Monk's] look. For a while that was a hip thing to do: to go to see jazz, to look at these guys. It had nothing to do with the music itself, which was a little challenging," Harry recalled.

While at the Jazz Gallery, a cavernous club with two large rooms, the group also played for ten days at the Apollo Theater. They did countless shows at the theater by day and went to the Jazz Gallery at night. "Those were very intense times. The show at the Apollo had

Miles Davis, John Coltrane, James Moody, Moms Mabley—an all-star show. So that was a hell of an experience," Steve Lacy recalled. Nica took them from the theater in her "silver pigeon" down to the Jazz Gallery every night.

"There was always something new I never heard him play before," Steve recalled:

> We played the same songs. The theme song, "Epistrophy," we played five or six times a day. It was always a thrill to hear his improvisations.
>
> By 1960, he had written most of his music. He wrote a little more in the '60s. But I don't really remember him ever showing up with new tunes. They were tunes that I had known before. Also, he didn't believe in showing paper to musicians. He wanted them to learn by rote realistically. He would play the songs over and over until we learned them. He wouldn't show us the paper, though he had it, and it was very clear. I think he was right. Some people later would play photocopies of photocopies of Monk's music, and they were wrong. It would be incredible the wrong information that would circulate about Monk's music. They should call fake books "mistake books."

It was a rather rare occurrence for people to play the right chord changes for Monk's songs, because musicians usually learned the songs by ear and, because they didn't have access to the sheet music, they thought it wasn't readily available. Many musicians gave up trying to play Monk's songs—especially those musicians who had a chance to play a tune for Monk and hear him comment that they had the changes wrong. The musicians could become too discouraged, or squelched, to persist.

While Steve Lacy was in the group, Roy Haynes left and Frankie Dunlop took over the drum seat. Steve thought Monk was absolutely happy and "at his peak" in those days. "He was enjoying life, having fun; he liked the band, the club. He was not troubled at that time." Monk did dabble in many substances, "over a long period of time,"

Steve noticed, "and combinations of certain things, too much bourbon mixed with beer, this and that. He liked everything. He was Rabelesian." Steve couldn't say for sure what Monk used. "There wasn't anything that I know of that he didn't like. He would have mixed them up, whatever showed up. I would think he knew about LSD, as far as I know. Heroin. These things were around. But he had an amazing force of character. When I knew him, he had control. He could handle just about anything."

Steve viewed his time with Monk as an opportunity: "He saw I needed it, and he gave it to me. It was like a postgraduate course where I learned what I was supposed to. And he went on with his business afterward. I wasn't fired. But the next time [he needed a group for another club], I wasn't hired again. He saw I had gotten what I needed from him. It would be easier for him to work with his quartet. He didn't need me. He was extremely generous. If someone needed something he could give, he would do it."

With his permit to play in New York clubs again, Monk could star in Birdland. Whatever problems he had had there before, they were completely finished. Johnnie Garry, who had spent the previous decade as Sarah Vaughan's road manager, became a manager at Birdland, where he watched Monk enjoy celebrity status. The club's dressing room wasn't very nice, Johnnie noticed. So he opened his more comfortable office to Monk, Miles, Dinah Washington, George Shearing, and others. Johnnie kept whiskey there, and he enjoyed sharing it and talking with them, mostly about music. Monk played at Birdland at least fifteen times between 1960 and 1965, when Johnny worked at the club. "The good guys would come in a couple of times a year," Johnnie said. Monk earned $1,000 and then $1,250 a week in 1960, and by 1965 he earned $1500 and up to $1750 a week—"big money in those days. He was a big draw with his quartet." The pianist Junior Mance found Monk in a good mood on his birthday, October 10, one night in Birdland. Junior said he, too, had been born on that day. Monk quipped, "No wonder you're so weird."

Monk had enough money to walk around all the time with a few thousand dollars in his pocket for bail money—"just in case he was pulled in somewhere," Harry Colomby recalled. "Most of the time he was aware of what he was perceived to be. At that time, the police were the enemy. That worried me more than anything. Jazz musicians were the target, the crazy, hopped-up jazz musicians. Once rock and roll came in, jazz musicians were ignored. But when I was with Monk, I was always worried about police. Because at that time, drugs were a big thing."

When Nat Hentoff went to Weehawken to interview the baroness for a long article in the October 1960 issue of *Esquire*, he met Thelonious there by chance. Nica talked candidly about her background as a privileged child in Europe and her growing involvement in the jazz world. By 1960 she was managing pianist Sir Charles Thompson and tenor saxophonist Hank Mobley, and helping out Thelonious. The previous year, Hentoff reported, Monk had called her from San Francisco to ask her to find replacements for his bassist and drummer. They had suddenly "decamped" from his group.

Hentoff didn't mention in the article that throughout his interview with Nica, Thelonious had sat in another room with Nat's wife and never said a word to her. Mrs. Hentoff thought he was very odd. Perhaps he was involved with his own concerns, was tired, or as usual simply had no taste for polite conversation and considered that it was Nica, not he, who was required to talk that day. Nevertheless, Nat would always muse that his wife's experience had real significance and augured something for Monk's future.

Monk's albums came out regularly, earning some rave reviews ranging from "an excellent set" to "For my money this is among the year's best releases," as Bob Dawbarn, always a gushing fan of Monk's music, wrote at the end of 1960 about *The Thelonious Monk Quintets* and *The Thelonious Monk Orchestra at Town Hall*. Dawbarn also raved about the reissues *Work* and *Thelonious Monk-Gerry Mulligan* and *Monk's Moods* in early 1961.

The attention of the press, though it could appall the sensitive man, reflected his commercial success. He was asked to contribute to general stories about jazz and told Gene Grove for the *New York Post* on Nov. 14, 1960, "I never tried to think of a definition [of jazz]. You're supposed to know jazz when you hear it. You can't talk it. What do you do when someone gives you something? You feel glad about it."

In March 1961 Monk played in Chicago's Birdhouse club and began to emerge as a fascinating interviewee, now that journalists were asking for private audiences with him. Gabriel Favoino, of the *Sun Times*, wrote that Monk was quite comfortable with the idea that "he had made modern jazz what it is." Monk himself said essentially that music had needed more sophisticated harmonies and a new conception of phrasing. When asked what he was trying to express, he said, "I don't know how to answer that," as he drank bourbon and Coca Cola. "Everything, I guess."

"When was the change of the 1940s complete?" he was asked, but he simply didn't answer. (The change of the 1940s would never be complete, in the sense that jazz would continue to evolve forever, always influenced by the bebop revolution. It's reasonable to speculate that something related to that idea went through Monk's mind when he was asked that question.) "What about Ornette Coleman, is that anything new?" Favoino asked. Monk replied, "I haven't listened to him that good. Like somethin' else was always happenin.' But I don't think it's going to revolutionize jazz."

A while before that interview, Monk had privately commented to Nellie, Nica, Harry Colomby, and a few other people at a gathering in Nica's house that he thought Ornette was very talented and could develop in an interesting way. Harry had noticed by then that Monk liked to be the center of attention all the time, and Harry thought that Monk's reserved reaction to Ornette might have been based on professional jealousy. To begin with, "All entertainers were like that," Harry said. And Monk didn't want anyone to upstage him.

He knew that Ornette played violin and trumpet and was into atonality, but not in a way that thrilled Monk. Ornette's first gig at the Five Spot, following Monk into "Monk's temple," Harry called it, had been explosive in 1959. Nobody could overlook the excitement of Ornette and that new thing. Musicians were attracted to the uproar and went to the club, where they reacted in varied ways. Some felt defensive because Ornette's group didn't have a piano. But his music was freer. "And a year or so passed," Harry Colomby recalled, "and Thelonious said Ornette sounded weird just to sound weird. I thought the same thing. He sounded odd and silly. However, his original quartet with Don Cherry, Billy Higgins, and Charlie Haden at the Five Spot was very exciting."

Monk usually found a way to give a noncommital endorsement to another musician. He never put down someone whose music he didn't like, but said instead, "He's good, he's good." But the matter of Ornette was complex—a musician about whom Monk exercised his righteous, personal taste and also responded with a bit of competitiveness. Monk didn't explain himself thoroughly to Favoino, the writer from the *Sun Times*, who commented, "And so it is always. Today's trailblazers are tomorrow's conservatives"—the kind of off-the-mark, critical comment that Monk had often had to deal with. Either he was too radical and "weird," or he had become too "establishment."

Despite his journeys to and from the edge of the abyss, Monk and Riverside made their marks commercially with his newly invigorated career. The loss of his cabaret card this time hadn't thrown him into a period of near oblivion as it had done in the early 1950s. Though Orrin Keepnews never became part of Monk's private life, the producer had an intense and sometimes exalted working relationship with Monk in the studios and in live performances. Keepnews experienced every aspect of Monk's approach to his career, from his stubbornness and perfectionism in the performances of his songs to his cavalier attitude toward the practicalities of studio costs when he was late. Once Monk walked into the kitchen of the Five Spot, after a set that the audience had loved, and, wiping his neck with his handkerchief, looked at his sidemen one by one, shook his head, saying, "That sure sounded bad."[*] Monk's high standards could make him seem irascible at times, especially when he expressed himself in his hoarse voice.

"Monk was very discriminating. He felt that discrimination was very important," Steve Lacy remembered. When Monk heard somebody play music that he had already heard Bud Powell play 20 years earlier, Monk said, "I can't be too impressed." Steve said, "He was discriminating historically and musically. And he always knew. One of his favorite sayings was 'always know.'" Monk told Lacy. The word "know" had special significance to Monk, because it was "Monk" spelled backwards, with the "m" upside down. "He liked to play with words, turn them upside down, things like that. He always wanted to know where he was and what he was doing and what everyone else was doing, and musically he was extremely oriented."

But Monk was agreeable about standing corrected when he realized he was wrong. One time, Orrin told him that if he ever came more than a little late again for a recording session, he shouldn't bother to show up at all; the costs were prohibitive. After he was reprimanded, he showed up ahead of time—even before Orrin—for a session, and he greeted Orrin by saying, mischievously, "What kept you?"

Nellie didn't go to the studios with him, nor did she go to his gigs in New York. But she traveled with him all the time. She believed that she and her sister Evelyn, nicknamed Skippy—for whom Thelonious wrote a song of the same name—were among his very few close and trusted confidantes. Success hadn't changed his values or his attitude toward his family and friends. He had always known his work was important, and he knew how hard won his success had been—and how suddenly his luck could run out, and his position could turn precarious. He did not leave any part of himself behind.

Nellie remembered how Monk had told her, when he was nineteen years old and filled with idealism about his prospects, that one day people would write about him the way they did about Beethoven and Mozart. She had thought that was impossible, but by now she had begun to learn never to second guess Thelonious. Monk was beginning to acquire that kind of regard. But his experiences had been too frustrating and humiliating, at times, for him ever to let himself be carried away by publicity. If anything, he had a sense of humor about it at times, as if he was aware and even expected that, if something could go wrong, it would.

Harry Colomby had always dreamed of arranging a lucrative contract for Monk with a bigger label than Riverside. In 1959, Monk had made his last recordings in a studio for Riverside. The live Town Hall concert album and the recordings in San Francisco were the last he made directly for the label. A major label, Columbia, had become interested in signing Monk after his success at the Five Spot. Riverside found it impossible to get Monk into the studio again, even though the label was entitled to a few more albums by Monk before he could record for Columbia. And so Riverside, learning of taped concerts played by Monk while on a European tour, at the Olympia Theater in Paris and Teatro Lirico in Milan in April 1961, acquired and released them.

Now Columbia was about to give Monk's career its greatest commercial boost on records, though nothing would ever eclipse the originality of his recordings for Blue Note and Prestige nor the added polish and artfulness of the sessions produced by Keepnews for Riverside.

In 1960, Monk played at Boston's Storyville jazz club again without any mishaps—except for a bad review. The *Boston Traveler* critic John McLellan found Monk's performance uninspired and thought the inclusion of the bassist Scott LaFaro (usually associated with Bill Evans) might have been the reason, his virtuosity—the beauty and subtlety of his harmonies and rhythms—notwithstanding. (LaFaro kept his strings very close to the fingerboard to enhance his agility; without the proper electronic equipment found in recording studios, he had an extremely soft sound.) McLellan didn't like the drummer Pete Mondrian for Monk's group, either. Also in 1960, Monk was booked again at the Newport Jazz Festival and gave splendid performances with his quartet at the Blackhawk club in San Francisco.

In 1961 Monk returned to Storyville, this time performing with Charlie Rouse, bassist John Ore, and drummer Frankie Dunlop, three musicians who would constitute his regular group for the next few years. Monk had sympathetic sidemen working closely with him, wrote McLellan. "Monk's own playing, which started off in a rather fumbling, disjointed manner, became progressively better co-ordinated and fluent as the set wore on. He has his own way of saying things. It's beautiful and brilliant, and there's not much more one need add to that." He played at the Newport Jazz Festival, then went on a tour in Europe with George Wein in 1961.

George Wein felt staunchly loyal to Thelonious. "I didn't hesitate to hire Thelonious again even after he left Storyville and ended up in a

Charlie Rouse, Monk, Frankie Dunlop, Butch Warren at the Five Spot, 1963.
Photo: Raymond Ross.

hospital. Everyone said I was crazy to take Monk to Europe, but he and
I built up a close relationship during that trip. We really became friends
to the end," George reminisced:

> It's always important to have some trust from the musicians. I got
> it from some and not from others. If I asked Monk to be some-
> place at 4 A.M. on a corner, he would be there. We used to go out
> for dinner together. I used to teach him about food. In Milan, we
> went to an Italian restaurant once. I told him to try fettuccine
> Alfredo, and he loved that. The second course was veal saltim-
> bocca. He loved that. Then we were showed the dessert carts.
>
> Monk said, "You mean it's time for dessert?"

I said, "Yes."

Monk said, "Can I have some more of those noodles—the fettuccine Alfredo?"

After a while he was gaining weight. And he saw me gaining weight. So he stopped eating. He was a proud man.

Monk's quartet and Art Blakey and the Jazz Messengers opened the tour at the Royal Festival Hall in London, all the musicians playing for the first time in Britain. The critics had fun in their preparatory articles writing about Monk's habits. Humphrey Lyttleton in the *Melody Maker* recounted how Monk had said one of his hats was "good for keeping the rain off." Monk's great admirer, Bob Dawbarn, wrote for the same magazine that Monk walked onto the stage wearing "an affable smile, a country squire's cap and a suit that would send the editor of the *Tailor and Cutter* into hysterics." Dawbarn praised Monk as a "true Jazz Great . . . During bass and drum solos, he lumbered about the stage, occasionally pirouetting, arms outstretched, with all the grace of a captive hippo. At one point, he lit a cigarette, handed it to a startled member of the audience before resuming his seat at the piano. Later he conducted a scientific experiment to discover the exact point at which his piano stool would topple forward." The critics, especially Dawbarn, liked Monk's singular music, too, although British audiences had mixed reactions to it. Monk and Blakey were booked to play in eight more cities; it's possible that at least one of those concerts was cancelled because of a lack of ticket sales.

George Wein noticed how much Monk depended on Nellie when they traveled. It was Nellie's job to coordinate everything for Monk from his clothes to his meals to his schedule for catching trains and getting to the stages at the right time. "He was crazy about Nellie," George recalled. George traveled with Thelonious many times after that. "For seven or eight years in a row, Monk went to Europe, Australia once, Japan several times, all over," George recalled.

Despite his occasional bouts of severe withdrawal, Monk liked to socialize with friends—and not just the people he met on his long walks or musicians he went to hear in clubs or who came to visit him at his house. After George Wein and his wife, Joyce, moved from Boston to New York in 1960, they lived in an apartment on Central Park West at 65th Street during the early 1960s. They told Thelonious, "Come by and visit us anytime."

Their doorbell rang one day. "It was Thelonious, beautifully attired," Joyce recalled. "He said, 'Hello.'" Joyce and George invited him in for a brandy. "And he played the piano and stayed about two hours. He did that again later in the 1960s," Joyce remembered with pleasure. "He was very intelligent; he didn't say much, but when he had something to say, it was correct and to the point. He was always following the conversations, even if you didn't always think he was."

On tours, Joyce noticed the close relationship between Nellie and Monk. Monk had some quirks, Joyce said, particularly about his wardrobe, which he loved. He would decide, as they were getting ready to leave a place, that he didn't like what he was wearing. Nellie would take things out of the suitcase and start to help him choose another outfit—or perhaps just a tie. "Thelonious was always impeccably dressed, due to Nellie. When they went on tour, everything was clean, right out of the cleaners," Joyce said. She knew that through all the years when the Monks didn't have much money, Nellie had made a cocoon for him, nurtured him and kept him going. "Being the wife of a musician means you're long-suffering," she said, speaking from years of observation of the arduousness and insecurities of the jazz life.

By the early 1960s, Monk had enough money, having signed with Columbia, in addition to all his other work, to afford things he had never been able to have before. He sent Toot to a private school, Cherry Lawn, in Darien, Connecticut for $7,000. a year in 1961, when Toot was eleven. (Harry Colomby found that school for Toot.) Randy Weston recalled that as Toot was growing up, he also went to the Windsor Mountain School in the Berkshires in Massachusetts, where both Toot and Randy Weston's son, Azzadine, played percussion; they had a ten-piece band there called Sahara East. Boo Boo—Barbara— also went off to a private school: Green Chimneys in Brewster, New York. In retrospect Toot would recall that Boo Boo was the really

Foreground, l to r: Thelonious S. Monk, III ("Toot"), Barbara "Boo Boo" Monk, unidentified woman, Thomas W. Monk, Jr. Photo courtesy the family of Thelonious S. Monk, Jr. &-ᴈ

talented child. He had to work hard for what he accomplished as a drummer, but singing and dancing at a superior level came easily to Barbara.

Toot thought that Barbara was especially beloved by her father, with the mystical closeness that sometimes happens between fathers and daughters. She was "the apple of my father's eye," Toot said. Barbara could talk about anything, even sexual matters, and confide in her father, who wrote two songs for her, "Boo Boo's Birthday" and "Green Chimneys."[9]

The additional money in the family gave the children the chance to escape from the intensity and complexities of their family life in their tiny apartment. The private schools put a distance between the children and their father, whose behavior could be so confusing for them. But Toot took with him, too, the positive memories of his immersion in the life of a musical genius and his milieu. There were even stacks of Mozart and Chopin records Monk had in the apartment.

Toot had become used to the visits in the 1950s by Sonny Rollins—"he was at the house everyday"—Art Blakey, and Max Roach. As he recalled in 1996:

> They were just daddy's friends, strange daddy and his strange friends. I knew they were special, and I knew my father was the most special, because all these special guys used to treat my father extra special. But I didn't know they were great musicians. I just thought they were a bunch of eccentrics, and I considered the level they played at as the norm. I was very shocked to find out everybody who played the tenor didn't play on the level of Sonny, Griffin, and Coltrane. My ears were spoiled by the time I was five. I thought if you played drums, you either sounded like Art Blakey or Max Roach or Roy Haynes. If you played the bass, you sounded like Pettiford or Paul Chambers or Charlie Mingus, or on trumpet like Miles or Dizzy—everybody on that level.
>
> But I also knew daddy was special, and this is something I just reconciled within the past few years. I went through a period when I was sort of mystified as to why my father was so different. I was upset about it. Why wasn't he doing what all the other piano players were doing? Because they were all working all the time, getting over all the time, and daddy only sounded like this different kind of cat. I didn't realize, I didn't understand the philosophy. I knew everybody was trying to play like Bud Powell, and I thought that was what you were supposed to do. And my daddy didn't. I didn't understand why he didn't. Was there something wrong with this guy that he's so different and so odd? Even compared to all these other odd balls, he's like far more odd. In

the beginning, I sort of hid that thought from myself—that I thought something was wrong. But of course a few short years later, I realized what he was doing.

When it was suggested to Toot that Monk might have been a little self-centered, Toot readily agreed that his father was the primary focus of his life:

> He was self-centered to a fault, my mother will tell you. However, I think two things on that subject. That's required of genius. Genius dictates that you have to be that way. You don't have control over it, particularly if you find an endeavor to apply that genius to.
>
> And second of all, he was absolutely dedicated to the cohesiveness of his family. So although he was selfish, he was big time for his family. I was out there. I never saw anybody's kids but my sister and me out in the clubs. I hung out in the Village Vanguard at ten years old and before that in the Five Spot when I was eight. I never saw the other cats with their kids. That's how I know the cats. I hung out because he took me around. He took us to the gigs. He was a very devoted family cat. He taught me to spin tops. He played basketball with me. He was there. He had a phone next to his bed, no matter where he was in the world, and I could call him. So I never did feel that I was stuffed away or out of contact when I was away at schools. My parents did a great job. Maybe that's why I'm out here, functioning.

During this period, Harry Colomby set up a music publishing company for the Monks, first called BarThel, named for the children. But a company already existed with that name, and so the Monks had to choose another: Thelonious Music, Inc. For that unique name, they had no competition. Harry got back all the rights to Monk's music from Prestige. Monk had recorded thirteen of his own tunes for Prestige, which were originally published by Prestige Music:

At that time, neither the musicians nor the record companies were making much money with jazz. The record companies were trying to get every penny out of jazz that they could. Prestige gave him only one-half of the rights. I got them all back from Bob Weinstock at Prestige. At the apartment, Nellie said, "Hey, you got the tunes back." She talked like that. She made me out to be terrific. And Thelonious didn't like that. He said, "What do I owe him, my life?" It may have been competition or a kind of rebellion. He may have resented me for doing that, because he needed me to do all these kinds of things. It wasn't because he was tight with a buck or selfish with money.

Harry assigned twenty percent of the publishing rights to himself as his payment, but the gentle manager never took a penny of it. Eventually he simply let his share go to Monk's estate.

Harry observed that Thelonious occasionally became a little angry with Nellie. "Nellie had to nudge him to do things," he noticed. "Men need their women but resent it. Sometimes I thought that Nellie said things at the wrong time, when he was going out of the house—for example, she might reprove him for some stuff. She was on his back and dominant. And he needed that." Harry thought that Nellie may have begun to get a little angry at Monk by that time. When she reproved him, she may have been getting back at him, because "she suffered a lot," and her reaction may have been simply "a human thing," Harry said.

Monk was also very afraid in those days of losing Nellie. He once tried to pick a fight with Harry over Nellie, at a time when Monk was having one of his spells of oddness. He accused Harry of getting Nellie addicted to heroin—a wild, delusionary idea. Nellie had never gone near it. That day, Harry left the apartment quickly, to avoid the possibility of a physical fight developing. That was the only time that Monk and Harry nearly fought about anything.

It seemed to Harry that each incident of oddness got worse than the last for Monk. Eventually Nellie got a prescription for Monk; Harry thought it was for Thorazine. Another close associate, a musician, thought Monk took lithium; perhaps he did take that, too, at some time. Both drugs existed, Thorazine for anxiety and lithium for manic depression; perhaps psychiatrists were experimenting to see if the drugs had any effect on Monk's withdrawal. It would take many years for psychiatrists to learn more about the effects of all kinds of drugs, prescribed or otherwise, that Monk took. "Nellie had an over-whelming job. I'm sure she was mad at him. 'Fuck it, I'm tired,' she must have said to herself," Harry theorized.

Toot recalled his mother talking about "what a wonderful, selfish individual Thelonious was," giving her "the greatest times in her life, every day exciting, every day a challenge." But Toot also thought she was "angry at" his father, because she didn't like him getting high. Toot said, "She felt he did himself in as a young man . . . and might have lived to be ninety-five if he hadn't taken ten million tons of drugs. She felt it changed his personality, and she was angry about that. And that's why [she considered that] he was so selfish. Because he was never giving enough to be the best that he could be in her estimation."

To catch Monk's attention and try to draw him into conversations, Harry always wanted to bring news to Monk, to stir things up, to get him going. "I told him that Marilyn Monroe was dead. I had the stage. Monk said, 'How do you know she's dead? Did you see her?' And when I told him they had landed a man on the moon, he said, 'How do you know? Did you see it?'" Harry thought Monk may have been competing for the limelight, as he seemed to have done to a degree in conversations about Ornette Coleman. Or Monk may have simply been trying to make small talk and stir up a little excitement himself. Harry wasn't sure. Paul Jeffrey thought Monk was saying he didn't believe everything that was written in the papers. They were part of an Establishment that did an African American genius little and belated good.

There were times when Monk's sense of humor washed away all Harry's worries and concerns. One time Harry said: "Erroll Garner had to sit on a telephone booth," when he should have said "a tele-phone book." Monk laughed "like hell" about that one. Another time, a percussionist visiting from Africa, who had an album out, went to visit the "jazz god," as he regarded Monk. Harry was at Monk's apartment during the visit and wound up taking the percussionist to his apartment on the Upper West Side. The percussionist, who never established a career in the U.S., invited Harry upstairs and went to undress in another room. Harry could see him doing that and walked out of the place. "When I described the scene to Monk, Monk went insane laughing. I never heard him laugh so hard before," Harry recalled.

Harry organized many matters for the family. He helped the Monks set up trust funds for Toot and Barbara and hired an accountant to do the Monks' taxes. "Ultimately, Monk and Nellie went through that trust fund money," Harry knew. Sometimes business went along smoothly; sometimes it didn't. Nellie didn't always mail the papers to the accountant on time. When Colomby went to the house, Nellie and Thelonious would call to each other: "Where are those papers?"; "Aren't they under there in that pile?"; "No, they're here, aren't they?"; "Where?"; "There!" Nellie had to go out to the mailbox when the family lived on West 63rd Street, which accounted for some papers being lost or never mailed. But even when the Monks moved later on, and the mail chute was right in the apartment building, she didn't always send papers to the accountant on time. "Oh, I didn't know where the chute was," she told Harry.

Harry was harassed and worried by the delays and problems they entailed. The accountant used to call and ask Harry where the papers were. But he didn't blame Nellie. He thought she was "just overwhelmed."

Many years later, when Harry learned that Nellie and Thelonious had not been legally married, he was very surprised; it would never have occured to him. She signed their tax papers, for one thing. Monk had come from a "stuffy background, and he was a gentleman at all times. Nellie came from a family of judges and lawyers. She was very bright," Harry said. He thought that by the mid-1950s, if Nellie had ever wanted to marry Thelonious, a legal ceremony might have been a very difficult project to organize. For example, Monk didn't concentrate on getting music to Harry, so it had to be transcribed from the records for copyright purposes. That was just a small detail to organize; Monk couldn't or didn't want to do it.

Nellie and Monk at Bud Powell's funeral, August 1966. Photo: Raymond Ross.

Perhaps Nellie enjoyed being a part of the "Nellie thing," the role she played, "Nellie Monk;" though at home she was in a very unglamorous situation, as the "mother-wife," Harry mused, she enjoyed sharing the life of a star and, by association, she was a star herself. But fame had not come to lighten her life until she and Thelonious had lived together for many years. By then his mental condition had to seem burdensome at times.

It's possible that Monk felt a genius didn't need to be married, and Nellie may have shared that reverence for Monk's status and her own independence of spirit to stand behind him in exactly the way she did—by her own choice. She and Monk knew how valuable he was and how well they worked together—a quintessential, free-thinking, unmarried couple with a high calling, who could live comfortably outside the legal norms of society. Intellectual and artistic couples had done the same thing in Greenwich Village for years.

In September 1961, *Harper's* ran a long article, "Monk Talk," by Robert Kotlowitz, paying serious attention to Monk's music and analyzing the audience factions, some of whom were true jazz lovers, and the rest status climbers and spectacle seekers. Kotlowitz described Monk's coats and hats, in which Monk sometimes hid during performances, and his goatee. His baritone voice "often liquid and soft in conversation, can be hoarse beyond imagination," wrote Kotlowitz. He was particularly adept at drawing the reader into Monk's private world, describing the grand piano located in Monk's kitchen, and the sound-proofed ceiling and walnut paneled front door, and Monk's ability to concentrate no matter what was going on in the apartment. "I find something almost every time I sit down at the piano," Monk said. "No matter what's going on around me."

Invited to witness a rehearsal with Monk and Charlie Rouse, Kotlowitz wrote:

> Monk feeds . . . Rouse . . . a note or phrase at a time, a mouthful to be digested to bewildered shakings of the head. It can take the entire two hours to get one full minute of music set between the two.
>
> Monk and Rouse say their notes, as though music were the simplest, most direct language available to man, and even more, as though B-C sharp, played on an instrument, means something as precise and unmistakeable as C-A-T. Throughout the rehearsal, Monk directs with short comments. "You're not making it," he says placidly after the seventh repetition of an octave jump. "Dig it." Well into the next phrase, Monk says, "Don't touch the note, hit it. And when you hit it, augment it."

When he was satisfied, Monk said slowly, "Solid." To Kotlowitz, who was listening to the repetitions, he said, "This dragging you?"

Relaxing after the rehearsal, Monk, wearing a black beanie from Chinatown, listened to jazz records, danced, rocking loosely to the music, and sipped fruit juice. "Jazz is America musically. It's all jazz, everywhere. . . . Maybe I've turned jazz another way. Maybe I'm a major influence. I don't know. Anyway, my music is my music, on my piano, too. That's a criterion of something. Jazz is my adventure. I'm after new chords, new ways of syncopating, new figurations, new runs. How to use notes differently. That's it. Just using notes differently."

The next month, *Down Beat* published a record review of the Monk-Coltrane studio collaboration done just before the first Five Spot gig. Martin Williams split hairs about which were the best of the great tracks. He thought the Five Spot performances had probably been better but wondered if nostalgia hadn't gotten the better of him. "However 'Trinkle Tinkle' very nearly is [up to the standards set by the group in the club]. The other two are fine performances. I think that in this way 'Epistrophy' is excellent, too. And 'Functional' is a near masterpiece."

Monk had at last achieved the distinction of constant scrutiny.

NOTES

Personal interviews: Harry Colomby, Steve Lacy, Paul Jeffrey, Maynard Ferguson, George Wein, Nellie Monk, Johnnie Garry, Junior Mance, Nat Hentoff, Joyce Wein, T. S. Monk Jr.

1. From the biographical documentary on Monk, *Straight, No Chaser*.
2. Gordon (1980).
3. Lapham (1964).
4. Hentoff (1960).
5. "The Night Monk Forgot the Music," *Amsterdam News*, Aug. 13, 1960.
6. *The New York Times*, Feb. 9, 1960.
7. Goldberg (1965). Monk would later record his arrangement of it for Columbia.
8. Reported in *Ebony*, May 1959. The story seemed credible to Steve Lacy.
9. Thelonious composed four songs expressly for himself, Toot said—"Monk's Dream," "Blue Monk," "Thelonious," and "Monk's Mood"—and one song each for Nellie, her sister Skippy, Nellie's niece Jackie, Ruby, and Pannonica. Monk also wrote the song "Little Butterfly," believing that Pannonica had been named for a type of butterfly that her father, apparently an amateur lepidopterist, had been unable to catch.

10 Monk's Dream

Monk began recording for Columbia in 1962. Harry Colomby was delighted. He had worked for about two years to bring that contract to fruition. "I just wanted to get him x amount of dollars for x amount of albums, for security. I told him, 'There's nothing written anywhere that you'll be working tomorrow. Of course it's likely that you will, but you want the security.'"

Sure enough, Monk's first album for Columbia, recorded in October and November 1962 and called *Monk's Dream*, wound up on the *Billboard* charts. "It had never happened to him before in his life," Colomby recalled. The album mixed Monk's original tunes with standards, one of them his staple "Just a Gigolo," as well as "Body and Soul."

Martin Williams took the occasion to write a retrospective about Monk's tortuous career and recording achievements.[1] If any critic was as good at analyzing Monk's music, no one was more astute. "[His] very individual music, plus [his] almost complete lack of interest in the niceties of music and nightclub business and publicity procedures, gained him a reputation for eccentricity that is only partly deserved. Monk waited, confident that an audience sincerely interested in his music would come eventually," Williams wrote. "The laurels . . . are deeply deserved."

Williams suggested that the combination of Monk's talent for communication and his penetrating wit drew listeners deeply into his creations. And far from being an inept technician, Williams wrote:

> Monk is a virtuoso . . . of the specific techniques of jazz, in challengingly original uses of accent, rhythm, meter, time and of musically expressive space, rest, and silence. It is also quite clear that he has won this expressiveness at a gradual sacrifice of conventional pianistic dexterity.
>
> Besides its highly original rhythmic subtleties, there is the question of Monk's quite advanced harmonic ear, which has led one critic to say that he has "pushed jazz to the brink of atonality." I am not sure that the term "harmony" is accurate with Monk; he seems much more interested in sound and in original and arresting combinations of sounds than in harmony *per se*. And this aspect has also saved him from the new Debussyian sentimentalities of many of his fellow modern jazz pianists . . . Monkian alchemy somehow distills granite from sugar water.

Williams thought that people should introduce themselves to Monk's music by listening first to his interpretations of familiar American pop standards. Monk himself thought people should simply begin with his earliest recordings and go forward chronologically; his instructions were "dig it." But Williams's idea was more practical, because it gave a neophyte a chance to practice listening to Monk's unique alterations and embellishments of familiar tunes. Then his alchemy became patently clear.

"Perhaps the masterpiece of such performances is the Monk version of 'Tea for Two,'" Williams wrote, aptly describing Monk's reworking of that song in his own musical language, "which Monk begins as if he were doing a wildly witty version of an old-style jazz pianist. But soon one realizes that the joke is not so much on jazz as it is on the kind of listener who thinks that the jazz pianist is someone who plays a ditty like 'Tea For Two' in a corny, ricky-tik style. One also realizes that everything Monk is playing is entirely and unfrivolously musical as well. Finally, the most brilliant stroke: by the end, Monk has converted the respectful joke into a performance of dramatic seriousness and penetrating sadness." Monk recorded that song for *The Unique Thelonious Monk*, a Riverside album with Art Blakey, and then he redid it for Columbia.

Williams next addressed the question of Monk's rank as a composer:

> [Monk] is, I think, a major jazz composer, the first since Duke Ellington. The same sensibility that leads Monk to make instrumental pieces out of popular songs leads him to compose compositions for instruments. His repertory abounds with intriguing melodies . . . truly instrumental pieces, a good test being that after encountering them we do not go away whistling their "tunes" ourselves so much as wanting to hear them played again. To play Monk properly, musicians justly testify, you have to know the melody and the harmony and understand just how they fit together.
>
> However, a jazz composition does not exist on paper or in the abstract. It lives only in performance, and it is a sign of the great jazz composer that his sense of form extends beyond written structure and beyond individual improviser, to encompass a whole performance . . . So it is with Monk.

Williams went on to analyze specific performances by Monk with virtuosic players, the shortcomings of the sidemen in his quartet, and the brilliance of Monk's style on several songs on his first album for Columbia: "Just a Gigolo," "Sweet and Lovely," "Body and Soul," and Monk's own "Bright Mississippi" (based on the chords of "Sweet Georgia Brown"). Williams was particularly enthralled with Monk's playing on "Five Spot Blues,"

> on which an archaic triplet figure is elaborated within a traditional framework. It is perhaps a measure of Monk's talent that

he is willing to undertake something so totally unpretentious. And yet in his solos, he stretches out that little triplet motif, then abruptly condenses it into half the space it is supposed to occupy, embellishes it until it is almost lost, then rediscovers it and restores its unapologetic simplicity. Almost anyone with an ear for melody and rhythm could follow him exactly, I think, yet in its small way "Five Spot Blues" is also a measure of his sense of order, of his rhythmic virtuosity, his originality, and his greatness.

Williams called Monk's Columbia contract "a final step in [Monk's] ascendancy." It was indeed a badge of his commercial rise—symbolic of the sales of his recordings, the crowds that gathered for him, and the enriched paychecks. By its very existence, Williams's article abetted that commercial success. Even more important for Monk's overall well-being, Williams's imprimatur acknowledged Monk's arrival in a niche from which he could never be dislodged.

In June 1963, as usual for the past few summers, Monk played at the Newport Jazz Festival, arriving rumpled, in a car, just in the nick of time for his concert. In those days, he was often hurrying from one gig to another. Harried by the commotion, he sometimes asked Harry Colomby to suggest the songs for the set. In July 1963, he went into the new Five Spot, which had moved from Cooper Square to Two St. Mark's Place near the Jazz Gallery. Monk's driver's license had been revoked, probably as early as 1960, and to his great dismay, he couldn't drive himself to the club or anywhere. He told friends how unhappy he was about that.

"The car sat across the street in a lot on Eleventh Avenue for years," Harry recalled. "It stayed there with flat tires, and it was costing him money, but he wouldn't get rid of it. He tried to get his license back with the help of a lawyer and Dr. Freymann, but he couldn't. There had been too many tickets, too many moving violations." Harry often sided with musicians in matters of laws and regulations, but he didn't lift a finger to help Monk get his driver's license. "If it was wrong, I said it was wrong," he said.

Driving Monk to the Five Spot one night, Harry saw Monk moving his fingers.

Monk said, "I feel like playing."

Harry was alerted by the remark. Usually Monk stared straight ahead, monosyllabic and unenthusiastic about work. It was the most unsatisfying aspect of the job for Harry, never really seeing Monk happy. "He never said, 'Great, I'm glad to be here.' I never saw him looking forward to a gig," Harry recalled.

Once Harry said, "Do you want to go back home or do you want to go to work?"

Monk replied, "I don't feel like working."

Monk never asked Harry to find him work. "He was never glad about a deal. When he got through working, and he had had a success, there was never any 'wow!' There was no fire. If they had stopped him from playing, he wouldn't have cared," Harry mused. "The feeling you usually get from other people, the happiness and sadness, you didn't get from him. If I told him a concert was going to pay him $25,000 instead of $2,500 [a usual fee Monk received for concerts for George Wein in the 1960s], he would have been mono-syllabic. He would have said, 'oh, yes, okay, uhuh,' as he usually did about everything else.

"I know he was okay with what we did. But he looked for nega-tives. He hated matinees. If he had to work a matinee on a tour of Europe, that was the first thing he noticed on an itinerary. I might explain that the place held only eighty people, and he would stop complaining. But he wouldn't be glad about it or really understand it." He thought of a matinee as an additional day's work, and he felt that people were taking advantage of him by forcing him to perform twice in a single day.

It was uncanny the way Monk could pick up a written itinerary as he was going out the door of his apartment, heading with Nellie to a European tour, and, within a second, locate the one matinee listed amidst all the concerts. Once the baroness was at the apartment when Harry was having a difficult time getting Monk out the door to travel. The baroness said, "Oh, look, a matinee." Monk hadn't seen it on the

itinerary yet. As far as Harry was concerned, the baroness could sometimes be no help at all!

But Monk as a musician, a group leader, and a stubborn, experienced man truly at the helm of his career, stood up for what he
believed in. Suddenly famous and under a great deal of pressure, he was
advised by some people of his own race to get rid of his white
manager. Monk did not let this advise influence him, and he added
quickly that the few times he had ever had trouble with club owners,
they were African American. At one place in Chicago, during a stifling
hot summer, he wanted to wear shorts to work, and the African
American club owner refused to let him enjoy that comfort. Monk
knew all about the problems in race relations; he wasn't naive. But he
was sophisticated in the way he judged people and handled them.
Monk liked to tell the tale that people had urged him to hate white
people, and just at the moment when he though he had succeeded,
someone came along and blew his whole idea to bits. "He was a decent
human being; otherwise I would have said to myself: 'Who needs
this?'" Harry recalled.

Several years later, Harry was at Shelle's Manne-hole in Los
Angeles, listening to a jazz group, where he recognized a musician
who played shrill music with which he tried to make a sociopolit-
ical statement. Harry introduced himself, saying, "You know, I used
to manage Thelonious Monk." The musician said, "Oh, yeah, and
took all his money." Harry said, "Why don't you ask him?" and he
started dialing Thelonious's phone number. The musician said, "You
don't have to do that." Harry knew Thelonious was a "straight-
arrow guy" and would stand up for him. In general Harry had
patience with all jazz musicians, because he thought they were brilliant. And especially Thelonious: "Thelonious was very important to
me. I thought he was a seminal influence on other musicians. And
I was right."

The gentle manager found running Monk's career fascinating—by
turns exalting, unnerving, and dispiriting. There were few dull
moments. But they did occur. Monk liked to eat plentifully and take
naps at the Five Spot, and sometimes his second set was delayed while

he slept. As time went by, Harry wanted Monk to use his newly composed tunes in his sets.

Monk told Harry, "I don't need new tunes."

Harry said, "People want them."

Monk said, "No, and the musicians don't know the old tunes yet. They have to learn those first."

"And so he stayed with what was," Harry said. "But he didn't look for players actively who could learn to play his new stuff and old stuff quickly. He worked with whom he worked with, and he did bring them up to his level."

In 1963, the Riverside releases of the Paris and Milan concerts and a second Columbia album, *Criss Cross*, came out, all garnering splendid reviews. Meanwhile, Monk continued to be a fascinating subject for interviews, always offering his own idiosyncratic answers to the critic's questions. Jazz critic Stanley Dance, an expert on the jazz masters of the Swing era, who arrived in New York from his native England in 1959, wrote a regular column for *Metronome*, presenting a set of identical questions to a variety of musicians. Though Monk hardly qualified as a swing era aficionado's darling, as early as 1944 Stanley had found Monk's work on Coleman Hawkins's recordings very interesting, and he had written about the young pianist for a British magazine, *Pick-Up*, the predecessor of *Jazz Journal*.

Responding to Dance in a 1963 interview, Monk gave candid, by turns serious and witty answers that could surprise only people who didn't know him:

Q: Whom do you consider one of the greatest Americans of the century?

Monk: George Washington Carver.

Q: Excepting New York City and Los Angeles, where in the U.S.A. would you prefer to live?

Monk: The moon.

Q: Outside the U.S.A., where would you prefer to live?

Monk: I'd have to make the whole world before answering that.

Q: Apart from jazz, what is your favorite art form?

Monk: Acting by great actors.

Q: Whom do you most admire in sports?

Monk: Paul Robeson.

Q: Which classical musician, alive or dead, composer or performer, do you most enjoy?

Monk: Iturbi.

Q: Who is your favorite songwriter?

Monk: I like all the great songwriters.

Q: What newspapers do you read?

Monk: I stopped reading newspapers.

Q: What is the greatest need in the music business?

Monk: Better listeners and better performers.

Q: What is your personal ambition?

Monk: To play better.

Q: If music were not your profession, which would you now choose?

Monk: To be a millionaire and do nothing but have fun.

Q: What do you regard as your greatest single achievement?

Monk: To have had a big hand in improving jazz.

Q: Who was your greatest influence?

Monk: Everybody and everything.

Q: Who is or was the greatest blues singer you ever heard?

Monk: I don't know.

Q: Who is or was the greatest dancer you ever saw?

Monk: Baby Lawrence.

Q: What is the biggest headache on the job?

Monk: Trying to get proprietors to have a good piano in tune on the stand.

Q: What other instrument would you like to be able to play?

Monk: If I intended or wanted to play another instrument, I would have learned.

Q: Name a record you play on that you especially like.

Monk: "Blue Monk" with the trio.

Q: Name just one musician you consider much underrated.

Monk: Kenny Clarke.

Q: What's your favorite brand?

Monk: A brand new automobile of the best kind made.

During his 1963 run at the Five Spot, Monk gave a performance at Philharmonic Hall on December 30, again with a big band.[2] Barry Farrell, a writer for *Time*, called the concert "the most successful jazz event of the season." Onstage, Monk greeted his triumph with grace and style. "At the piano he turned to like a blacksmith at a cranky forge—foot flapping madly, a moan of exertion fleeing his lips. The music he made suggested that the better he is received by his audience, the better he gets," wrote Farrell.

At the time of the concert, bassist Butch Warren and drummer Frankie Dunlop played in Monk's regular quartet with Rouse; the rest of the personnel for the ten-piece orchestra included Thad Jones on cornet, Nick Travis on trumpet, Eddie Bert, Steve Lacy, Phil Woods on alto saxophone and clarinet, and Gene Allen on baritone saxophone, bass clarinet, and clarinet. Monk presented a new composition, "Oska T," named for the way he heard someone in Britain say "Ask for T," meaning *T* for Thelonious.

This was the first time Monk had led his orchestra with arrangements by Hall Overton since 1959; only a handful of musicians in the new group had played with him at Town Hall. The higher-voiced clarinets and soprano saxophone gave the new arrangements a different texture, wrote critic Ira Gitler, who had been involved with Monk's recording career at the Prestige label. Gitler's review found fault with the other musicians for uneven performances and with the hall for its acoustics, but never with Monk. Gitler thought Monk's simple theme for his new piece had a nursery-rhyme quality, but as usual Monk's imagination and angular style made the music beautiful, emotionally exciting and intellectualy stimulating. The ensemble enhanced the impression of the piece, and Gitler hoped the group would play more concerts and develop.

Time magazine had planned to run a cover story on Thelonious for its November 29th issue, but instead replaced it with one on the new president, Lyndon B. Johnson. The story on Monk ran on February 28, 1964. Writer Barry Farrell traveled with Monk and interviewed and observed him assiduously for the piece. Just meeting with Farrell for the first time had been a hurdle for Monk. Harry Colomby noticed that Monk started to exhibit signs of one of his spells of oddness, a withdrawal from communication, on the way to their appointment with Farrell. Inside the *Time* office, Monk walked around the room and stared out the window. Harry, knowing the signals well, held his breath, hoping the writer wouldn't notice Monk's strange behavior and have the article cancelled. If Farrell noticed Monk's detachment, he didn't let it fluster him. Exactly why the session upset Thelonious wasn't clear to Harry. Perhaps Monk was thinking about something else. But he had suffered for decades through a stream of articles and reviews riddled with the word "weird." Perhaps he expected, with malaise, that it would come up again in *Time* (and it did). Or perhaps Monk was simply lost in his own reveries.

The article turned out to be a mixed bag of brilliant insights, observations, and witticisms, including "It's always night or we wouldn't need light," supposedly a "mystic utterance" by Monk. Barry Farrell said Monk's compositions were being studied at Juilliard. He described Monk's hectic tour of Europe in 1963—a tour that interrupted his seven-month stay at the Five Spot, which ended in January 1964. In Europe, enthusiastic audiences greeted him in sold-out concert halls in Amsterdam, Dusseldorf, and Stockholm. Swedish television broadcast his concert live. He played in other cities from Helsinki to Milan. "Such European enthusiasm for a breed of cat many Americans still consider weird, if not downright wicked, may seem something of a puzzle. But to jazzmen touring Europe, it is one more proof that the limits of the art at home are more sociological than esthetic," wrote Farrell. Farrell didn't shrink from mentioning the racial prejudice that kept Americans at that time from acknowledging jazz as a major, original American art form.

Time said Monk's Columbia contract called for three albums a year—but didn't add that his producer, Teo Macero, the saxophonist, sometimes had the problem of getting Monk into the studio—and that Monk earned about $50,000 a year. Farrell called Monk's compositions "a diabolical and witty self-portrait," so complex that only Monk and Bud Powell were able to improvise freely on them. Altogether the *Time* story was a gold-mine of the stuff that legends are made of, putting

Monk's survival and showmanship into perspective. His rise had been painful and arduous; he had outlived and outlasted more socially scintillating and flashier musicians who had been felled by the traps and pitfalls of the jazz life. Now Monk was facing his success "gladly but without surprise," Farrell wrote.

Farrell described the dark, moody-looking, smoke-filled Five Spot, Monk's variations and explorations of his usual repertoire, and his shuffling dance filled with twirls and jerky body movements as he stroked his goatee into a point. "His eyes are hooded with an abstract sleepiness, his lips are pursed in a meditative O . . . he is absorbed in a fragile trance, and his three sidemen play on while he dances alone in the darkness. At the last cry of the saxophone, he dashes to the piano and his hands strike the keys in a cat's pounce." It was a fine description of the way Monk always hit exactly the right note on the piano at the exact moment he should come in.

Ben Riley, a young drummer about to join Monk's group, would eventually reveal that "when the music was happening, Monk would get up and dance. When the music was swinging, he said he didn't have to play; the group was making it happen." (3) The dancing was a part of the piano playing, and Monk used both to guide the musicians and inspire them to find the right groove.

Farrell knew Monk's champions assigned spiritual strength to the pianist, whom Farrell, unlike musicians, perceived as selfish and moody offstage. And Farrell didn't hesitate to explore Monk's dalliances with drugs: "Every day is a brand-new pharmaceutical event for Monk: alcohol, Dexedrine, sleeping potions, whatever is at hand, charge through his bloodstream in baffling combinations. Predictably, Monk is highly unpredictable."

Farrell also learned that Monk was at times a very happy, even gleeful man. One day Monk went to his brother's apartment and danced in front of a mirror, wearing a boutonniere made out of a collard green leaf. Farrell also noticed Monk's periods of muteness. Even so, Farrell thought Monk was far more witty than wacky, and he theorized that people became confused when they tried to analyze Monk's personality because he had developed a method for teasing

Monk waiting to use phone at the 5 Spot, 1963. Photo: Raymond Ross.

"squares." "Monk is proud of his skill," Farrell wrote. "'When anybody says something that's a drag,' he says, 'I just say something that's a bigger drag. Ain't nobody can beat me at it either. I've had plenty of practice.'" Farrell wrote that Monk had become more "mannerly" and "conventional" lately—apparently unaware that Monk had been that way all his life. Farrell also added: "He says he hates the 'mad genius' legend he has lived with for twenty years—though he's beginning to wonder politely about the 'genius' part." And Farrell recounted how Nellie had supported the family and nurtured Monk through a period Nellie would call their "un-years."[4] Then the baroness became a patroness and family friend to Monk and a benefactor to other musicians, too.

"Now that Monk is being heard regularly, he seems more alone than ever," Farrell wrote, attributing the situation in part to the splintering of jazz into many styles. Other musicians had far more bizarre personalities than Monk's and cultivated and exploited their images more assiduously than Monk did. Racial woes and the financial insecurity, long journeys, and hardships of jazz musicians in general added to Monk's lonesomeness, Farrell suggested. Monk bemoaned his lack of companions among musicians by the mid-1960s. He used to have more time to see them, in the days when all of them were struggling even harder. Now his contact with Bud Powell had dwindled to sending money to Bud in a tuberculosis sanatorium near Paris. Steve Lacy was under the impression that people had stopped going to Monk's apartment to visit him and take walks with him. Monk needed that company; without it he was too isolated. But Monk didn't wallow in self-pity; he was very clear about his mission; he told Farrell, "All you're supposed to do is lay down the sounds and let the people pick up on them. If you ain't doing that, you just ain't a musician. Nothing more to it than that."

Farrell wrote, "When he is playing anywhere near New York, the baroness comes to drive him home, and they fly off in the Bentley, content in the knowledge that there is no one remotely like either one of them under the sun . . ." Then Monk "skips out and disappears into his old $39 a month apartment. The baroness then drives home

Thelonious with Nellie in their apartment, November 1963. This photo ran with the Time magazine story. Photo: David Gahr.

to Weehawken, where she lives in a luxurious bedroom oasis, surrounded by the reeking squalor her thirty-two cats have created in the other rooms."

At home, Monk spent time "layin' dead," as he called his rest periods to Farrell. The children were at boarding schools. Nellie wended her way rapidly through the narrow pathways in the clutter of their possessions. "Monk's grand piano stands in the kitchen, the foundation for a tower of forgotten souvenirs, phone books, a typewriter, old magazines and groceries." (It was not unusual for people who had suffered through poverty to save everything on the theory they might someday need it.) When Monk shouted to Nellie—"Nellie! Ice cream!"—as he lay in bed, she rushed to serve him, but she muttered to herself in a gentle voice, "Melodious Thunk."⁵

Farrell wrote: "Nellie and the few other people who have ever known Monk in the slightest all see a great inner logic to his life that dignifies everything he says and does. He never lies. He never shouts. He has no greed. He has no envy."

Harry Colomby echoed that praise: "Monk was never conniving. He was never planning to get someplace by doing something. He was preoccupied, overwhelmed by himself. I can't blame him. He was emotionally immature; he never grew up. He was not a father who lay down in bed and worried about his kids, for example."

Farrell wrote, "His message, as Nellie interprets it to their children is noble and strong. 'Be yourself,' she tells them. 'Don't bother about what other people say, because you are you! The thing is to be just yourself!' She also tells them that Monk is no one special," but the children believed their own eyes and ears and knew differently. And Nellie said, "After all, if Thelonious isn't special, then what is?"

Around this time, Monk developed a peculiar habit onstage at the Five Spot. He played one tune with the group. Then he called for a solo number from each musician. He would not play again with the group until the end of the first set, after which he would rejoin them for the final number.

Harry often said to Monk, "You can't do that."

Monk answered, "People want to hear solos. They guys want to play. They tell me they want to solo."

Monk just didn't feel like playing, Harry knew. That routine happened only during the first set, when "Monk went through a period," Harry said. "I don't know how long it took for him to get over that. It seemed like forever. For the second set, he'd play. When he handled the first set that way, I used to pace back and forth. It wasn't so interesting—no brilliant solos. I didn't tell him that. But that was true. And it was the only time I can remember his going to the microphone and saying, 'Now I'd like you to hear a nice solo from the drummer,' or whomever. And he would go offstage and have a drink and a sandwich." This odd behavior eventually ended. "Thank God," Harry said.

Frankie Dunlop was about to leave the quartet, and soon afterward so would the bassist Butch Warren. Warren had gotten his job through the recommendation of a very respected bassist, Sam Jones. After filling in for one gig at Birdland, Butch stayed with the band for a year, noticing that Nellie showed up for a performance once in a while, and Nica arrived every other day. Though he recognized Monk's genius, he didn't have a close relationship with his boss. "I just made the job," Butch recalled.

There were no rehearsals. On the bright side, Butch found that Monk gave the bass plenty of space; it stood out and played a dominant role in Monk's music. But Monk didn't like Butch to use the bow, and so Butch wasn't very interested in the gig. A few other bassists would also suffer from the same constraint with Monk, who wanted the group to swing first and foremost. After a world tour under George Wein's auspices, the long run at the Five Spot, and the Town Hall concert, Butch quit to go home to Washington, D.C. The group next went through a succession of about five bassists, until Monk finally asked drummer Ben Riley to pick someone he liked; Ben picked Larry Gales.

Ben, thirty years old in January 1964, had played in both Woody Herman's band and later Sonny Rollins's group for almost a year, as just two examples of his important gigs in the years when he was developing into a strong, soft-voiced drummer capable of powerful subtleties. He could wrest more music from two drums and two cymbals than many other drummers could produce from ten-piece drumsets. (His astounding ability is demonstrated clearly on the video, *Monk in Oslo*.)

When he returned to New York after the Rollins job, he went into the Five Spot for six weeks and played in successive trios with pianists Junior Mance, Walter Bishop, Jr., and Bobby Timmons. Every time a trio changed, Ben remained with a different group as the warm-up group for Thelonious's band. Ben had no idea Thelonious was listening to him. Every night Thelonious looked at Ben and walked right by him into the kitchen without saying a word.

Larry Gales, 1965. Photo: Raymond Ross.

"One night, he came in and said to me, 'Who the fuck are you, the house drummer?' And he walked into the kitchen. Those were the first words he spoke to me," Ben recalled:

> Some of my friends there that night asked me how I liked listening to Monk. I said, 'The greatest. I'm going to be in that band.' I just felt it. After we closed on a Sunday, his manager called me the next day. [It was January 29, 1964.] He said they were in a Columbia recording studio, and Thelonious wanted me to finish a record he was doing. I had a friend. We used to play a joke on each other. We'd call each other and say, "Come on down, Ellington wants you to play with his band." So I thought it was a joke, and I hung up on Monk's manager. He called right back and said, "I'm serious. We're here. Please take a taxi and come down."
>
> Sure enough, Charlie Rouse, Butch Warren [still with the group at that moment], and Monk were there. Monk still didn't say a word. As soon as I set up, he rushed in and started playing. I thought, "It's a good thing I've been listening for six weeks." After we played, Monk finally spoke to me. He said, "You need money?"
>
> I said, "No. I'll wait for the check."
>
> He said, "I don't want anyone in my band being broke."
>
> I said, "What?"
>
> He said, "I don't want anyone in my band being broke. You got a passport?"
>
> "No," I said.
>
> "Hurry up," he said. "We're leaving Friday for Europe."
>
> So I had to rush to get a passport. The rest is history. I stayed with Monk for almost five years. I learned from him, and I'm still learning from him. I didn't understand a lot of things he said to me at the time. Now things happen, and what he said pops into my head. "Oh, that's what he meant." He was way ahead.

Thirty years later, Ben reflected on some of the lessons he learned from Monk:

He said, "When you play with small groups and big groups, don't change the way you play, because all you're doing is trying to force things to happen."

He made me think melodically.

He taught me about playing in between the beats. He said most guys play slow, fast, and medium—only three tempos, and we're going to play between the three. To make that clearer, we played either slow, medium, or fast, too, but sometimes we played a little faster or slower than other people. Monk never tapped it off the way you would expect it to be. And that's when I started playing between the beats.

Also he said, "Just because you're the drummer, you think you have the best beat. But nobody likes all the songs. You have to listen to the one who likes the song the best. He has the best beat. Listen to the bass player. If he likes the song best, that's who you play with. Sometimes it will be me." I've been listening ever since.

And he used to play things he knew I didn't like. He made me listen to other musicians. "Blue Monk" used to drive me crazy. Monk played it slowly. And he wouldn't force me beyond a point until I was comfortable there, and then he'd take me to another level.

He actually taught me how to be inquisitive. And he was a very definite person. When he made up his mind, he was definite. Even if his decision rubbed you the wrong way, he went ahead with it.

He made me think. He made me realize you have to make mistakes to learn. Mistakes were positive. He made me be creative. He made me use mistakes, and then not make them again. He taught me to take chances. He didn't tell me that in words, but the music dictated that I take chances.

Monk had always liked the gifted, versatile drummer Billy Higgins, who had played with his quartet only briefly. Nica had wanted Billy Higgins to follow Frankie Dunlop into Monk's group. Higgins had played a great deal of experimental, modern music. Nica admitted to Ben that she had preferred Higgins to him when the group was playing in San Francisco. But by that time, she said, she understood why Monk wanted Ben for the group.

Ben, who became a close friend of Monk's, never wanted to discuss their personal relationship. Ben said that sometimes Monk talked so much that he told him, "Why don't you shut up?" But Ben also thought, in retrospect, that Thelonious kept his troubles to himself. He didn't unburden himself to other people. Ben would say that he thought everything eventually "caught up with him."

Some people liked to joke that Monk didn't talk much except to cuss. But there were times when Monk seemed to wax virtually talkative with interviewers, revealing the scope of his intellect. He could be downright hilarious and candid in a way that, for all its succinctness, gave the impression of chattiness, about his experiences. He understood that people were interested in what he was doing. They were standing in line to hear him. He knew he was one of only a few jazz musicians who had ever appeared on the cover of *Time*, and he understood the significance of the exposure for his career and for jazz. He knew he was winning honors in the jazz magazine polls.

At times it may have seemed as if Monk couldn't muster a great deal of enthusiasm for his celebrity. "Ain't that a bitch?" he would say rhetorically when Bob Jones, on George Wein's staff, told Monk a few years later that he was included in a *Who's Who* book. Monk had a sense of humor and a modesty about his fame. He remained down-to-earth. The hard times had been hard for a very long time. He would have kept living without all the attention he had finally won, despite those people who had failed or refused to accept and acknowledge the African American genius in their midst—a true *rara avis*, an even greater pariah for a while than a white genius would have been. Barry Farrell had been perspicacious enough to write that Monk had seemed to be a member of "a race of strangers."[4] But he had lived to have the last laugh on any unfriendly audiences and critics such as the one who had written in the 1940s that Monk "played bad." And Monk was enjoying his life, having a good time in his own way, staying focused on music.

NOTES

Personal interviews: Harry Colomby, Eddie Bert.

1. Williams (1963).

2. He was supposed to have performed there on November 29, but President John F. Kennedy had just been assassinated. Concerts were cancelled and rescheduled. Monk seemed unworried by the postponement, joking with his musicians in a rehearsal, as trombonist Eddie Bert remembered, "I told him to stay in the bulletproof car."

3. From the documentary *Thelonious Monk: An American Composer*, © Toby Byron/Multiprises, 1961. All rights reserved.

4. From an interview by Valerie Wilmer in *Down Beat* (1965); revised version in *Jazz People*, (1977).

5. Two years later, in Canada, Monk told Warren Gerard, of the *Globe and Mail* that Nellie had never said any such thing. "That's a lie, man. It's those reporters, man, you can't trust them." Though it's unlikely that the witticism was trumped up, it did appear to be a joke at his expense—even if, for his demandingness, he probably deserved it.

6. A reference to the preface of *This Man from Lebanon: A Study of Kahlil Gibrans*, by Barbara Young; the full quote is given as one of the epigraphs to this book.

11 Deity and Target

Back from Europe, Monk was touring in the United States and Canada with his quartet and planning another concert with the ten-piece band for Philharmonic Hall; he seems to have been fairly constantly on the move in this period of commercial success.

When he performed at Massey Hall in Toronto in April 1964, the critics paid rapt attention. Patrick Scott, of the *Globe and Mail*, called the performance brilliant: "Monk especially achieved greater swing with his right foot than the entire Thompson ensemble [a band that shared the bill with Monk] managed to contrive all evening." Scott lauded the beauty, drive, and warmth of Monk's style, and called his introductions "miniature jewels." As usual, Helen McNamara, of the Toronto *Telegram*, who had never accepted Monk's music wholeheartedly, found fault with the group. The headline for her piece read, "Monk Show Flies Low." Though Ralph Thomas of the Toronto *Daily Star* agreed with Scott, he muttered about Monk's shyness with the audience; Monk didn't seem to acknowledge the exuberant applause. So Thomas called Monk a "strange one . . . hulking and brooding."

Monk could never shake that image; it had become part of the socially awkward musician's claim to fame. Lewis Lapham, who had the chance to interview Monk in his own apartment, tried to dispel some of the mystery surrounding Monk. Lapham had expected to find Monk hidden away in a dark, back room but instead discovered him in his homey, perenially cluttered, little ground-floor apartment in a tenement. The title of the story, "Monk: High Priest of Jazz," reinforced the old image.' But Lapham became the first writer to describe Monk as "a sentimental man with kind eyes." Lapham looked for the familiar and positive in Monk's personality:

> Contrary to prevalent gossip, Monk is neither crazy nor putting on an act. The story of his life is the story of an honest man in a not-so-honest world. In many ways naive, believing—as he once told a trumpet player—the truth is not supposed to hurt you— Monk never learned to tell the convenient lies or make the customary compromises. That he should have been proclaimed the complete and perfect hipster is an absurd irony.

Lapham conceded that Monk was a man who lived according to his own instinctive schedule and yet remained a creature of habit. Monk, for example, had refurnished his family's apartment, which had been damaged twice by fires (in 1956 and 1961), rather than move out of the neighborhood or out of town to places that seemed to him "foreign and uncertain, inhabited by unreliable people who, for no apparent reason, one day ask for your autograph and the next day want to put you in jail."

Although Monk was wearing different clothing than he had for the Robert Kotlowitz interview, this time "an elegantly cut sharkskin suit, a purple shirt made of Japanese silk, a dockworker's cap and a diamond ring on the little finger of his right hand"—Monk often wore a big diamond ring on each hand—he treated Lapham to the same scene that Kotlowitz witnessed in the kitchen on West 63rd Street. Monk had just returned from a recording session at midnight. He took a can of grape soda from the icebox and sat down at his piano. "While he played 'Lulu's Back in Town,' Nellie rummaged through the bedroom in search of his slippers. Married to Monk for seventeen years, Nellie watches over him as if he were one of the children, even picking out his clothes in the morning. 'We don't talk much,' she said, 'but I just like being with him,'" Lapham wrote.

Monk began pacing the room, occasionally stopping at the piano to play some chords, constantly lighting cigarettes with gold lighters he took out of various pockets. "Monk stands steadfastly erect, carrying himself with a dignity that marks him as a man of serious purpose. He speaks in a soft drawl, slurring his words and ending his sentences with the question, 'You dig, man, you dig?'" Lapham recounted.

"He began with the subject of his reputation. 'That's a drag picture they're paintin' of me, man,' he said. 'A lot of people still think I'm nuts or something . . . but I dig it, man; I can feel the draft.'" Lapham thought that Monk's music had always saved him from the effects of ridicule. Monk said he was bewildered by complaints from some night club owners about his dancing and idiosyncratic stage demeanor. "'I don't imitate anybody,' he said. 'I have my own way of walking and talking. They want me to smile at the audience or play every forty minutes like a train schedule or something, but I can't be grinning at somebody's face for nothing, man. I'm thinking about how to play, and I ain't got time for that fancy stuff.'" To encourage his musicians in his group to be themselves, he had once told them, "A man is a genius just for looking like himself."

"The fierce intransigence of his convictions," wrote Lapham, "also hurt him commercially and often frightened people. In a milieu where departures from conventional morality are considered proper if not obligatory, Monk remained embarrassingly square. After quitting work at 4 A.M., he would go dutifully home to Nellie. 'He's so straight, it makes you nervous,' [his manager] said. 'A man's not supposed to be that way in this business.'"

Lapham noted that Monk was a dyed-in-the-wool New Yorker:

> Monk's talents have won him global acceptance, but he still feels easiest in New York. Asked 'What is jazz?' he once answered, "New York, man. You can feel it. It's around in the air."
>
> The first time he played a concert in Switzerland, he was asked how he liked the lakes. He said he preferred the lake in Central

Park. . . . He believes his 1954 Buick is the best car in the world, that he is married to the best wife, lives on the best block in the best town, and, despite his various troubles with established authority, is a citizen of the best country. A critic soliciting musical opinions once asked him to name his favorite vocal group. Monk nominated Fred Waring, on the ground that "he's the only guy that sings the 'Star Spangled Banner' right."

Monk has accepted his success without surprise, but he remains slightly suspicious of the attendant publicity. 'I was playing the same stuff twenty years ago, man,' he says, 'and nobody was painting any portraits.' He nevertheless enjoys his new affluence. He likes traveling first class on airplanes and usually carries a bill of large denomination, either $100 or $1,000, on the theory that "you never know when you're gonna run into a bargain." (Or when he was going to need bail money, as Colomby knew.)

Lapham said that Monk kept experimenting musically. While Nellie was asking him whether he wanted to take his green suede shoes to Stockholm, "Monk gazed at the ceiling and said, 'The only cats worth anything are the cats who take chances. Sometimes I play things I never heard myself.'"

At 3 A.M., Monk decided he wanted to buy a quart of strawberry ice cream around the corner, and after asking Nellie if he needed to change shirts—she said "no"—he promised to return in half an hour. At the front door, he remembered his boots. "With the apologetic smile of an absent-minded but obedient husband he went meekly back to fetch them," Lapham observed.

Monk's insistence on always looking fine was not so much vanity, though he advised younger musicians to be sure they dressed in fine clothes, because it was a survival instinct to dress well in a racist society. A much younger pianist, John Hicks, recalled how he and a friend were carrying an upright piano along a street on the Upper West Side, when they saw Thelonious. He offered to help them carry it to John's apartment—up the stairs in a building with no elevator—then he sat down to test the piano's sound. He didn't give John any advice about playing but told him to be sure to always look "fine." Monk himself didn't want to be mistaken for a less-dignified and worthy person than he knew he was. He used his finery as protection against disrespectfulness, resentment, and attacks on his genius.

Lapham ended his story: "Outside in the street, walking in the shadows of the warehouses on 11th Avenue, the lights of the Jersey piers glowing cold and far-off across the Hudson River, Monk listened to the wind rattling empty tin cans in a vacant lot. He looked at the sky and said: 'You know what's the loudest noise in the world, man? The loudest noise in the world is silence.'"

Jules Colomby produced, in association with Marc Smilow, Thelonious Monk and Orchestra at Carnegie Hall on June 6, 1964, at 8:30 P.M., with ticket prices ranging from $2.50 to $5.00. Once again, Hall Overton wrote the arrangements, and rehearsals took place at his midtown loft three steep flights above Sixth Avenue. In the group were Rouse and Riley with bassist Spanky DeBrest, and six other musicians: Eddie Bert, Nick Travis, Jerome Richardson, Steve Lacy, Phil Woods, and Thad Jones. For a 10 o'clock rehearsal, some of the musicians came late, with Monk arriving latest of all, "staring rather vaguely in front of him and not looking at anyone in particular," wrote Martin Williams, who attended the rehearsal: "[Monk] returns Thad Jones' greeting and twirls around in a kind of dance movement. Lacy approaches him, and they exchange greetings. Then for a moment he looks out of the back windows of the studio. Soon he speaks to Overton: 'How's it going?'"

Overton said it was going all right, except for some problems with the horns. Overton said, "I scored out some chords at the end of 'Rootie Tootie.' When you hear them you might want to pick a couple for backgrounds for the solos."

Monk nodded, and the group played "Thelonious." Williams continues:

> Overton turns to Monk and says, "That goes faster than that, doesn't it?"
>
> Monk moves to the piano, apparently to give the question a complete answer, and begins to play the piece himself, a bit faster,

very forcefully, and with fascinating harmonies and successions of sounds pivoting off that one note [that is the basis for that song]. At the end, Overton asks: "Are you going to take all the blowing on this?" [Monk said,] "Anybody can blow it if they know the chords." [Overton said,] "Well did it sound okay?" [Monk said,] "Was everybody in tune? Yeah, it sounds okay."

" . . . Okay, let's go to 'Rootie Tootie' again," Overton says. "Monk, I'd like you to hear those chords now. Maybe you could think about how you would like to use them for background?"

Monk nods. And paces. And turns. His tread is becoming heavier and more varied.

"Okay, here we go, chord number 1," said Overton. . . .

Monk kept stepping and turning as Overton worked on more chords and finally called out: "Hey Thelonious . . ." trying to get him to return to the piano, but Monk seems uninterested. Monk had never removed his overcoat and hat and with all his movement is perspiring. It was, after all, a warm day in June, but the man stayed hidden in his coat. Overton went to play the piano himself with the band. Williams reports, "At the end, Monk says, 'Everybody ought to hold that last note.'

"'But fade it out gradually, right?' [Overton asks].

'Yeah.'"

Overton led them to work on backgrounds to the solos. Williams continues:

> Monk's movements, feet complemented by flying elbows, are developing into a kind of tap dance. At the same time, he still seems to be executing counter-rhythms and special accents to the piece as they play it. Overton crosses over to him for a quiet discussion—a discussion on cigarets, one might think from the concentration with which both of them are smoking.

Moving back to the group, Overton announces they should work on "Four in One" in their last half hour of rehearsal time, but the musicians choose "Rootie Tootie" and play the choruses. Williams describes the scene:

To the rear, Monk is decidedly tap dancing now, in an unorthodox but effective way. The collar of his raincoat is quite wet. His face is still expressionless—or perhaps a bit solemn. He seldom looks directly at anyone unless he is speaking to them—as if he were too shy to but not quite admitting it. He is listening, and his movements still seem to be a way of participating in the rehearsal—encouraging, feeling if it's right. From time to time, one or two of the players will turn to watch him briefly after a particularly heavy stomp or tap or a triplet.

The group plays "Rootie Tootie" from the top. "The only thing missing is Monk," wrote Williams. The men decide to meet again for a rehearsal only on the morning of the performance and not over-rehearse and get tired.[2]

Monk received good notices for his narrow-brimmed, cream-colored, ten-gallon hat and gray suit from John S. Wilson of the *New York Times*, but only the final moments of the program had a zestful exuberance from the ensemble, Wilson said. He didn't like the rhythm section or Rouse at all. Though other musicians had great respect for Monk's sidemen, their very position in the group sometimes made them seem like fair game to critics. It was not that they were inferior players, but they were interpretative artists subordinate to the leader-genius.

Perhaps the performance would have received a better review had Monk played through the rehearsals with the band and supported that effort, even if he didn't need any rehearsals himself. One wonders if he knew he would stand out above all by maintaining his aloofness. If people wanted to consider him apart, he would play that role to the hilt and upstage everyone. That was the way he had conducted his entire life. Most likely he had considered himself as the composer, and that view of himself, plus his shyness and his distaste for arranging, led him to assume a shadowy role in the preparations.

After that concert, Monk continued working primarily within a quartet. A critic named Jo McDonald gave a jewel-like but curious review to Monk at the Village Gate in August 1964. "Thelonious

Monk, saturnine and hatted . . . slipped on to the piano stool, struck a few chords, and we were transported immediately to his own special kingdom, with Charlie Rouse, Ben Riley, and Bob Cranshaw on tenor sax, drums and bass. I was reminded, watching Monk play, of Segovia, since both men have such command of their instruments that their hands alone move, leaving their bodies immobile." It was the first time anyone had ever seen Monk play without using at least one foot as a rhythm prop.

The next month, he shared a Sunday afternoon with bassist Charles Mingus at a Monterey Jazz Festival concert in California. By March 1965, Ben Riley's friend Larry Gales was playing bass in the quartet, when Monk set off on a world tour oranized by George Wein. It began in London and moved on to Italy, Germany, Holland before switching to the eastern hemisphere: Japan, Hong Kong, Manila, and Australia and New Zealand.

In a room at London's Hilton Hotel, Monk, in a mellow, talkative mood, made himself available to writer Valerie Wilmer for one of his more striking interviews.[1] He discussed his history, including the "dark days" and the "un years" as Nellie dubbed them to Valerie, when he didn't have "the prospects of a dog," she said.

Wilmer asked Monk about his technique, questioning the unorthodox way he held his hands. "Was he ever taught to hold his hands in the formal manner?" she asked:

> "That's how you're supposed to?" he asked, feigning wide-eyed surprise. "I hold them anyway I feel like holding 'em. I hit the piano with my elbow sometimes because of a certain sound I want to hear, certain chords. You can't hit that many notes with your hands. Sometimes people laugh when I'm doing that. Yeah, let 'em laugh. They need something to laugh at."

By dancing in performance he could dig the rhythm better, he explained. (It was possible he liked to dance as a way of mastering his shyness, too. Louis Victor Mialy, a French journalist and record producer, once remarked that Monk danced "for the joy of it.")

"Somebody's got to say something about everything you do!" he commented and added that he didn't read what people wrote about him. "People write all kinds of jive."

When Wilmer suggested that Monk didn't live the way other people did—for example he had always lived at home in the family apartment—Monk said:

> I don't know what other people are doing; I just know about me . . .
>
> I've got a wife and two kids to take care of, and I have to make some money and see that they eat and sleep, and me, too—you dig? What happens 'round the corner, what happens to [someone else's] family is none of my business . . . I don't be around the corner, looking into everybody's house, looking to see what's happening. I'm not a policeman or a social worker—that's for your social workers to do. I'm not in power. I'm not worrying about politics . . .

Monk's response is revealing of his personality and also his view of himself. Monk always listened very carefully, as few people did, and was a very literal person, addressing himself to precisely what people said. Furthermore, it's curious that he singled out policemen and social workers in his answer; his mother had been a social worker, and his brother Thomas had worked for a while for the police. Monk was declaring himself unlike them; he stood apart from his family, and he wasn't like anybody but a musical genius. That kept him busy.

Wilmer continued, ". . . and just as he refused to concern himself with politics, Monk is, on the surface, equally indifferent towards racial problems:

> "I hardly know anything about it," he said, brushing the subject aside. "I never was interested in those Muslims. If you want to know, you should ask Art Blakey. I didn't have to change my name—it's always been weird enough! I haven't done one of those 'freedom' suites, and I don't intend to. I mean, I don't see

the point. I'm not thinking that race thing now, it's not on my mind. Everybody's trying to get me to think it, though, but it doesn't bother me. It only bugs the people who're trying to get me to think it."

Harry Colomby and Monk had watched the civil rights march on Washington in 1963 on television together. Though Monk had never been involved actively in the civil rights movement, he remarked to Harry, "I think I contributed as much with my music. I don't have to be there marching." Harry knew that people might go to Harry Belafonte or later Bill Cosby, if they wanted to ask for advice or help in the struggle. But Monk didn't articulate the matters involved in the movement. "People didn't go to see him for that," Harry knew. Perhaps Monk might have felt a little guilty about his inaction, and that may have prompted him to say he didn't have to march. "But he contributed to the movement by what he symbolized. And he stood up. He was a proud man," Harry said.

After the riots in the 1960s in Watts and other cities, several faces were painted on a public mural in Chicago:; one was Patrice Lumumba; another was Malcolm X; another was Thelonious Monk—"stoic and different," said Harry. He was one of the "gods that inner city folks looked up to because of the strength that emanated from him . . . Monk symbolized a black man who was strong . . . It was important for a black man to be strong. He had a stern look. Even his smile was wistful . . . Monk represented a guy not satisfied with the status quo—but not angry."

Nellie told Wilmer, "We live music everyday. Thelonious has never attempted to do anything else except play music. He's always been optimistic." Monk had said, "How can I be anything other than what I am?"

The increase in his income made no difference to him, Wilmer elicited from him. "If I feel like it, I'll spend it, but I spend it on what anybody else spends it on—clothes and food. My wife and kids spend a lot of money, but I really don't know how much I make. I'd go stupid collecting and counting my money. I worked for seventeen dollars a week when I was a kid, make thousands now . . . Everything's all right. I don't look like I'm worrying about anything, do I? . . . I don't talk much because you can't tell everybody what you're thinking. Sometimes you don't know what you're thinking yourself!"

Nellie said, "You wouldn't know whether he was happy or not at any time. He's always been very agreeable. Even in the direst situations you can't see if he's worried from looking at his face. Maybe you can tell from a chance remark, but he isn't a worrier. We have a theory that worry creates a mental block and prevents you from being creative. So worry is a waste of time."

Monk said he liked to walk and dig the scene, and at home he watched television. He suggested that was the way he took his vacations, since he didn't have to pay to watch television, but he could still experience the world. He could fall asleep in his bed at home while watching television; he didn't have to pay to go to a movie where he would fall asleep in his seat.

He candidly recalled about his drug arrest in 1951, relating that:

> being in jail was a drag. I'm sorry for anyone that's in jail. . . . In the United States the police bothers you more than they do anywhere else. The police heckle you more. You don't have that much trouble anywhere else in the world. . . . The police just mess with you for nothing. They just bully people and all that kind of shit. They carry guns, too, and they shoot people for nothing.
>
> New York violent? It has to be violent if the cops are making the trouble. . . . You don't run into trouble so much if you're kind of famous, but people that is kinda down, they just pick on them. But New York changes. Anyplace changes a lot because you have different generations coming up with new ideas. The police ain't quite as bad as they used to be, but they'd probably get better if they put more intelligent people on the force.

Monk said he kept playing his same tunes over and over again "so somebody will hear them." Once, when he was asked to bring a new Monk song to a recording session, he brought "Abide with Me," the hymn written by William H. Monk; it turned out to be a fine, surprising inclusion on the recording. He laughed when he found out that Valerie Wilmer thought his music was easier to listen to than it used to be. He said she was essentially getting used to it. Furthermore, he wasn't changing anything because he wanted to reach people with what he had already done. "Because you might be changing and then stop playing, and they'd not get a chance to hear it."

"The massive, bearded figure leaned back in his chair and grinned expansively," Valerie wrote. "'But,' he added, 'I never be noticing these things; I just be trying to play.' He sank back into an untidy heap, looking for all the world like a huge, well-dressed grizzly bear who had somehow found a home in the recesses of a plushly padded armchair at the London Hilton. For Monk, it was time, indisputably his time. He closed his eyes. He slept," ended Wilmer.[4]

Monk went into the Columbia studios in February and March 1965 but made no more recordings for the label that year. For one thing, he was on the road, working. Life on the road, especially a road that led around the globe to play performances at night, could be nerve-wracking, disorienting, and exhausting for any musician. And Monk was already in his late forties.

Several documentaries from this period, the mid-1960s, particularly *Monk in Oslo*, showed Monk in brilliant performances with Rouse, Riley, and Gales. When Monk stood up and stopped playing, watched his group with his eyes blinking in deep concentration, and then turned around to start playing again at just the appropriate moment, the audience got the ideal opportunity to see his reliance on the group playing exactly as he had bid, to express the music exactly as he heard it himself.

The documentary *Straight, No Chaser* portrayed Monk as a man who knew exactly what he wanted, without any confusion or wasted motion in the ways he dealt with his music, sidemen, and producer Teo Macero. Monk could talk to Teo, a saxophonist, as one musician to another. Viewers of *Straight, No Chaser* saw Monk as a vital, bright, witty, and commanding leader. As if to alleviate tension for himself, Monk showed up in a CBS studio wearing a hat given to him in Poland—a hat with corners like a graduation cap's. Monk added his own witty touch—little wire-rimmed glasses with no glass in them. "Invisible glasses," he said in good humor when Teo Macero noticed them. When Macero suggested he wanted to hear something a bit complicated or different, Monk said, "I want it to be as easy as possible so people can dig it, and it will still be good, you know, the melody, the time."

Monk began playing a song, "Ugly Beauty," thinking that Teo was recording it. Then Teo interrupted the group. "Why did you stop us for?" Monk said with a bit of irritation. "Unnecessary to stop." He then told his group to start playing again as it had been when it was so "rudely interrupted." Then, having played again, Monk said, "I'd like to hear how that sounds," and he became truly aggravated when he found out it hadn't been taped. He had specified that he wanted it taped. "Why don't nobody want to do what I asked them to do!" he said, meaning Teo (with whom he actually had a good relationship; he once wrote a song called "Teo" in his honor.) Monk collected himself with the cool head of a professional, saying, "I didn't say that. I didn't say nothing! Can we hear it?" But it didn't exist. Burying his pique, he persisted with the song.

Also fascinating in the film was the chance to see Monk teaching a composition, "Boo Boo's Birthday," in his classic way to Charlie Rouse, giving Rouse a choice of notes to hit—whatever Rouse thought might sound best. Rouse had to write down the notes himself.

Returning from one tour in Europe and Asia, Monk played at the Five Spot again and did a share of traveling in the United States. Then he had one bout of terrible trouble that involved LSD, probably in 1965. Nellie remarked to Harry Colomby that the incident was the worst thing that ever happened to Monk. He was playing in a Minneapolis club—Davy Jones's Locker, as Harry remembered— where a young man introduced himself during intermission and invited Monk to a party. The fan then slipped LSD into Monk's drink. "Monk couldn't finish the night's work. He went out and walked on top of cars. He was sick in bed for a week or two, with delusions and hallucinations," Harry remembered.

Harry thought the kid, like many fans, usually college-age kids, had probably wanted to prove how hip he was by turning on a famous musician. "It's like a feather in their caps. They can socialize with their friends and say, 'Hey, I turned Monk on.'" (Someone once gave Dizzy Gillespie a dose of a drug in the Village Vanguard, and he nearly died from it.) "It's the weirdest kind of reaction, almost a sexual thing," Colomby said, that led people to do these kinds of things. Colomby didn't think the young man had really wanted to hurt Monk. But the damage was done.

"Monk was the worst guy in the world to give LSD to," Harry said. Monk seemed to recover eventually, but he had a relapse one night when he was playing in the Village Vanguard the next year. "He played the first song of a set for about an hour; he kept repeating it, although the guys in the group kept signalling him to stop." Harry thought he detected a deterioration in Monk's mental condition after the incident in Minneapolis. Harry had been watching Monk for years and was sensitive to small changes.

But so powerful was his talent and quick his reflexes and intellect that Monk, at that time, could still survive his setbacks on his feet, as it were, and come back dancing.

Clark Terry recalled playing at the *Boston Globe* jazz festival one year when Monk played; on the bus back to New York, Clark and Monk were sitting across the aisle from each other, near the driver. Displaying his impish sense of humor, Monk called out, "The toe bone connected to the foot bone." Everyone was quiet when Monk spoke. He went to sleep for a while, then woke up and said, "The foot bone connected to the ankle bone." He kept doing that, going to sleep for a while, then awaking and calling out the next line, about the shin bone, the thigh bone, and so on. "And when we went through the tunnel, coming into New York, he was at the head bone and the skull bone. It was hilarious." Clark would say years later.

Monk continued to display his sense of humor in performance and backstage, although some would interpret his behavior as bordering on the bizarre. Monk played in Chicago at the Plugged Nickel in February 1966. A critic in attendance at the show recalled that a long-haired man who looked like a hippie called out from the audience, interrupting Monk as he was dancing around the stage, yelling "Whatever happened to Frankie Dunlop?"

Monk smiled, his feet still dancing, said, "Scubbie doobie ah ah ah ooorampah, mackareenie," and danced away.

The club owner told the critic, "I was introduced to him the night he arrived, and all he said, was, 'Hey, you the man got my bread.' He hasn't said anything since."

When Monk arrived to play one night at the Village Vanguard in New York,, Max Gordon, the club's owner, complimented him on his new suit. Monk assured him it was an old suit, and quipped, "I don't wear any of my new shit."[5]

Whether he was still suffering from the dose of LSD or feeling testy for another reason, Monk presented himself as unfriendly and self-absorbed—and driven, opinionated, and witty, too—during a blindfold test conducted in Los Angeles in 1966 by Leonard Feather as part of his regular series for *Down Beat*; Monk had little patience with the test.[6] Perhaps he hadn't been able to forget Feather's—or other critic's—earlier harsh opinion of his music. And here he was, putting his precious time for free into publicity for an Establishment that had aggravated him so much for so long.

Monk started by wandering around the room, saying, "The view is great, and you have a crazy stereo system." Feather thought he might catch Monk's attention with a recording of his own music. In a version of "Rhythm-a-ning" led by Art Pepper, Monk detected an added note—"A note that's not supposed to be there," he said. He refused to rate the recording by stars as was the custom in Feather's column, telling Feather to ask Mrs. Monk. "It's your opinion I'm asking," Feather said. Thelonious ended the debate: "I gave you my opinion."

For a medley including "'Round Midnight" led by Dizzy Gillespie, whom Monk recognized right away and praised as an influence on everyone, he said, "Everybody sounded good on there. I mean, the harmony and everything was crazy . . . play it again." He also thought an arrangement by Bob Florence for "Straight, No Chaser" was "top notch," though he didn't recognize any of the musicians. Yet he commented, "It sounded so good, it made me like the song better!" He was annoyed by Phineas Newborn's version of "Well, You Needn't": "[Phineas] hit the inside wrong—didn't have the right changes," Monk said. He didn't recognize Phineas's brilliant playing; he knew the recording wasn't Bud Powell but someone trying to sound like Bud. "I enjoy all piano players," Monk said, instinctively retreating from the brink of criticizing another musician publicly. "All pianists have got five stars for me . . . but I was thinking about the wrong changes, so I didn't pay too much attention to the rest of it." For Bud Powell's version of "Ruby, My Dear," Monk commented on Bud's general condition: "He's just tired, stopped playing, doesn't want to play no more. I don't know what's going through his mind." Feather asked if the recording was Bud's best work. "Of course not," Monk said, impatient with the obvious.

While Oscar Peterson's recording of "Easy Listenin' Blues" was playing, Monk asked, "Which is the way to the toilet?," then waited for the recording to end before he went. He didn't recognize the piano player and, as for Herb Ellis, the guitarist in Peterson's trio, Monk said, "Charlie Christian spoiled me for everybody else."

He loved Denny Zeitlin's "Carole's Garden," however. Surprised, Feather asked, "You liked that one?" Monk answered, "I like all music." Feather commented, "Except the kind that makes you go to the toilet." Monk said, "No, but you need that kind, too . . . [Zeitlin] reminded me of Bobby Timmons, and that's got to be good. Rhythm section has the right grove, too, Drummer made me think of Art Blakey. Hey, play that again." After hearing it once more, he said, "Yeah! He sounds like a piano player. You can keep changing keys all the time doing that. Sounds like something that was studied and figured out. And he can play it; you know what's happening with this one."

At the time the article was published, Monk was in the middle of another world tour produced by George Wein and scheduled to appear in Paris, Caen, Lyons, Nantes, and Amiens, in France; then Geneva, Bern, Zurich, Lugano, and Basel, in Switzerland; the resort city of Lecco in northern Italy; Brussels, Belgium; and Warsaw, Poland, where he gave two concerts and appeared on television. During this tour

Monk and Nellie visited a palace in Poland. The palace security guards were so meticulous about preserving the floor and rugs that they gave the visitors soft slippers to wear over their shoes. Monk was shown a bedroom that had belonged to a queen. On the ceiling were painted angels and cherubs, and the bed itself was a lavish concoction, with velvet ropes around it to protect it from the intrusion of visitors. Monk climbed over the ropes and lay down. Nellie screamed. On another floor, Ben Riley heard her and went running to the royal bedroom.

"What are you doing, motherfucker?" Ben said, very excited. "You can't lie down there. This is a national treasure."

Monk replied, "I just wanted to see what the bitch saw." Rules were not for Monk. Intrigued by royalty and aware of his own majesty, he felt he was entitled to take liberties and satisfy his curiosity.

"Thelonious Monk did exactly what he wanted to do when he wanted to do it," Nellie would later reflect.

The group went to all the Scandinavian capitol cities, to Frankfurt, Germany, and Amsterdam, the Netherlands, and England—where Monk appeared at Royal Festival Hall for the second time in his life—and proceeded to Birmingham and Manchester. He also did a B.B.C. television show and visited several universities, then flew to Tokyo on May 4 for a nine-concert tour. By May 16, Monk had returned to the United States, played on the West Coast, and from there went to do two concerts in Minneapolis and another concert at the first Atlanta Jazz Festival, which was produced by George Wein in conjunction with the Atlanta Braves baseball team. On July 2, Monk played with his quartet on a Saturday night at the Newport Jazz Festival.

By August, he was appearing at the Village Vanguard, where his display of energy was astounding. Critic Bob Micklin marveled at his performance:

> As he plays, elbows flapping, long fingers held stiff as they literally attack the keys, Monk radiates raw power. His right foot smacks the floor in a strange, out-of-tempo solo dance, he grunts to himself, punctuating each dissonant chord with rhythmic body english. The music sounded from the piano is not reflective, not even pianistic. It is more like Monk's piano is a big band in itself,

with segmented riffs punched out one after the other to make a separate composition out of his solo. And when his solo is over, as [Charlie] Rouse steps to the microphone for his turn, Monk leaves his seat and dances by himself next to the piano. A kind of twist, but in a Monkian way—powerful and jerky. As you watch him, you have to wonder what he's thinking about.

Monk received his usual hero's welcome in Toronto in late 1966. In November 1966 critics flocked to his two-week engagement at Toronto's Colonial Tavern, and their reactions to Monk's showmanship, even more than his music, fueled his legendary reputation. "Let's Rejoice: Monk's back in town" read the headline for Jack Batten's review[7]:

> Thelonious Monk made an entrance into the Colonial Tavern at 10:50 last night, stalking [into] the room with a kind of ominous grace, like some wise and dark Old Testament prophet.
>
> He's a large, strong man, heavy across the shoulders. He wears a pointed, graying, black Talmudic beard and his eyes are black and heavy as lead. He seems surrounded by an arrogance he must have earned a long time ago. "Are you going to play that thing or not?" a nervous, strident lady asks. "I'm going to do what I feel like doing," Monk says, looking at her, leaning on the bandstand.
>
> The drummer finished setting up at 11:24, and Monk begins to play a quirky, cranky melody line. One of his own, of course. Charlie Rouse, Monk's tenor saxophonist, has the first solo, and behind him Monk rises from the piano bench, opens a gold case and lights a cigarette. Monk solos; mostly he plays around with some rhythmic figures that suggest a Count Basie gone wacky. He ends all this with a sudden, long, funny, higgledy-piggledy run and lets the bass, Larry Gales, and the drums, Ben Riley, have their say.
>
> Monk starts the second tune, his "Rhythm-a-ning," over the applause for the first. Backing Rouse's solo, Monk plays some grandly eccentric runs at the bass end of the keyboard. Rouse must be the fastest thinking tenor man alive. He is also a master,

as on this solo, at fitting fragments of melody into a nearly seamless whole. Monk begins his solo with some queer, delightful, surprising ascending runs that he alternates with the melody and then he builds to a climax with giant clusters of notes that nearly overwhelm everyone, including Monk, who almost crashes off the piano bench. Everything's all right, though . . . Monk introduces "Blue Monk" with some full-blooded stride piano, and after Rouse's fine solo, he begins to tinker with the melody, pushing, shunting, reshuffling, nudging it this way, that way, filling it with startling new directions. He gives the impression he might have discovered these chords for the first time. . . . Then he roars into "Jackie-ing" with a boogie beat. He just states the theme, says, "Now buy some booze" to no one special and glides off the stand. End of set at 11:58.

Patrick Scott, a longtime admirer of Monk's music, who often wrote serious analyses of Monk's performances and recordings, adopted a witty attitude this time for the *Globe and Mail*. When the gig was supposed to begin at 6 P.M., Monk was nowhere in sight. The time was changed to 8:30. At that hour, Goodie Lichtenberg, the man in charge of the Colonial Tavern, arrived, as Scott recounted in his column done in a telegraphic style, "bleeding at elbows from chewing fingers nails, customers' as well as his own." "I never panic!" Lichtenberg screamed at 9 P.M. Someone called from the airport at 10:10 to say Monk had just arrived and would reach the Colonial in forty-five minutes, which Scott estimated actually would be sixty-five minutes. After the first set—despite all the delays—Scott wrote that he had "turned into a greater Monk fan than ever."

Warren Gerard, who was writing a feature article for the *Globe and Mail*, had the opportunity to visit Nellie and Monk in their Royal York Hotel room. Monk was drinking bourbon chased with Coca Cola and watching television, but was leery of the impending arrival of a photographer and his girlfriend who were bringing a Capuchin monkey to his room; the photographer wanted Monk to pose with the monkey. Gerard suggested to Monk that it might turn out to be a gorilla. "'A gorilla, man?' Monk asked with mild alarm." He asked Nellie, who was in bed with a cold, "'Are they going to bring a gorilla up here?' Nellie mumbled something and Monk sat down again. He thought a minute. 'I'd like a gorilla to sit on my piano, man. Wild!'"

Nonetheless, the photo shoot came off well, with Monk obliging the hokey idea that the photographer said had been inspired by a Monk album cover depicting Monk with a monkey. Monk didn't remember that photograph at all.

Although Gerard went through the journalist's obligatory description of Monk's comportment on stage, he also recounted Monk's gentle conversation at the bar between the sets with a drunk woman in her fifties wearing a green dress. The woman announced she was drunk. Monk told her she wasn't drunk or she would be out cold:

> "You know what?" she asked, grabbing Monk.
>
> "What?" Monk said.
>
> "I'm different," she announced.
>
> Monk thought about that and said, "Everybody's different, man."
>
> "What do you know?" she asked.
>
> "I know a lot of things, man," he said.
>
> "Can you sing?" she asked.
>
> "Everybody can sing," he replied.
>
> She sang a cowboy song for Monk who sat very still, looking ahead, expression unchanged.
>
> "What's music?" she asked.
>
> "Music is any pleasing sound," he said.
>
> "Your music is wonderful," she gurgled.
>
> "I make a whole lot of noise, man, and everybody claps," he said.

Gerard thought that autograph hunters interfered with Monk's drinking, cutting it down to four shots of bourbon: "Each person told him with touching sincerity how great they thought he was and how much they would like his signature. Monk listened, always politely, and signed."

One sweet-looking young woman complimented Monk. He nodded, and she didn't know what else to do, so she started to leave. Monk gestured to her to sit down. But she fell off the chair onto the floor. Monk sat there, looking at her, and then jumped up to go back to the piano, saying, "That's the coolest fall I've ever seen."

After witnessing Monk's varied behavior during the show and at the bar, Gerard concluded:

> Monk is a gentle person. He's quiet and shy. He doesn't like to be alone, nor does he like to be bugged—especially by reporters who ask him . . . questions about race or Vietnam or God and the future of all mankind. He is a TV and bourbon addict, although he complains in a sad voice that the juice hasn't done anything for him in years. Monk is at the summit; he is recognized not only as a great jazz pianist but also as the grand wizard of all the cultist hippies of the world. His beard makes him look like Othello, the mad Moor, and his crazy hats endorse the high priest image. Monk wears hats because people give them to him. "I like to stand out, man. I'm not one of the crowd. If the crowd goes that way, man," he said, pointing ahead, "I go the other way," he pointed over his shoulder with a thumb."

Another writer, Charles Gerein, a staff writer for the *Toronto Daily Star*, got into a verbal contest with Monk, when the writer introduced the world "cult" into the conversation. Monk said, after a pained silence, "If you want to use that word . . . it sounds like something bad. It sounds evil. I don't approve of the word 'cult.'"

"Mystique? Fanatic fans?" the writer tried; Monk replied:

> "Just describe them as fans. Some people [not meaning his, neces-sarily] are just natural fanatics."
> "Eccentric?"
> More silence. "Yes, I'm eccentric musically."
> "As a person?"

"If the music is eccentric, I have to be. Anybody talented in any way—they're called eccentric."

"Arrogant?"

"You can write what you want to . . . I'm not arrogant. Do I seem to be? I never felt arrogant."

Monk said he supposed that people came to see him because he had the reputation for being eccentric, but he didn't care, as long as they kept coming.

The critic responded, "Isn't that cold and business-like for a genius to be saying?"

"You have to do business to make money," Monk replied.

The interview degenerated into chaos, when the writer asked about where "humility entered into the philosophical order of things." Monk could bear it no more and said he didn't know about "humble jazz," directed the writer to stand up on the bandstand to talk philosophy, and excused himself to go to work.[*] ("If you picked at Monk, he would pick at you," Ben Riley had noticed about his boss.)

Given the chance, Monk provided erudite interviews for journalists, his insistence on vernacular grammar notwithstanding. For the *Telegram*, Monk and Dolores Wilson, a star of New York's Metropolitan Opera who was appearing at the O'Keefe in *Fiddler on the Roof*, did a joint interview. Monk seemed fascinated with the opportunity, and said he liked opera, because he liked plays, "and that is what opera is," he said. He had never been to the opera, he regretted to say. Miss Wilson had never sung a jazz song and thought that jazz and opera were miles apart. The interviewer said "in a way, today's jazz has sort of taken the place of yesterday's opera." Miss Wilson said, "Yes, it seems that that was just what I was trying to say."

Monk offered, "But I wouldn't quite say that. They're both all alone in their field, although they're related to each other. But you see, take musicals, that's today's opera in a sense."

The interviewer asked Monk: "How do you see your form of expression? What is it?"

Monk said, "Making it sound as best you can. And to improve on it as much as you can."

The interviewer asked, "Is it sound or the experience?"

Monk said, "Well, it's both. It's mostly the sound, I mean . . . you know music is sound, what happens to sound."

Interviewer: "But is there another reason beyond the sound? Is the sound not just a means to an end?"

Monk: "Well, I enjoy doing it. That's all I wanted to do anyway. I guess, you know, if I didn't make it with the piano, I guess I would have been the biggest bum."

The interviewer went on to expound upon modern composers. Monk didn't like modern classical music. "'There's no expression in its soul, and I don't want to sit and listen and say, "Listen to that scale, listen to the treatment he gives." I just want to go and be moved by the beauty of it. I want to feel it.' Mr. Monk does that beautifully with his music. There is soul, there is expression, but some of our modern composers now are just trying for just plain sound."

Monk said, "I agree with you wholeheartedly because in jazz they're doing the same things, what they call avant garde, they do anything, make any kind of noise. A lot of young musicians are doing that."

The interviewer remarked on the lyrics in rock and roll.

Monk said, 'I wouldn't call that advanced. Rock and roll is . . . digressed."

Wilson and the interviewer said rock and roll gave them headaches. Monk said it gave his wife a stomach ache. "I can listen to it, but as [Nellie] explained it, it doesn't have that tone and it don't tell a story."

Interviewer: "What do you do for relaxation—apart from playing the piano?"

Monk said he lay down, rested, and played pool and ping-pong. He said he spent a lot of time in New York. His daughter, who wanted to be a singing star, sang rock and roll and other types of music. His son was a drummer. Closing the interview, Monk made sure to say his club had been packed all week. "And your city hall . . . beautiful, beautiful . . . Oh, yes, the sculpture by Henry Moore? it's crazy. I dig it. It's modern . . . If everybody's as hip as the city hall, this is a very modern place."

The Toronto press danced attendance upon him when he returned to the Colonial for two weeks in August 1967. Patrick Scott found Monk "at the top of his form," and while some people called Monk "an abominable showman," Scott reported he "remains the dominant performer, whether as soloist or accompanist." For an appearance at the O'Keefe Centre during a jazz festival in June 1968, Monk received a wonderful review from John Norris writing for the *Daily Star.* "With a few deft touches at the keyboard, Thelonious Monk reminded a large audience . . . why he is one of the pre-eminent musicians in jazz." Monk arrived early for the performance, wore a small hat, and played for sixty minutes, and altogether thoroughly satisfied the reviewer. Only Helen McNarmara of the *Telegram* kept her mind closed to Monk's spell, calling his playing "ponderous" and "clumsy." She admired, instead, his polar opposite as a stylist, John Lewis, of the Modern Jazz Quartet, who was on the same program for the festival. She considered Lewis to be articulate, crisp, and swinging, a "sheer delight." Lewis's light touch was a standard most pianists admired, though it was within the context of the MJQ that he attracted the most fans; as a soloist, he could sound as if he were playing in a distant room. Solo, Monk was mesmerizing.

Monk's energy for these extensive tours, with their late night hours, came, undoubtedly, from a combination of medicines and drugs—and, of course, food; Monk enjoyed meals. Also many people noticed that Monk smoked a great deal of marijuana, and bourbon was his drink of choice.

He may not have known how much money he was earning. But in 1967, he and Nellie were well able to afford to move out of their West 63rd Street apartment and into Lincoln Towers on West End Avenue. It was only a few blocks away, but in essence the fancy, high-rise apartment was in a world removed from San Juan Hill. Harry Colomby had to coax and cajole until Monk agreed to move. "It was hard to get them to say yes to moving." And, of course, they took their clutter with them.

"Thelonious seemed to like the new place," Harry Colomby recalled. "He looked out the window. They painted the apartment in blues and reds. He and the doormen were friendly. But when he walked out the front door, there was a wind, an updraft [that disturbed Monk]. Monk was living among strange people"—that is, neighbors he didn't know. All his habits had to change. No longer did he simply walk into his ground-floor apartment; he had to go up and down in an elevator." Harry concluded, "He felt safer on West 63rd Street. He had an emotional connection to it. It was ineffable."

Eventually the Monks moved to another good apartment nearby on West End Avenue. Thelonious still wouldn't release the apartment on West 63rd Street, in part because he was unable to forget the days when, as Nellie would sum them up, "They didn't give black people a break." The apartment on 63rd Street, which had cost only about $37 a month in the 1960s, rented for $76 a month in the 1970s. He knew he could somehow afford the rent there and keep a roof over his family's head, if he had to—if the balloon burst, and the unreliable world made him face terrible exigencies again. He didn't want to be left without a tiny corner of the world to repair to.[9]

So Monk was enjoying prestigious engagements and luxurious living quarters. But in July 1967 Harry Colomby decided to accept an offer in Hollywood and leave Monk. Harry had always wanted to go to Hollywood and work in films. Furthermore, he was under the impression that Monk wasn't as interested in working as he had once been. He was traveling so much on Wein's tours that he didn't need Harry's hard, day-to-day care anymore. The challenge of managing Monk had evaporated for Harry. As it would turn out, Harry would later be able to look back on the years he managed Monk as the majority of the glory years of Monk's performing career. For Harry, the son of refugees from Hitler's Germany, the years had been an idealistic adventure, during which he had helped a musical genius escape from his own prison of circumstances.

NOTES

Personal interviews: Lewis Lapham, John Hicks, Harry Colomby, Nellie Monk, Clark Terry, Ben Riley.

1. Lapham (1964).
2. Williams (1970).
3. Wilmer (1965; 1977).

4. Giving the lie to his claim that he didn't read stories about himself, he later quibbled with her about one tiny thing in her story—the time he bumped into her in the Village Vanguard—Harry Colomby remembered. Harry didn't know what it was, but it had stuck in Monk's mind.

5. From the documentary, *Straight, No Chaser.*

6. Feather (1966).

7. Toronto *Daily Star,* November 1, 1966.

8. Gerein (1966).

9. When Toot finished school in 1971, he lived alone in the tiny West 63rd Street apartment, staying there until 1975, after which his sister Barbara took it over.

Monk with all-star Newport Jazz Festival group, including Milt Jackson on vibes
and Dizzy Gillespie on trumpet, 1967. Photo: Raymond Ross.

12 North of the Sunset

George Wein, the founder/impresario behind the Newport Jazz Festival, was a major force in the jazz world as a promoter/packager in the sixties. Monk became a regular on his packaged tours, and in many ways they provided him with the financial security he couldn't find merely playing small clubs. Sometimes George Wein himself went on the tours with Monk and other musicians, and sometimes he sent his trusted staffers—Bob Jones, for one, who became a great admirer of the musician.[1]

After working with Monk at the Newport Jazz Festivals, Jones took charge of a tour called the "Schlitz Salute to Jazz" that traveled around the United States in 1968. Performing on the same bill with Monk for some or all of the fifteen cities were alto saxophonist Cannonball Adderley, vibist Gary Burton, organist Jimmy Smith, pianist Dave Brubeck, pop vocalist Dionne Warwick, pianist Ramsey Lewis, singer Miriam Makeba, drummer Art Blakey, bandleader, singer, and clarinetist Woody Herman, pianist Ahmad Jamal, trumpeters Dizzy Gillespie and Hugh Masakela, and, in a concert or two, Lena Horne. The schedule called for the groups to do a weekend in two or three cities—for example, Dallas, Austin, and Houston, Texas—and then go on to another place and stay there for a full week.: Ben Riley was still playing in the group with Monk, Rouse, and Larry Gales.

In cities where they stayed for a week, Bob Jones got to know Monk better, though Bob saw Monk and Nellie only at night; they stayed in their room during the days. Rouse explained, "[Monk's] just more comfortable at night." Jones knew that some people said they were night people, but Monk was the epitome of that. One of the few times Jones saw Monk out of his room by day was at a pool table in a hotel probably in San Diego. Monk and Jimmy Smith played pool; Monk did it so well, Jones thought, that he realized, "The man has done other things than play the piano."

Also in San Diego, the musicians got together at a bar for a long discussion about music, particularly Herb Alpert and the Tiajuana Brass, who was on top of the charts at the time. Monk said, "How can this guy be so well known, and a trumpet player, and I don't even know who he is? How can this guy have sold a million records? It's impossible. If he's that great a trumpet player, I would have known about him."

"And everyone was trying to tell him, 'That's not true, Thelonious,'" Bob Jones recalled. "It wasn't that Alpert had to be a terrible player, but Monk didn't understand the pop scene. He had tunnel vision about jazz. He didn't really understand how pop music could become popular."

But Monk wasn't just a closet genius. For example he had become well-aware of the Beatles, telling Harry Colomby "They're just imitating Nashville"; in other words, they were just copying, and not copying American blacks but white country and western musicians. Monk didn't think the Beatles had anything to do with black American music. And Monk understood Dr. John, the New Orleans-born pianist who at the time often performed in elaborate costumes, including feathered head dresses. "I remember when he played a date for Bill Graham in San Francisco," Bob Jones said, "and Dr. John and the Nightrippers were on the date. Monk said, 'That name is a motherfucker!' He loved it [because it alluded to nighttime, night people,] and he thought [Dr. John] was a good piano player." Bob thought Dr. John and Monk had in common the aura of seeming a little crazy. "But when you got to know Mac [Rebennack, Dr. John's real name], you found out his interest was his music, and he didn't care if the world was falling apart beside him. I had that feeling about Monk. As long as he could play, he was fine," Jones said.

Monk and the other musicians on the tour also had a very long discussion about how record companies conspired among themselves and decided who would sell a million records. Jones didn't agree with the musicians, because he believed that record companies would want everyone to sell a million! And popular music was popular because the public liked it, whether jazz-world people did or not, in Jones's opinion.

Later in the year, Jones went on a George Wein-arranged European tour with Monk leading an octet to play Hall Overton's arrangements. "He was nervous about the trip," Jones recalled. "Joyce Wein and I went to his apartment to take him to the airport, and he wasn't going to go. He wasn't going to let the music out of his hands, either. Nellie spoke to him in endearing terms, not forcefully, saying, 'This will be okay. Bob is with us. He'll make sure the music is all right. George looks after you.'" Jones didn't think Monk really wanted to leave New York City: "He was at home in his own place. He wasn't just physically at home; he had peace of mind in New York City."

Bob was unaware if Monk took any medication for any physical or mental illness. "I never considered him mentally ill. The things he did seemed fairly logical. The fact that he might twirl around in the airport in London" (as Monk was seen doing in the documentary , dancing in the airport the way he did on stages), didn't fluster Jones at all. "He was an artist. He might have been doing it for publicity."

Much later, Jones found out, in addition to his uncanny knack for showmanship, Monk had a mental disturbance of some kind. All Jones knew at the time they were leaving for Europe in 1968 was that Monk seemed very nervous. Jones thought Monk's anxiety stemmed from his logical concern about the music. Monk didn't know what was going to happen to it. "He probably felt a little lack of control," Jones said. The music had been written for a ten-piece group; Monk worried that the arrangements wouldn't work well because he didn't have enough horns in the octet. "The voicings were not all there. So he was afraid.

He knew what it should sound like. And in giving the music away to the musicians, he was taking a risk. He didn't know what it was going to sound like." Jones cajoled the music away from Monk on the plane and gave it to Phil Woods, Jimmy Cleveland, and Ray Copeland, so they could rearrange it for the smaller group; Phil in particular worked with it, Jones observed. Jones thought that, like Monk, Phil could look at a score and know what it was going to sound like.

Jones recalled:

> And that's what they did on the plane on the way to London; they transcribed the music. "You play this part, I play this part." In London, we went directly to the rehearsal and then the gig at night at Odeon Hammersmith Hall, not even to the hotel. Monk sat in an overcoat in the audience during the rehearsal, and then he went to the stage at the end and played a few chords. It appeared as if Phil Woods or Charlie Rouse was running the rehearsal directly, but Monk was listening all the time. When he finally got to the piano, he went to the few parts he felt needed attention. He said, "No, no, we have to do it this way," and made a few statements with his hands on the piano. He was just adjusting the parts he felt needed corrections. He had only a few tunes scored out for the octet and the rest of the tunes for his regular quartet. At the end of the rehearsal, George Wein called me from someplace, perhaps Paris, and I remember saying point blank: "I have no idea of what's going to happen."

Monk did the first half of the concert with the quartet. There were slight rumblings in the audience, which was expecting a large-band show. Then the octet appeared for the second half of the concert. Jones recalls:

> The men ended the first tune, a pretty good stomper. And the place went crazy. The audience gave Monk almost a standing ovation. At that point, he became—"oh, my God, what we're doing is great here!"—he seemed to be saying that to himself.

Suddenly he was standing up, counting the band off, transfixed. He seemed to be saying to himself: "I'm the leader of these guys, and they're all playing their asses off!" And he's calling out solos; the ensemble work became less and less. He wanted people to solo more in this larger bebop structure. At the end of the concert, which was a big success, he was suddenly smiling as if he had won the lottery.

The tour went on to several other major European cities. Bob recalled Monk enjoying playing a marvelous concert in La Fenice, a gorgeous theater in Venice; he also liked playing in a fine hall in Barcelona, where the architecture and sculpture impressed him. "He was taken by that kind of stuff," Jones recalled. At Tivoli Garden in Copenhagen, Monk wandered off. Jones went looking for him during an intermission. It seemed as if a long time passed until he heard Monk playing a gospel hymn alone in a room. Monk explained, "I saw this book, man."

In Berlin, Monk suddenly decided he wanted to do two other tunes. Bob had to find a copyist. "We had four days off before we had to play in Mainz," he recalled:

> I said to him, "Why? We only have one concert left." But by then he felt, and it was true, the group had really bonded. The concerts were really strong. He wanted to hear what the group would do with his other tunes. I brought the copyist to Monk's room, where there was a small piano. The copyist didn't believe that Monk could actually read music that well, and so the copyist was surprised. Monk was one of those people who could tell what music will sound like when he sees it written. And the group ended up playing the tunes. This was one of those rare occasions.

After the Berlin concert, where Monk was a big hit, he said he wanted to go to East Berlin:

> T. called me himself and said, "Bob, I want to go." He wanted to see in person what he saw of East Germany on T.V. He was

fascinated by the colors. I'm not sure what he saw, but he thought the colors of the neon lights were different in East Germany because of the way they showed up on television. So I told him: "You have to go to the border, change money, it's a big deal." He said he wanted to go. He was in high spirits. So he, Nellie, Jones, and Charlie Rouse took a taxi to Checkpoint Charlie, where they had to declare all their money.

Nellie and Thelonious were the types that always had all their money with them. He had a good chunk of money with him. I told him he had to declare all the money. He didn't want to. When he got tired of counting, he gave it to Nellie to count. The guard said, "If she's counting it, she has to declare the money." So they changed the papers. You also had to buy a certain amount of German money—perhaps twenty dollars worth. They wouldn't change it back to dollars when you returned to the west. And we drove into East Berlin and stopped in a bar and got a beer. Thelonious said the green of the neon lights was definitely different. We took a little tour. The taxi driver pointed things out. This was during the day.

When we got back to the border, Nellie handed her things over to the guard. The guard asked for all her money. But she had given the major part of the money back to Thelonious. She said to him, "I need to have the money to put on my slip." He said, "No." They got into a little argument. "It's not your money," Thelonious said. The East German guard didn't understand. Finally Thelonious took this wad of money and threw it on the counter. "Fuck it, count the money," he said. The guard was laughing. Another guard came in and knew it was Monk, the piano player, and told the first guard. Nellie put all the money in her bag. Monk said, "You may think that's your money, but when I get in the car again, I'm taking it back."

Charlie Rouse and Jones were greatly amused by this scene.

Though Nellie and Monk never discussed their relationship in front of Jones, Jones noticed how Nellie looked after Thelonious, and how

Thelonious was concerned about her. Several times Monk came down in the elevator in the Schwitzerhof Hotel in Berlin, got out of the elevator, and had a discussion with Nellie about the tie he had on. Was it a good match with the suit and shirt? If she didn't like it, he would go upstairs and change his tie. He might go back three times before he got the tie right. Monk's comment about this ritual to Jones was on the order of: "Nellie knows best."

"Monk always liked to look spiffy. He had a Burberry raincoat. Nellie made sure that he dressed well. He traveled with five or six huge suitcases, though he never carried anything himself; he always traveled in a suit and tie and looked dignified and hip. And when getting on planes, he was concerned that she got on. They waited for each other. One was not going without the other," Bob noticed.

Despite the suggestion from their wardrobes and luggage that they were prosperous, the Monks clung to habits of frugality. One time they carried empty Coca Cola bottles with them from one continent to another, and the tour paid the overweight charge for their luggage. Nellie explained they had to bring the bottles back to the United States to collect the deposits on them.

Jones went on one more tour with the Monks, to the Montreal Expo, sometime in 1970, where Monk was performing as part of the U.S. day. Afterward, Jones and several musicians gathered at a little subway station that took people from the Expo to the main departure station, from which they could travel back to their hotel. The only way to get to the departure station was by the little subway train. "All of us were waiting for the train to come. Monk was there, and so was Herbie Mann, signing autographs," Jones recalled. "Then the train came. Monk had disappeared." They found him already in the train, with his arms out, saving seats for them. "We New Yorkers know how to get on subways. Why are you looking for me? I got the seats," Monk said. Jones was very amused.

He knew that Monk "smoked pot like it was going out of style. The band smoked pot, they lived on pot, Larry Gales and Rouse and Monk did." But Jones never thought that Monk or the band were drug addicts.

In these years, Monk was also a frequent visitor to San Francisco, where he played at a number of clubs. Marion Williams, who with her husband, Richard, had owned several jazz clubs on the West Coast, set aside studio apartments for visiting musicians in their three-story Victorian house at 729 Oak Street in San Francisco. Musicians called it the Happy House. Monk often visited the Happy House, between 1963 and 1970; his sidemen stayed at the house for ten dollars a week, plus dinners, while Monk stayed in hotels. Marion became inured to Monk's idiosyncrasies and, furthermore, thought he was well aware of what he was doing at all times.

Once, while standing up at the dinner table, Monk accidentally poured milk from a pitcher on the table, while he was aiming for a glass. He was so tall that it was hard for him to get the milk into the glass while he was standing up. Marion thought he spilled the milk accidentally on purpose, as a kind of sight gag. "I think that kind of thing just doesn't set well with me sometimes," Marion explained.

Another time, invited to the Happy House for dinner with "Nell," as Marion called Nellie, Monk eyed the Williams's Steinway in the living room. He looked at it all night but didn't ask if he could play it. Later he complained to Ben Riley that the Williams family hadn't asked him to play. Marion said they had refrained from imposing on him.

She noticed that Nellie, the few times she visited, was very quiet, while Monk did all the talking, mostly about gigs. He complained about the small size of the Jazz Workshop's stage. Monk was so big, Marion always noticed, and Charlie Rouse was tall, too; when they got on stage, with Ben Riley and his drums, the bassist had to search for a bit of space. The Black Hawk hadn't been much better.

In between the sets at the Jazz Workshop, Monk liked to go outside "in the middle of busy Broadway," Marion recalled, and conduct traffic. "San Francisco is a very tolerant city. The police were used to some of the things that artistic people did, and they didn't bother with him. I enjoyed the man, I admired him as a person," she added. "He was a lovely man, but different."

Once Ben Riley was awakened in the Happy House by a phone call at 6 A.M. from Monk's hotel. The hotel's manager told him that Monk was in front of the hotel holding his hand in the fountain. Ben quickly went to the hotel, where, sure enough, Monk was holding his diamond ring under the fountain water. He told Ben that he liked the way the ring looked submerged in the water. But Monk had a more pressing matter in mind. He wanted Ben to go to the hotel and order drinks for them. The hotel had stopped Monk from drinking that night. "I don't want to get drunk with you," Ben told Thelonious. He refused to start ordering drinks.

"When he did these things," Marion said, "he did them with the attitude: hey, this is okay, this is me, I can do this. He knew what he was doing."

Another time Monk was staying in a San Francisco motel where the rooms had ceilings with flimsy coverings. Monk took a piece of glass and cut the ceiling cover in his room. The motel manager, taking a dim view of Monk's antics, called the baroness. She flew to San Francisco to pay for the repair of the ceiling.

Ben Riley left Monk's group in the late sixties, abandoning the music business entirely, going to work in the audio visual department for the school system on Long Island, and then for a few summers with the YMCA in the parks. "I'd had enough," he explained. "I was tired of the business, tired of being taken advantage of. And I wasn't taking care of myself. I might have had a nervous breakdown if I didn't get away from it." It took him about four years to return to playing. John Coltrane, who had occasionally played with Monk's group—once when Charlie Rouse had been late, Coltrane, who was on the same bill, had volunteered to play—called Ben Riley and brought him back into the jazz-world fold.[1]

Most musicians loved and respected Thelonious. Despite his bearish appearance, rough-hewn voice, and perfectionistic, demanding temperament, he could behave with grace and warmth toward them. It was not so much what he said, nor the terse, even succinct way he said it—when he said anything at all. But they sensed a sweetness in his approach toward them. Riley left Monk and the complex gig with an everlasting feeling of love for the man.

Maynard Ferguson, who sometimes found himself on the same festival bills with Monk, showed up to lead his big band for a concert at the Newport Jazz Festival in 1963.[4] Maynard decided to play "'Round Midnight," which was on one of his albums, with an arrangement by trombonist Slide Hampton. Maynard loved the arrangement, because Slide had such good taste that he knew exactly how to write for Maynard's strengths as a high-note player. "All the writing was directed as a tribute to Monk and used the talents I had in my band," Maynard recalled.

But Maynard found out that Monk's group was going to precede him at the festival. So Maynard called his band into the dressing room and told the musicians, "Guys, pull 'Round about Midnight.' Monk is going on right before us. We'll play another ballad."

Maynard felt a hand slap him on the shoulder. Monk had come into the dressing room, and he said, "Oh, don't do that, man. I want to hear what you guys have done to my tune."

Maynard thought that was very sweet. He said, "Are you sure, man?"

"Yeah, yeah, yeah," Monk said.

Maynard had been trying to be polite, but that was exactly what Monk didn't want. He stood just offstage, listening, and was delighted with Slide's arrangement.

NOTES

Personal interviews: Bob Jones, Ben Riley, Maynard Ferguson, Marion Williams.

1. Jones, who had met Monk at a festival in the mid-1960s, had overheard a reporter there ask Monk if he liked all music. Monk said, "Yes." The reporter pressed him: "Country and western?" Monk said, "I think the fellow is hard of hearing," not letting himself be badgered.

2. The tour lasted from June 21 through August 18, and traveled to Winston Salem, Philadelphia, Dallas, Austin, Houston, Omaha, Denver, Oklahoma City, Phoenix, Oakland, San Diego, Rochester, N.Y., Madison, Wisconsin, Detroit, Kansas City, St. Louis, Cleveland, Chicago, Cincinnati, and Memphis.

3. If Riley, a sideman, could become that exhausted in the group, one can imagine that Monk, the leader, felt countless times more pressured to maintain the level of everyone's performance and survive on the road. All the while he was playing at night and indulging his "Rabelesian appetites," as Steve Lacy had dubbed them.

4. Monk played at Newport in 1958, '59, '60, '62, '63, '64, '65, '66, '67, and '72, '75, and '76.

13 A New Saxophonist

After breaking with Harry Colomby and losing Ben Riley from the group, Monk faced new challenges while encountering new audiences. The late 1960s and early seventies saw a rise in rock and roll venues that were interested in featuring jazz acts. Meanwhile, Monk had to break in a new group, including saxophonist Paul Jeffrey, who would become an important member of his last groups. And, Monk's behavior, always eccentric, was becoming increasingly strange and erratic.

Monk continued to play in a variety of clubs and theaters, showing up in such places as the Fillmore East, probably in 1969, and for the final program at the Garden State Arts Center in Holmdel, New Jersey on September 6, 1970—booked, managed, or both by Jules Colomby. Harry Colomby, who confined his activities for Monk to bookings in the Los Angeles area, wanted to get Monk a musical director. But that idea never worked out, because Monk was not interested in rehearsing.

Harry also thought that Monk's music was sounding a bit stale. Some critics were inclined to agree. John S. Wilson of the *New York Times* reviewed the Holmdel concert, and he referred to the stars—Miles, Monk, and the Modern Jazz Quartet—as the three Ms who had dominated jazz in the 1950s. Miles was the only one whose playing had

Paul Jeffrey. Photo: Raymond Ross.

changed notably over the years, Wilson said. The MJQ had achieved refinement, becoming one of the most polished jazz groups in history. But for Monk, time had stood still, in Wilson's opinion. The sound of his quartet hadn't changed in 12 years. And what had "once seemed odd and angular in his compositions and performance has now become so familiar as to seem almost routine . . ." wrote Wilson.

The musicians Thelonious worked with usually had a different opinion of Monk's playing. Though his repertoire remained the same, it always thrilled them. George Wein kept taking him on tours, and audiences still showed up for the pleasure of hearing him sound exactly like himself. Then all the personnel changed in 1970.

Tenor saxophonist Paul Jeffrey, who had been born in Harlem Hospital in New York on April 8, 1933, had studied music at Ithaca

College. Paul Jeffrey finished college, went to Atlantic City, and led a group including a teenaged pianist destined for stardom, McCoy Tyner. When the club owner found out how young McCoy was, the group lost its gig. Paul returned to New York, where he met Charlie Rouse in the 1950s at a Monday night jazz session at Small's in Harlem, and subsequently went to Rouse's house to study with him.

Paul also went to the old Five Spot to listen to Monk and overheard Coltrane asking Monk about the tune "Skippy." Paul didn't know Monk at all. "I was just hanging around. I was completely nobody, just glad to get back to the kichen where they were. And I asked Monk, 'What note is it?' Monk had a briefcase with his music written out. He gave me a copy of 'Skippy.' So I copied it and gave it back to him." Paul used to go to the Five Spot all the time in 1957 when Coltrane was in Monk's band.

"Then, when Rouse was in the band, in the 1960s, I had just enough money to go into the Vanguard and buy a beer at the bar one night. Monk came dancing back through the club and told the bartender to give me a drink. After the guy poured the drink, Monk said, 'April Fool.' It was April Fool's Day, and I had no money. The bartender felt sorry for me and let me have it. Later on, Monk and I used to laugh about it."

Rouse and Monk had a quarrel at the Vanguard one night. Someone in the audience asked for a tune. Rouse said he didn't remember it. Monk, forgoing any pretense of diplomacy, and presenting himself as a high and mighty priest of bebop, told him, "Learn it now." Rouse quit the group. It was his moment to start a new chapter of his life. Jeffrey wasn't sure but thought the tune that served as the catalyst might have been Monk's composition, "Locomotion." It was hard to remember all those tunes, Paul would come to know. No one could remember them all, and many musicians had a difficult time matching the tunes with their names. Pat Patrick, a baritone saxophonist who worked with Sun Ra and picked up the tenor just to play with Monk, replaced Rouse.

At that time, Paul Jeffrey was hanging out with Wilbur Ware, whom most people were afraid to hire, because he had become so chronically unreliable. But Ware, a wonderful player and somewhat of a mentor for

Jeffrey, played club dates with the young saxophonist. Wilbur told him, "Look, I'm going to get you a job with Monk."

Jeffrey said, "I can't play with him. I don't know the music."

Nevertheless Ware brought Jeffrey to Monk's apartment at 65th Street and West End Avenue in 1970.

Monk said to Jeffrey, "We've got plenty of time."

Jeffrey didn't know what he meant. But he soon found out one Saturday when Wilbur called him and said, "I got a job for you, young man."

"Where?" Jeffrey said.

"With Thelonious Monk."

Paul almost died of fright.

"We're going to work in Raleigh, North Carolina, for ten days," Ware said.

Jeffrey started to turn the job down because he didn't have enough confidence to take it. But something told him: "You've got to," he recalled. So he took some reeds and a horn and met Monk at La Guardia Airport.

Monk looked at him and said, "Solid."

Monk, Jeffrey, Ware, and drummer Leroy Williams flew to the job at the Frog and Nightgown club together. Monk had retained his attachment to Ware ever since the days they had played together with Johnny Griffin in Chicago in the mid-1950s. Monk's instructions to Jeffrey were: "Just play the rhythm that I play but any note's good." Jeffrey didn't laugh then, but later he laughed heartily at the memory. For the first set, the group played "Blue Monk," "Hackensack," "Bright Mississippi," and of course "Epistrophy," which Monk had adopted as his theme song in the 1950s.

For Jeffrey, the gig was an incredible experience. After the first set, none of the men in the group spoke to each other. Wilbur went into one corner.

Jeffrey said, "Don't anybody speak to Monk?"

Ware said, "Well, he doesn't say anything."

So Jeffrey went to Monk and asked him, "Do you drink?"

Monk said, "No, I don't drink. Well, maybe some orange juice."

Wilbur Ware, 1963. Photo: Raymond Ross.

Jeffrey ran to the bar and got a glass of orange juice. Monk didn't say anything to him. Jeffrey asked himself, "Gee, what am I doing?" But just then a trumpeter was playing on a record during the intermission. Jeffrey said, "That's Jonah Jones."

Of course, it was Sweets, Jeffrey found out. He said to himself, "Oh, I'm not doing so good tonight."

Monk said to Jeffrey, "I invented the jazz waltz, 'Carolina Moon.' [Actually other composers had also written jazz waltzes—Fats Waller for one, Benny Carter for another]." Then he started talking to Jeffrey—a couple of words.

After that gig, the group went back to New York and into the Village Vanguard, with Pat Patrick on tenor instead of Jeffrey. When Jeffrey went to the club, he said "hello," and so did Monk. But Monk remained distant. Then Count Basie hired Jeffrey to substitute for Eddie "Lockjaw" Davis in the band, since "Jaws" wanted to take a month off. Jeffrey let Thelonious know when he left town and came back, mostly as a matter of good form.

Monk said, "You want to go to Japan? Talk to Nellie."

Jeffrey told her he had a passport. She asked him, "Will you go by George Wein's office and pick up the other passports?"

Jeffrey brought the passports to Monk's house. "I jumped at the chance to do it," he recalled, "because I had been scuffling with the music in North Carolina, and I wanted to learn it really correctly."

He asked Monk for a rehearsal.

Monk said, "I don't try to mess up anybody. I could have really fucked you up if I wanted to." Then he said as an afterthought: "Okay, how about tomorrow?"

Jeffrey came to the apartment and waited a long time until Monk came out of a back room.

Monk said, "Let's see what we'll play." He started playing "Ugly Beauty." He wouldn't give Jeffrey any written music and required him to learn it by ear. Monk played it over and over. When Jeffrey finally got the melody to Monk's satisfaction, Monk said, "Make a solo." When Jeffrey finished, Monk said, "That's pretty good. Sometimes when a guy learns the changes, he plays a worse solo." To Jeffrey, it meant that he really had to hear the music. Then Monk disappeared into another back room.

Jeffrey stayed in the living room for two hours, sitting in a chair, holding his horn, not knowing if he had measured up for the job or not. Monk came back, all dressed up, and said, "Let's go for a walk."

They walked around the neighborhood for a long time, with Monk introducing Jeffrey to people; soon it was three in the morning on Sunday. Monk said, "Are you coming back tomorrow?" That would be only a few hours later.

Jeffrey returned to stay with Monk for three days. The Baroness picked them up and took them to her house, where they played ping pong and whiled away the time. Jeffrey finally telephoned his wife, who was so angry at him that she was ready to divorce him. Monk took the phone and told her, "He's with me." That calmed her down. Jeffrey felt so grateful to Monk, and thought the man really cared about him to help him with his wife. Throughout the summer Paul and Thelonious often went to the Baroness's house, played ping-pong, and rehearsed "Ugly Beauty."

Jeffrey had to learn "Evidence," too, in a room full of people at Monk's apartment. One day, Monk simply said, "Let's rehearse." Jeffrey began learning that Monk did things on the spur of the moment. "You couldn't panic, playing with him," Jeffrey learned. One time Monk even told him, "Working with me is pressure." But Monk prepared Jeffrey for the stress by rehearsing him in a room full of people, never writing anything down, and always requiring Jeffrey to learn the music by ear. Monk played it. "And then I got it. I used to write it down myself, but he never handed me a sheet of music, except for the time years earlier when he had handed me 'Skippy.'" It was difficult for anyone to get information out of Monk, Jeffrey learned.

Jeffrey played a wrong note in "Epistrophy" for a few months. Finally Monk said to him, "You know, that note is wrong." Jeffrey said, "Monk, why didn't you tell me during these months?" Monk said, "Well, sometimes I like to hear a guy play wrong shit."

Another time, in Monk's apartment, Monk told Jeffrey, "Transcribe this," and gave him his Riverside recording of "Pannonica." Jeffrey began scuffling with it. Finally he said, "It just seems to keep going into different keys." Monk smiled. It did. Jeffrey thought it was a test of his honesty. Another time, they went to King Arthur's Pub, a little club in the Bronx, where George Benson was playing. Monk liked guitar players, Jeffrey knew, and Monk liked Benson very much but said, "Nobody has a sound like Charlie Christian." George and Monk talked for a while. Then Monk took Jeffrey for a walk to a place about eight blocks from the club. Monk said, "The music sounds very good from here." Jeffrey said, "I can't hear it." Monk said, "I'm hip." Perhaps it was just a joke; Monk liked to joke in that mischievous way. Jeffrey thought the incident was another test of his honesty. Perhaps someone else might lie, not wanting to disagree with Monk. But Jeffrey was afraid he might actually lose the job if he didn't tell the truth.

All summer, Jeffrey hung out with Monk, possibly learning about "Zen and the Art of Ping Pong," as well as how to relate to Thelonious as guru and to play his music well. Jeffrey enjoyed Monk's company; Monk sometimes burst into song or said something funny. Once Paul made the remark that Ringo Starr had made more money than Buddy Rich, Philly Joe Jones, Max Roach, and Art Blakey, all the jazz drummers put together. Monk paused, then said, "But if Ringo was in a room with all of them, he would have to feel weird." Monk was putting it into perspective, in a witty way. Despite all his money, Ringo would realize that the other guys were the ones really playing the drums. "Monk had sound philosophies," Paul learned. "He didn't believe everything he read in the newspaper. He was a stickler for accuracy." That was why he always asked for proof of anything that people offered as a fact after reading it in the papers.

Just the way Monk conducted his ping-pong games was amusing in its own way. Normally Monk trounced Jeffrey. But if Jeffrey ever got ahead of him, at a score of, perhaps nineteen to twelve, then Monk would win one point and say the score was nineteen to eighteen. "How are you going to argue with him?" Jeffrey asked himself. The few times that Jeffrey beat Monk, Jeffrey knew he was going to have to play thirty more games to even the score, and Monk would never let him quit. Monk liked to win. He was good-natured when he lost, but then he made sure he trounced an opponent for many games after that.

If Monk was working in town, Jeffrey traveled all the way from Coney Island, where he lived, to escort Monk to his gig, even if the baroness was also coming to take Monk in her car. Jeffrey stayed at the gig and took Monk to his door afterward.

One night they played a concert in a hotel in the mountains, where Wilbur Ware got drunk before the job. "Monk was not too happy," Jeffrey recalled. In October, when Monk's group prepared to go to Japan, Wilbur Ware was held back because of visa problems, and Leroy

Williams had a complication, too. So Wein hired bassist Larry Ridley, a man he had hired for other tours before this one, as the bassist, and a Brooklynite, Lenny McBrowne, as the drummer.

Ridley had gone to hear Monk at the Five Spot as early as 1958, when Monk played with Johnny Griffin, and, though in awe of Monk, Ridley had never had any hestitations about walking up to him and striking up a conversation. "He wasn't very talkative, but we had a good rapport," Ridley would recall. "He was interesting to me because he was a master of understatement in his playing and his conversation. Thelonious could say a lot with a few words; he was a true genius. When Thelonious hit that piano, it had a range to it; he could make a piano out of tune sound good. It was his touch."

Ridley, who later became a professor on the jazz faculty at Rutgers University in New Jersey, explains that there's more to learning Monk's style than simply learning the tunes:

> It's not just about learning to play Coltrane's licks, or all of Bud Powell, or even attempting to think you can imitate Thelonious's licks. There's a personal touch involved, part of an individual's signature. Every individual has to find his own identity. Jazz is a language. Understanding the vocabulary, syntax, everything involved, and putting it all together—that's what jazz musicians have to do. And that's the kind of genius that a person like Thelonious had.
>
> He had a very angular approach to melody. He was very individualistic about putting sounds together to express himself in his compositions, in the way he voiced his chords, used space, sound and silence. Thelonious could play just two or three notes, and you could think you heard a lot of them—[the overtones]. Some people will say: he didn't have the technique of an Art Tatum. Well, he didn't need it, because Art Tatum had a different voice and signature—a different way of expressing himself. He used more words to tell his story. Thelonious told his story with subtle innuendos and implications and with dynamics—all of these kinds of things.

And one of the things that Thelonious made me so aware of—I learned it by playing with him—is the importance of consistency in time and tempo. And I really emphasize that, because people have a tendency to want to rush or drop the time. But Thelonious was almost like a Swiss clock. Once he set the tempo, that time was right there—like tick tock, tick tock. And he could play in some of the most interesting tempos. They would stay right there, with him never rushing the time or dropping the tempo. He was very consistent. So the idea of pacing—that was one of the things that John Coltrane got from him, I think, when he was doing all that experimenting with fast runs. I think he got that kind of equilibrium from Thelonious. If you believe in astrology, and I do, then Thelonious was a Libra and a believer in balancing. I think John's playing was like a lava flow. It looks innocent, but the torrent! It's like seeing a tornado coming at you. John used to comment about a lot of things he acquired from his association with Thelonious. I'm paraphrasing John, but that whole idea of pacing and taking chances came from Thelonious.

I remember something about taking chances that Thelonious once said to me, when we were playing "Evidence," which is based on the chord changes of "Just You, Just Me." In the course of one of my solos onstage somewhere, I worked in part of the melody of "Just You, Just Me." And when we were walking off the stage shoulder-to-shoulder, Thelonious said, "Larry, next time don't make it so obvious." That's another classic example of his understatement. It had far-reaching implications—the idea of keeping a kind of mysteriousness. The title even, "Evidence"—keep the evidence slightly cloudy, keep an aura of intrigue. That's what I got out of it. Yeah, he was something.

Larry would work with Thelonious on and off for several years after the trip to Japan. The group played only the pieces already in Monk's repertoire. Larry never got sick of them: "Misterioso," "Straight, No Chaser," "Evidence," "Crepuscule with Nellie," "Ruby, My Dear," "Blue Monk," "Little Rootie Tootie," "Thelonious," "Epistrophy," and

"Bright Mississippi" (based on the changes of "Sweet Georgia Brown"). "Each time we played a song, it was a work in progress." Larry thought that Ellington certainly had an influence on Monk for the clusters and sophisticated dissonances and harmonic risks, "because Ellington defined 101 arranging concepts and focused on sound. The sound was the important thing. Thelonious did the same thing."

Monk always showed up on time for performances in Larry's experience, and Larry never thought Monk's behavior was peculiar. "People used to say it was, but I never thought so. I always thought that he seemed reflective and introspective," Larry recalled:

> He was cool with me. We'd talk about a lot of things. He would always have interesting kinds of ways of being very succinct and candid about his insights. One time someone made a comment to us—during the civil rights days, and things were pretty touchy, black power and all. I had a big Afro and dashikis. We were very conscious of this whole movement. This white guy said something about "you boys" this and "you boys" that to me. I turned to Thelonious and said, "I'm tired of these motherfuckers calling us boys. They don't have to go through all that. We're men." Thelonious said to me, "Ain't no drag, Larry, because everybody wants to be young." I said, "Okay, I'll think on that one." So he could really turn things into nothing with a few words. And there I was, upset, with my fist up in the air about respect. It was interesting.

Sometimes in rehearsals, Monk would stop if he didn't like the way the music sounded. But Larry didn't remember Monk ever saying anything directly to him about what he was doing or how he should approach things.

Paul Jeffrey noticed that Monk felt well on the trip to Japan. They toured there and even made a recording of "Evidence" and "Straight No Chaser" with a Japanese big band for Express Records. But because of Thelonious's contract with Columbia, the recording never came out in the United States, Jeffrey said.[1] He eventually got a copy of the Japanese release as a gift. Monk also recorded "Don't Blame Me" solo in Japan. And there was film footage made of the quartet playing "Blue Monk" with the Japanese big band.

Ridley never saw Monk in any dire mental or physical trouble. But once in a while, something curious would happen. They were sitting in the back of the Golden Getsukai in Japan, a restaurant-club with entertainment, where the group was playing. Monk was sitting across from Ridley; there was an elevator to Ridley's left. "The next thing I knew, Thelonious, who had been drinking Coca Cola, sent this Coke bottle flying in front of me." Larry recalled asking Monk what the hell he was doing. Paul Jeffrey, who was also in the room, thought he may have been the one who asked. Other people may have been there, too; it was difficult for Paul to remember exactly. But everyone there was "shook up," he said. The bottle smashed when it hit the elevator button.

Monk said, "I was just trying to call the elevator. I hit what I aim at."

Ridley recalled, "Suddenly I had seen this Coke bottle thrown in front of my face. But it wasn't directed at me. He had suddenly got this [urge] to call the elevator." When he hit the elevator button, the elevator came to the floor. "I can't remember if it opened," Paul said. "It must have. Nobody got on it."

After the tour ended, the group was heading for the Jazz Workshop in San Francisco to play for two weeks. Thelonious wanted Larry Ridley to go there, but Ridley hadn't known about the San Fransciso job in advance; he had already signed up to do something in New York after the tour of Japan. Years later he couldn't remember exactly what it had been, he said, but it may have been a gig. He was also attending classes at New York University, from which he would receive his degree in music education the next year. As they were flying over the Pacific Ocean, Monk came back from first class to talk to Ridley in the coach section; Ridley had an aisle seat.

Monk said, "Larry, we got to make this gig, man."

But Larry refused to cancel his gig or cut his classes in New York and stay on the west coast with Thelonious. Ridley later explained that he wanted to be known for keeping his word. Monk may not have understood the nature of Ridley's commitments, or else he was under the impression that Ridley could postpone his plans. Monk went away, then came back and nudged Ridley, who was falling asleep. Monk said, "Wouldn't it be something if this plane fell in the ocean right now?"

Ridley thought the comment was a little bizarre. He knew Monk was very angry because he didn't like anything to get in the way of what he wanted for his music.

Bassist Putter Smith, the younger brother of bassist Carson Smith, was recruited to come up from Los Angeles and play with Monk's group. Putter had transcribed many of Monk's songs for the love of the music, but he had never thought he would actually get a chance to play with Monk. When Putter arrived at the club, Monk, Jeffrey, and McBrowne were in the dressing room, waiting for him. Monk was smoking and pacing the floor. He looked at Putter, who was white, and said, "You the new bass player?"

Putter said, "Yes."

Monk said, "White is right."

Putter recalled, "That's how I felt. Everything is going to be all right," I told myself, "and it was."

Russ Wilson, a critic for the *Oakland Tribune*, gave the group a wonderful review: "Thelonious Monk, a major innovator in jazz who remains, after twenty-five years of activity, one of the most unmistakeably original talents in his field, is back in the Bay Area after a protracted absence. The massive pianist began a two-week stay at the Jazz Workshop in San Francisco on [Oct 16] Wednesday night with three associates who have not been heard with him out here. It is a most felicitous meld."

Wilson discussed the background of Monk's group in detail. "I cite this background," he wrote,

> because it is important to the music Monk currently is playing. As has always been the case, it is highly personal and it carries no great new revelations. But because the expressions of his sidemen differ from their predecessors, the pianist's playing reflected a similar freshness. On a couple of tunes, for example—a romping, stomping "Epistrophy" and an uptempo blues—Monk's solos had

the fervor he must have shown during his salad days when he was touring the country with an itinerant evangelist. Additionally he displayed his too often unremarked technical fluency at the keyboard.

One night Monk danced for a whole set. A lady sitting in the front called out, "I paid good money to see you."

Monk didn't wait a millisecond. He said, "Are you blind?"

Putter, who enjoyed the gig enormously, thought Monk had a wonderful sense of humor. And he perceived Monk as a very shy man, who simply looked aggressive—a big, strong man, with a majestic appearance. "I was on the stage at the Workshop. He came in through the audience. Everyone in the club turned around to look at him." Later people went backstage to pay their respects to him. Monk seemed to emanate a sweetness to them—and to Putter, too. "He seemed loving, not because of anything special he said, but because of the way he conducted himself," Putter recalled.

Several times, during breaks at the job, Putter and Monk went to Mike's Pool Hall on Broadway. Putter was captivated by Monk's style of shooting pool. "He played randomly with a lot of force. He shot into a pile of balls with something in mind rather than shooting at one ball. I read profundities into him perhaps," Putter thought in retrospect.

Paul Jeffrey recalled something that Monk used to do in a restaurant at night after the gig at the Jazz Workshop. To Paul, it synthesized Monk's spirit as a prankster and a persistent, patient artist—all qualities that evidenced themselves in his music. He liked to order a cup of tea, add lemon, and then milk. Each time the milk curdled, because of the lemon. Monk kept saying he was sure he could add the milk and not have it curdle. Each time he tried it, he failed. The waitress used to get annoyed, because she knew she would have to bring him another cup of tea. "He just kept saying it could be done," Paul said. Finally one night, Monk did get his experiment to work.

"Nothing disturbed him," Paul said, recalling a tale he had heard about Monk's ability to concentrate. "One time David Izenson was playing bass as a subsitute in one of Monk's groups, and he was playing very strongly to impress Monk. His bridge collapsed. When that happens, it sounds like someone shot a rifle. Monk acted as if he hadn't heard it."

On a Saturday night—Putter thought it was during the second weekend of the two-week gig—Monk didn't show up to play. Another pianist, who did a poor job of interpreting Monk's music, was recruited. That was the last night of the gig. Putter didn't think the incident of the missed performance was very important. He heard some kind of rumor about Monk's mental condition but didn't pay much attention to it. Trying to recall events, Putter actually thought the gig lasted one more night and that Monk showed up to play. But Paul Jeffrey knew that was not so: Monk had been hospitalized again.

It's unclear exactly what happened—whether Monk simply withdrew for a little while, as he had habitually done, or for longer than usual. Or perhaps he had actually suffered something as severe as the symptoms he had once gotten from a surprise dose of LSD in Minneapolis. It's conceivable that someone had done the same thing to him in San Francisco, or that he had done something similar to himself knowingly or not. But something terrible had happened. Monk went to a hospital, probably the Langley Porter in San Francisco. Doctors may have discussed giving him shock treatments there. [*] This may have been the first time Paul Jeffrey had seen Monk extremely upset. Paul assisted Nellie, taking her back and forth from the hospital.

Putter stayed in San Francisco for a while after the gig ended and saw Monk one day in an apartment, which belonged to Jules Colomby's girlfriend (Jules was managing Monk at this time). Putter played his own transcription of a song by Monk at the piano. Monk was very surprised that Putter played the piano at all. Putter was under the impression that Monk had liked the effort.

Putter went back to Los Angeles; for the entire month of December, the drummer Clarence Becton (replacing Lenny McBrowne) and bassist Raphael Garrett played with Monk and Jeffrey at the Both/And Club in San Francisco. Becton, who thought Monk sounded fine and gave no special sign of feeling ill, met Monk just as the gig was about to begin without a rehearsal. Becton, who knew the songs, set up his drums. Monk sat down at the piano and began to play. If Becton ever had questions about the music, he asked Jeffrey, who was serving as de facto musical director, and Jeffrey relayed them to Monk. The only time Becton found Monk at all sociable was at a Christmas party given by a friend of Becton's in Berkeley. Otherwise Becton didn't see Monk at the bar or Nellie in the club. Monk didn't seem to talk to anyone except Paul and didn't even get up and dance his usual dance for joy during that gig. Mostly Monk stayed in his dressing room between the sets, while Becton stayed at the bar and socialized with people whom he knew.

Sammy Mitchell, reviewing this engagement, suggested that Monk showed symptoms of withdrawal.[1] Mitchell wrote:

> This wasn't exemplary Monk. Subdued from a bout of illness and thinned down in appearance and output, he seemed introspectively-deep in a nirvanic cocoon, occasionally emerging with a message, sometimes cryptic but worth waiting for (below par Monk can still shine)—before retreating into detachment until the next call, leaving the tenorist to carry most of the solo lead.

The reviewer praised Jeffrey's extroverted style and even said:

> though Monk's solos were sparse in comparison to Jeffrey's heroics, his essence came through unimpaired—the absorbing stylist no one comes within miles of emulating. "I Mean You" and "Nutty" were among the best because he was at his least hermetic ... [Rafael] Garrett and Becton supplied the pulse of good professionals, slickly pushing the beat along ... Shadowy at times, Monk was still substantial listening.

If Monk had suffered a period of severe withdrawal—and that seems to have been the case—it was likely to have frightened anyone who had never seen him go through such a spell before. Paul Jeffrey decided to stay with the group despite Monk's breakdown. He told Becton that the group was going on the road and asked if Becton was available to travel. But he was attending San Francisco City College for music courses. That was the last time Becton worked with Monk.

Soon afterward, Monk went to Los Angeles, where Putter Smith played with the group at the jazz club, Shelle's Manne-hole. Putter was impressed with how many famous people came to visit Monk back-stage—comedian Flip Wilson, singer Abbey Lincoln, maybe even Bill Cosby—and musicians, too, among them Candy Finch, Dizzy Gilles-pie's drummer. With Candy, the conversation turned to the subject of martial arts, in which Candy was involved. He remarked that bullets did more damage if they were fired into a man's back instead of his front. Thelonious, who had been very quiet, suddenly said, "Next time, when you're running away from the police, maybe you should run backwards."

To Putter the music sounded even better in Los Angeles than it had in San Francisco. Ndugu Chancler, then nager beginning his career as a drummer, played with the group. Even though he clearly admired the modern style of Tony Williams—and Putter, among so many others, preferred Monk's work with Art Blakey—Putter—and Paul Jeffrey, too—thought Ndugu sounded fine in the group. Putter thought Thelonious had some great moments in Los Angeles; he played more and danced less than he had in San Francisco.

So if Monk seemed withdrawn during the gig with Becton, he was coming closer to approximating his usual self by the time he was playing in Los Angeles. That's not to say that Putter thought Monk was absolutely down to earth at the time. "I thought of him as being in a zone," Putter would recall. "He had a Tourette's syndrome kind of thing. But a zone is not a mental illness." Putter knew that Monk returned to Los Angeles to play in succeeding years, too, though Putter had to go to Europe and didn't hear Monk play in person again.

There are other tales of Monk's encroaching instability that are diffi-cult to place in exact chronological order, dating back to the 1960s. Writer Grover Sales recalled seeing Monk in a coffeehouse near the Jazz Workshop in the 1960s. Monk was late in getting ready to go on the bandstand. Furthermore, he was dancing in the coffeehouse, where the wife of the owner went up to him and said, "You can't dance here." That puzzled Monk. Just then, the bouncer from the Jazz Workshop went up to him and said, "Are you ready, Monk?" Monk said, "I'm always ready." He went back to the work.

Grover Sales noticed a great difference between Monk's playing at that time and in 1959, when Monk had appeared at the Blackhawk jazz club. Sales thought Monk was not nearly as exciting nor as excited himself at the later date, nor did he sound as wonderful nor appear as healthy as he had at the Monterey Jazz Festival earlier in the 1960s. Now everything sounded predictable. Furthermore, Sales took some people down to the dressing room to meet Monk at the Jazz Workshop and found Monk seemingly under very heavy medication.

Sonny Buxton, who had seen Monk play at the Blackhawk with Billy Higgins years earlier, was surprised later in the 1960s by a bizarre incident at the Jazz Workshop. Monk's group was playing on stage, but Monk was nowhere in sight. Then he came dancing down the aisle, wearing a tweed topcoat with the collar pulled up on a warm night. His entrance was thrilling. When he got up on stage, he started conducting the group. But none of the men in the band paid any attention. They just kept playing. Monk sat down at the piano as if he was going to play. But he didn't. Instead he made a couple of gestures and "sashayed" out of the club and out the door, Buxton recalled. Monk didn't return. Buxton, a jazz fan and a broadcaster hoping to get an interview for his station, was very disappointed.

After the set, Buxton went across the street to a deli, where he was surprised to find Monk sitting at a table. Sonny went up to him and found Monk very friendly. So Sonny said, "What was that all about in the club?" Monk said, "What club?" Sonny said, "The Jazz Workshop across the street?" Monk looked away. Sonny sat there a moment more, then said, "It's beautiful to meet you," and got up and walked out.

Monk and Jeffrey stayed on the west coast until March 1971, "hanging out" during February, as Paul Jeffrey accounted for the time. The group wasn't working all the time, "and I wanted to stay out there all the time," Jeffrey recalled:

Monk asked me, "Am I sticking?" I wanted to stay more than anything else in this world. So I figured out ways to supplement [my income] as a copyist. Herman Lubinsky of Savoy Records, in Newark, sent me gospel records. And I would take music off the records and tell [Lubinsky] to send the money to my wife. My expenses out there were being paid by the Monks. Monk was very generous in a way, looking out for his sidemen. He'd always ask you if you liked your accommodations and different things like that.

When he returned to New York, Monk took a group, still managed and booked by Jules Colomby, to play a concert opposite Blood, Sweat and Tears, then a very popular rock band that employed a jazz-style brass section, in Avery Fisher Hall in April 1971. Wilbur Ware and Philly Joe Jones joined the band at that time. Afterward, both groups played a concert in Quebec City. Jules and Bobby Colomby, the drummer and the youngest Colomby brother, who was playing drums in Blood, Sweat and Tears, thought it would be a great idea to send Monk's quartet and Blood, Sweat and Tears on a tour, Paul Jeffrey recalled. The first concert took place in Washington, D.C., but the rest of the tour never materialized. Paul thought that politics and competition between a couple of members in the groups put an end to the project. From a commercial point of view, it could have been ideal.

Monk had not recorded for Columbia since 1968, and during this period, Monk's contractual relationship with Columbia ended, although exactly when it ended isn't clear. Teo Macero thought it might have ended even before 1968, but that is the year of Monk's last recording for Columbia. Macero did recall very clearly, however, that Columbia ended the relationship because Monk's recordings weren't selling well enough to suit the company. Macero also recalled that the company didn't renew Duke Ellington's contract and turned down chances to record John Coltrane and others. When asked why Columbia passed on these opportunities to record jazz, Macero replied, "They're idiots, that's why."

"Toot," Larry Ridley, and Thelonious performing in Mexico. Photo courtesy Nadine Markova.

Even a musician as venerated as Monk was affected by the public's lack of interest in acoustic jazz at a time when rock reigned. According to Paul Jeffrey, Columbia wanted Monk to do an album of Beatles songs with Blood Sweat and Tears; Monk refused. Jeffrey thought that someone had shown Beatles music to Monk and even suggested that Monk might need help in reading it! However, Teo Macero never heard of the idea of an album of Beatles songs for Monk, and Bobby Colomby has no memory of it, either.[4]

From Washington, Monk tacked to Syracuse University in New York State, then over to Saginaw, Michigan. Lenny McBrowne was supposed to replace Philly Joe, but then Thelonious Jr. took over the drum seat. Larry Ridley played with the group for a while at that time. They went to the Village Vanguard. All Jeffrey could remember of the group's gigs during the rest of 1971 was a trip to Mexico, for which Ridley and Thelonious, Jr. went along.

On October 10, 1971, *Down Beat* ran an article by Pearl Gonzalez that reported on Monk's trip to Mexico City. Preparing for that visit, Thelonious read about Mexican history and the Aztecs, George Wein somehow discovered! Monk apparently enjoyed seeing this new culture.

"Thelonious Monk came out from the wings alone and played a bawdy house blues version of 'I Love You' to an audience that didn't want to go home," Ms. Gonzalez began her article. After the performance, she asked him if that was his way of showing appreciation to the audience, and he said "yes." She asked him what the importance of jazz was, and he answered that it was stimulating and inspiring to musicians. Then she asked how he selected musicians, and he answered, "just hire them." Seeing that Thelonious looked tired, she suggested they continue the interview the next day at his hotel.

The next day, Monk seemed in very good spirits, and , patiently answered Gonzalez's questions about his background. When she asked if classical composers like Bach and Beethoven had any influence on him, he said, "Oh, you mean Rachmaninoff, Stravinsky and guys like that." And she recounted that he laughed and added, "I only mentioned their names because you're wearing a red jacket [an oblique, and amusing, reference to the fact that these were Russian composers]."

His blatant humor was so unlike him in other interviews. He seemed milder and more playful in public now. Ms. Gonzalez laughed at his joke and called him a "really sweet, warm man." He kept toying with words for her. She asked him, "What do you think your sound is?" He said, "Music." She said, "Let's face it. You have your own style." He said, "Face? Is there a face in music? Isn't there a song like that? 'Let's Face the Music?'"

She and Paul Jeffrey laughed heartily, and Ms. Gonzalez called Monk "our cornball friend." In response to her question about how he felt about his influence on jazz, he said he was surprised when people dug it and asked him for particular songs. He had always been humble before, parrying jovially with reporters who tried to get him to call himself a genius, but he had never before expressed wonderment at receiving attention.

Ms. Gonzales asked him what his other interests were.

"Life in general," he said.

"What do you do about it?" she asked.

"Keep breathing."

"I hear you don't give out too many interviews, why is that?"

"I can't figure that one out myself. Sometimes I talk, and sometimes I don't feel like talking."

"Why?"

"I don't know, I'd like to know, too."

Remembering that response years later, Paul Jeffrey laughed softly.

"Moods?"

"I don't know what makes people talk. Maybe it's whisky. A lot of people talk a lot [when they're] full of whisky, in other words."

He said that the majority of addicts to many legal and illegal substances weren't musicians. When asked how he relaxed, he mentioned playing ping-pong. He answered questions about his children—his son, a drummer, who was traveling with him in his group, and his daughter, a singer and dancer. Expressing a fully realized, succinct analysis of the joys of the creative process, he said that when he himself wrote music, he felt as if he had "accomplished something. Feel as if it's a fulfilment. Something's been pulled through."

In response to Gonzalez's curiosity about how he had acquired a yellow, belted, silk suit that he was wearing, he said he preferred more casual clothes, but his family had forced him to buy that suit in Tokyo. He had also bought a beautiful opal ring in Hong Kong, and had designed his black onyx and diamond ring with the name Monk on it. The rings excited him more than the clothes.

Asked how he regarded money, he said he didn't worry about it; he just let the family spend a quarter of what he earned.

Gonzalez asked, "Had he ever thought about writing a book?"

Toot on drums, July 2, 1972. Photo: Raymond Ross.

People had suggested it to him, he said, but he hadn't made a decision.

"And what did he want to do with the rest of his life," Ms. Gonzalez asked.

He said, "I want to enjoy it."

"How?" Ms. Gonzalez asked.

Monk said, "That's what I want to find out from reporters. If you know the best way to enjoy life, I'd like to know. I believe everybody would like to find out."

He didn't want to bring religion into the discussion. His formal religious affiliations had ended, he suggested, though he still thought about religion—"at all times," he said. "You just know everybody goes for religion." But asked his opinion of the value of the then-popular Broadway "rock opera," *Jesus Christ Superstar*, he said it was a "gimmick." That prompted his son, then about twenty-two, to put in his two cents. "It's gone too far for just a gimmick," said Toot. "I think it's healthy. The kids do not accept just anything. This is just another fight of the young."

Monk Sr. refused to comment on Toot's opinion.

But then Toot said, "The people who are running the church are saying one thing and doing another. Why, the Catholic church can pay off the national debt."

His father said, "How do you know? Have you seen their books?" That was the kind of skeptical statement that Harry Colomby and Paul Jeffrey had become used to from Monk, who always wanted to have people report what they had seen with their own eyes.

Toot pressed on, "The Catholic Church owns everything inside the Catholic churches and all kinds of property."

Jeffrey would later recall that Monk had tried to guide Toot by saying, "What you say sticks [in other words, be careful to say exactly what you mean, because others will take it seriously]." Ms. Gonzalez quoted Monk as saying, "This is a Catholic country, you know."

Toot persisted: "I can't help that. Look at Harlem. The church isn't helping the people; they throw people out. This is not an opinion, Dad, this is a fact."

Monk said, "Well, I'm not a preacher."

Ms. Gonzalez asked, "Do you discuss these things at home?"

Monk said, "All kinds of things come up. Mostly they talk with their mother. You know, I did a gig in the Catholic Church way back, in the Village. Played the same kind of music last night," he said, trying to convey a feeling of tolerance in the face of his son's youthful idealism and loquaciousness. Perhaps Thelonious, Sr. was even concerned about how his son would fare should he be detained by the police.

The interview continued. The writer asked Monk Sr. if he thought music reflected its time. Paul Jeffrey said, "Yes." Monk Sr. took the question personally, saying, "It's not the same kind of music.

You don't have as much fire and enthusiasm. It happens to everybody with age . . ."

Ms. Gonzalez said, "That wasn't exactly my question."

But she could have been alerted by it.

Toot said, "I think more than my Dad about what he said. There are changes a man goes through. You don't have to get old with years. You can get old because you get on something."

The conversation was taking a particularly tantalizing turn. Monk was fifty-four years old—in a decade in life when most people begin to think profoundly about their mortality. They consider what they have done in their lives; what they have left to look forward to, how much time they have left on earth, and what they want to do with that time. But instead of pursuing that topic with Monk, or asking his son what he meant by "get on something"—drugs perhaps—Ms. Gonzalez let the musicians veer off to the subjects of good music, commercial music, and rock and roll. Thelonious, Sr. said, "Good music is something you enjoy. It's pleasing to you. It's good to your ear. Anything that sounds good to your ear, a nice type of sound, is music."

Toot said, "I agree. But I'll go one step further. Good music has a tendency to last."

Thelonious Sr. made no effort to hold junior back or compete with him for center stage.

The interviewer asked Toot, "What are you studying for?"

"I've graduated [from] a prep school in Darien, Connecticut, and I'm going to study music and continue playing drums."

Charlie Bourgeois of the George Wein organization interrupted the interview at this point, saying Monk had to go to work again in the International Jazz Festival in Mexico. But Monk didn't want to stop the interview and said, "There's still time. It's only across the street," referring to the place where he was going to play. Ms. Gonzalez, preparing to leave anyway, watched Monk as he listened to the sound of mariachis when the door of his suite opened. "B flat," he said about a note they were playing.

Then Ms. Gonzalez asked him a very grand question: "What do you think the purpose of life is?"

Thelonious Monk Sr. said, "To die."

She said, "But between birth and death, there's a lot to do."

"You asked a question. That's the answer," he said in his familiar style, with his back to her, reminding her of who was being interviewed, and, as she wrote, "staring out of the 12th floor window that overlooked a valley once conquered by another kind of sound led by a chief with relatively few forces in his band."

If he had suggested that he was a depressed or at least still a very solemn, intense man at times by pronouncing the purpose of life was to die, he also sounded less driven, less perfectionistic, and, oddly, far more amiable, less edgy, and softer in manner and attitude than he had in previous interviews. As a father, he was ideally encouraging. He displayed himself as the introspective man that his intimate friends always said he was. Paul Jeffrey knew that Monk talked candidly to his family and close associates at times, but the public rarely had a chance to know about his private thoughts; he had often become so annoyed with journalists for denigrating him in his early years and misquoting him that he tended to speak guardedly, protectively.

A Japanese journalist had once asked Monk in what form he would like to return to earth, if he could be reincarnated. Monk said, "The devil." The Japanese writer asked why. Monk said, "Because the devil has the most fun." The journalist wrote that the devil has *more* fun. Monk became very annoyed because he had been misquoted. He had said "the most fun," not "more fun"—more was *not* the most. Gonzalez had managed a great victory, bringing off an interview in which Monk suggested he was tired and definitely searching and thinking about his mortality. So many of his friends and supporters had died by then: Ellington, who had praised the spirit of innovation and defended Monk early in his career, Denzil Best, Coleman Hawkins, Bud Powell, and pianist Elmo Hope, to name a few. Paul Jeffrey thought Monk had never shrunk from the idea that he would die one day, but this was the first time that Monk had mentioned his mortality to the public. He usually shied away from philosophizing about his personal life with journalists.

Jeffrey, so deeply attached to and protective of the Monks, enjoyed that interview. Monk liked Mexico—hearing the mariachi band, the interview, and seeing a ballet for which they got box seats. For Jeffrey, Monk's talk about death was nothing very new. "I think Monk was realistic," Jeffrey would muse later. "He never mentioned being disturbed by the finality of death. He said whatever happened was supposed to happen."

Larry Ridley, who had gone with Monk to play in Mexico, went back to New York very ill. He was heading out the door to keep a date to play with Monk's group at the Vanguard, when he suddenly realized he had better go to the bathroom quickly. At the same moment, Monk was having the same experience in his apartment. Neither of them ever got to the gig. They had apparently contracted dysentery in Mexico. Nellie and Nica treated both of them with an herbal remedy that exacerbated their illness. It was Larry's understanding that the women thought the men had to clean out their systems. They got well eventually, though Ridley was alarmed by the amount of weight he lost. In retrospect he couldn't remember why he had simply gone along with the medical collaboration of Nica and Nellie. Sometimes they worked together as a great team, sometimes just as a team. In any case he knew them, and they certainly meant well.

NOTES

Personal interviews: Paul Jeffrey, Larry Ridley, Putter Smith, Clarence Becton, Grover Sales, Sonny Buxton, Teo Macero, Bobby Colomby, Bob Jones.

1. It's unclear whether Monk was still under contract to Columbia at the time of this tour; in any case, there may still have been some unresolved issues in his contract, even if he had been dropped by the label.
2. A trumpeter named Eddie Henderson, who was studying to become a doctor and working at the hospital at that time, later told several people about Monk's stay at the hospital. Some people thought that Henderson said he had prevented the hospital from administering shock treatments to Monk, and some people thought that Henderson said Monk actually had been given shock treatments.
3. Mitchell (1971).
4. In 1972 or '73, Bobby wanted to do an album of Monk's music, with Monk, strings, and arrangements by Hall Overton. But Bobby was discouraged from pursuing the project; as he recalled many years later, he may have been told that Monk wasn't feeling up to the project. Monk may have had little interest in recording at that time (or record-industry executives, cognizant of the small sales of jazz artists's recordings, may have discouraged Bobby).

14 Drug Use and Brain Damage

Later in 1971, without Paul Jeffrey although accompanied by Nellie, Monk went to Europe on a "Giants of Jazz" tour organized by George Wein, playing in a band including Dizzy Gillespie, Art Blakey, Al McKibbon, alto saxophonist Sonny Stitt, and trombonist Kai Winding. First they flew to Australia, then to Japan. Sonny Stitt was *persona non grata* in Japan at that time for legal reasons probably connected with his narcotics use, and so he had to fly to Europe and wait for the group there. Stitt was replaced in Japan by a well-known, highly regarded Japanese tenor player, Sleepy Matsumoto.

The Giants of Jazz played and recorded in Paris at a hall—no one seems to remember which one—then went on to London and gave two concerts in mid-November at the Victoria Theatre, where Atlantic recorded the group. For the concerts in Paris and London in November, Monk played very little; Dizzy played both trumpet and piano on the recordings. But the day after the last Victoria Theatre concert, Monk recorded in a studio with Al McKibbon and Art Blakey and also as a soloist for a mixture of standards and his own compositions for the British Black Lion label. His solo recordings were very highly praised in England.

George Wein had no compunctions about taking Monk along on that tour. In retrospect, it wasn't the memory of Monk's problems but the general atmosphere of the touring group that remained with George. "I'll never forget the cooperation," he said:

> Most [of the players] usually went first class with their own groups; they were all leaders. But all of them agreed to go tourist class to make that tour possible. And they did a lot of wonderful things like that . . . I think Thelonious like Duke Ellington was very impressed by royalty, riches. Those things meant something to him. The baroness was a Rothschild and devoted to him. He talked about her and her Rolls Royce. Quality was very important to him. In England we got him a Rolls, and he genuflected to the people, tipped his hat to the people. The guy was very nice. I loved Thelonious.

George Wein reflected, "There's no question [Monk] was a genius, and the only man I know of that, if he had had a different attitude and control of his life, would have been a challenge to Duke Ellington, a great man like Ellington. Monk wasn't into jazz as business. He was a real jazz composer. But he never had the organizational ability to keep a band or orchestra together."

Paul Jeffrey met the plane that brought Monk and Nellie back to John F. Kennedy airport, where, Jeffrey observed, Monk wasn't feeling very well. He had leaned on Nellie to help him through the tour. Jeffrey had been surprised that Monk had gone on the tour. The band had been surprised, too, and yet it had turned out to be a very successful one. "But I thought it took a lot out of him," Paul recalled.

Soon afterward, in December, Monk seemed so upset that Paul telephoned an old friend whom he had met while attending Ithaca College, then a resident in psychiatry at Beth Israel Hospital. The psychiatrist made a house call at Monk's apartment. "At that time it was already unusual for doctors to make house calls," Paul recalled, but this doctor did it as a favor to his old friend from their student days.

The doctor decided that Monk should be admitted to Beth Israel, where the doctor worked with him for a while, preparing a report that took into account past diagnoses and treatments. He concluded that Monk had been misdiagnosed and wrongly treated previously.

Although this psychiatrist would not share his report without the permission of Monk's family—and this permission was withheld—from conversations with other doctors familiar with Monk's case it was possible to formulate an interpretation of Monk's mental history. Monk emerged as a genius beginning in his teens, and his habit of disconnecting from his surroundings suggested nothing more myste-rious than his total absorption with music. It was unlikely that Monk was either schizophrenic or manic depressive, nor that he suffered from a depression that led to hallucinations.

At the time of his hospitalization in 1971, Monk couldn't play the piano at all. The quality of his music had deteriorated at that point, and his hands were stiff—possibly as a side effect of some medication or a mixture of different medications.

One doctor who discussed Monk's case with seveatl physicians at the time of his treatment was Dr. Everett Dulit. As the years passed, Dr. Dulit, an amateur jazz saxophonist with an interest in Monk, was able to analyze Monk's condition. Dr. Dulit elaborated on the case:

> Thelonious Monk was a drug user, and every piece of evidence that we had suggests that what happened at the end of his life was probably brain damage from too much drug use. We can't know what he used, but if I had to make a bet, it wasn't aging, it was some kind of a syndrome similar to Alzheimer's disease [that afflicted him]. People with Alzheimer's fall into a mute state and die. Now, Monk didn't have Alzheimer's. The similarity between Alzheimer's and Monk's condition has to do with pervasive brain damage, and one of the ways you can damage your brain is by using the wrong drugs too much.

Monk returned home from Beth Israel, but soon entered Gracie Square Hospital, a private hospital located in the East Sixties in

Manhattan. Several people, who had known him for years, saw him there, because Ray Nance was hospitalized there at the same time. Drummer Ray Mosca, pianist Sir Charles Thompson, and Duke Ellington's nephew Michael James were among those who visited both musicians.

Ray Mosca had first met Monk in the 1950s, probably before Monk lost his cabaret card, because at the time Monk was playing at Cafe Bohemia in the West Village, in a group led by Miles Davis, with Kenny Clarke on drums and Oscar Pettiford on drums. Mosca played opposite Monk many times in clubs after that, when Monk had drummers Roy Haynes and then Frankie Dunlop in the groups.

In 1971 Mosca worked for violinist and trumpeter Ray Nance, who was leading a group for a four-week gig at the Top of the Gate in the Village Gate club on Bleecker Street. One night, the Gate's owner Art D'Lugoff threw a big party for Nance and his wife in honor of their twenty-fifth wedding anniversary. Duke Ellington and his band arrived, after finishing their uptown gig, and jammed for the party. Nance had played as a very important member of Duke's orchestra for years. On Sunday, Nance flew to Europe for a record date on Monday and returned to New York on Tuesday, in time to play at the Gate at 10 P.M. He had been on methadone for quite a few years by then, after using heroin for about thirty-five years, and he was drinking vodka, too. When he got off the plane from Europe, he was "ripped," Mosca recalled.

Nance went to his apartment on Charles Street, behind the Village Vanguard. Unable to find his keys, he couldn't get in the front door. However, "there was a little guy who had been hanging around the Nances for quite a while," Mosca said. "He lived next door to them. Nance had thought he was gay, and so did I. But Mrs. Nance suddenly had left Ray Nance for the little guy over the weekend. She opened the window from her lover's apartment and said she wouldn't throw the keys down to Nance. He broke the door down. The police came and took him to Bellevue. So he missed the last week of his gig at the Gate, where his group played as a trio." Duke Ellington, who did not forsake his former player, arranged for Nance to go to Gracie

Square Hospital, where he was put in a room next door to Thelonious Monk's.

When Mosca and Sir Charles Thompson visited Nance, they found him terribly angry and cursing at Thelonious. Thelonious was "sitting on the floor, wearing a hat and listening to music on a little Victrola," Mosca recalled, "and he wouldn't talk to Nance." He and Monk had never been close friends, but they had known each other. Nance didn't know that Monk sometimes withdrew. That was his trouble. "What's wrong with this guy!" Nance yelled. Mosca and Sir Charles couldn't help laughing very hard, because Nance was so frustrated. Mosca recalled that Nance got out of the hospital soon after that. Monk stayed a little longer.

Michael James noticed that Monk repeatedly listened to one tune: his own recording of "Ruby, My Dear" with Coleman Hawkins. Michael read a great deal into Monk's choice. Monk had recorded the song with John Coltrane and Charlie Rouse, too, but appeared to prefer Hawk's sound. Furthermore, Hawk, who had been Monk's very important early mentor, had died only a couple of years earlier.

Another visitor was Reverend John Gensel, pastor of St. Peter's Lutheran Church with a special ministry for the jazz world, who was called the "Shepherd of the Night Flock" by Duke Ellington. He found Monk to be "perfectly all right, not in bed, and very appreciative of the visit." Thelonious talked about having toured with a church group early in his career. He had told Reverend Gensel about that once before, when the pastor had paid a friendly visit to the Monks at their apartment. Reverend Gensel, who knew Ray Nance quite well, didn't see Nance in the hospital at that time; Nance had probably already left.

When Wilbur Ware, the bassist, and Leroy Williams, the drummer, visited Monk, the hospital personnel brought him down to the lobby. Leroy was working in Yusuf Lateef's group and was heading out of town. Monk said, "I hear you're going out of town." Leroy was surprised to hear that Monk knew what was going on. He was well connected by then. Leroy said, "Yes. I'm just waiting for you to get out of the hospital." Monk said, "I don't know how long I'll be here."

Leroy knew that Monk sometimes withdrew, and he also "talked when he felt like it," Leroy recalled.

Monk not only left the hospital but went back to work. On March 10, 1972, an article by Colman Andrews appeared in *The Staff* about Monk's performance with bassist Al McKibbon, Paul Jeffrey, and Toot on February 17 at Shelly's Manne-hole in Los Angeles. The critic echoed the opinion that Monk's music had become very familiar to jazz listeners by this time: "If he sounds less than shocking (less than exciting, for that matter) today, it's only because he's been playing pretty much the same thing for a very long time. To see and hear Monk in 1972 is not a thrilling, convention-shattering experience. It's more like paying homage to a legitimate, living American musical tradition."

This review was in a sense predictable. It could have been written about any star with a long career, and actually it was the type of review that would soon be written about Dizzy Gillespie, Ella Fitzgerald, Sarah Vaughan, Count Basie—jazz stars who had become legendary figures by doing what they did so well repeatedly. Critics weren't actually saying that Monk couldn't play well anymore, only that they had already heard everything he was doing. Musicians were still enthralled by Monk—though occasionally some detected a coldness in his sound.

In 1972, thirty-one-year-old bassist Ron McClure was teaching at Berklee College of Music in Boston, when his old friend, Jules Colomby, telephoned him. Ron had met Jules in a class taught by Hall Overton at the New School in New York. Colomby asked Ron to work for a week in Monk's group, with Paul Jeffrey and Toot, at Lenny's on the Turnpike in Boston. Ron was delighted at the chance. Jeffrey, whom Ron knew slightly from classes at Charles Colin's studios in Manhattan, sent some of Monk's music to Ron before the gig. "Like most musicians my age," Ron recalled, "I knew a bunch of Monk's tunes and had heard him play in New York clubs and on records."

McClure enjoyed the job. Jeffrey played in a style reminiscent of Charlie Rouse's with Monk. McClure recalled:

Toot was just a nice innocent kid at that time, and he played good. I had some solo space. I remember the pianist, teacher and composer at one of the Boston music colleges, Ran Blake, coming up to me after a set and complimenting me because I had improvised in the style of Monk's music. I had never really thought too much about it, but I did try to play in accordance with whatever is going on in the music that I happen to be playing, including my own. And it is always nice to know that someone with an understanding of jazz—like Ran Blake—hears what you are playing . . . I was the talk of Berkelee College that week. "Fuckin' McClure got the gig with Monk!"

Ron played again with Monk for a week at the Village Vanguard in New York, then two weeks at the Aqua Lounge in Philadelphia, and another week at the Vanguard. Monk almost never spoke to Ron directly, nor did the baroness, who was at the gig at the Vanguard every night. If Monk had anything to say to Ron, Jeffrey acted as the go-between. "The baroness wouldn't even say hello to me. I didn't exist," Ron recalled. "She was attractive; she looked like a beagle or a blood-hound, with her long face and long, hanging hair . . . A baroness where? Not in America. You're in New York now. She wore her money," he said. A remarkably good, strong bassist, McClure did not appreciate being snubbed by the baroness.

All in all, McClure enjoyed his dates playing with Monk:

One night—in the Aqua Lounge—Monk was swinging, and I was looking at him, smiling, with such appreciation in my expression. He noticed and gave me a great big smile. He knew he was really hooking up. Sometimes he really played great. He'd go in and out.

I was the only white person there in any direction . . . that was not an unfamiliar experience for me, since I had already played at the Gold Coast in Brooklyn, New York with Wynton Kelly and Jimmy Cobb . . . Wynton had told me of the comments he received from black people for having hired me as his bass player after Paul Chambers died. "Come on down and hear Ron McClure play," he told them. They did. And no one ever said or did anything less than friendly and complimentary to me during that phase of my career. In fact, my experience has been quite to the contrary of what one might expect. It has most often been the white people who have overlooked me because I wasn't black when it came to who gets the nod to play . . . [But] I've always found plenty of people with open hearts, minds and ears to play with.

One Saturday night at the Aqua Lounge, Ron got up his nerve to play a bowed solo. He had never done it before with Monk. The audience seemed to like it. But at the Sunday afternoon matinee, Monk walked directly to him, cleared his throat "like a self-conscious teenager," Ron thought, and said, "Can you leave the bow alone?" Ron said, "Sure, but why? Is there something you don't like about it?" Monk cleared his throat again and said, "Uh, the sound." Monk simply thought a bowed bass sounded boring, no matter who was playing arco. He wanted the music to swing, and the sidemen had to maintain the time in their solos.

From the Aqua Lounge, they went back to the Vanguard for another week. Monk liked to dance on the bandstand. And Ron saw him in the bathroom a great deal:

> Monk was always doing coke. If I went into the bathroom, he put it away. He never did it in front of me. Monk looked so tall, about six feet one or two, and he had a presence. There was a largeness about him . . . with his goatee and little hats. People would goof on him. That is, they would just watch him. He was a charismatic character. He had the expression of a little boy who had just stuck in his thumb and pulled out a plum [Ron looked out of the side of his eyes to imitate a man with an ultra-mischievous look] a cat that had caught a canary. He was thinking about other shit. You could see it in his eyes. And he'd get up from the piano and dance around. He was show biz. He was very aware of himself and how

he looked. On the street, he was very aware of the attention he was attracting.

At the end of the first week at the Vanguard, Monk motioned Ron to follow him into the men's room. Ron, who had never used coke at that time, thought Monk was going to offer him some. But instead Monk was trying to take advantage of the privacy of a men's room stall to pay Ron. "He handed me one bill at a time and grunted and stared at me until I acknowledged how much he had given me. It was pretty weird. We were jammed into a stall together. I was looking way up at him.

"He payed me $250 a week for six nights a week.

"It was one of the greatest experiences of my life."

Ron didn't play with Monk again, though Jules Colomby passed along the word that Monk sometimes asked, "How's Ronny?" That made Ron feel very good. Paul Jeffrey knew that Monk, who had a vast number of people ready and eager to play with him, had liked Ron's playing, or he wouldn't have kept Ron in the group.

A number of different bassists worked with the band after that—Dave Holland for one, Reggie Workman for another—at the Village Vanguard, the Village Gate, and the Aqua Lounge. Monk didn't travel much. He did go back to Shelly's Manne-hole that year, where he felt well, working with Jeffrey, McKibbon, and Toot, then played with Larry Gales on bass in San Diego, and then at Fresh Air, a club in Seattle, Washington, for which Adolphus Alsbrook, a very unusual, little-known but highly regarded bassist joined the group.[1]

That summer Monk played in the Newport Jazz Festival and went back to Europe with another "Giants of Jazz" tour, featuring the same musicians who had gone in 1971. They recorded in Switzerland on November 12, and Monk played on all the tunes.

By that time, Monk was living full-time at Nica's house in Weehawken. Nica would recount in the documentary, *Straight, No Chaser*, that, as she and Monk were driving to her house one day, he told her he thought he was "seriously ill." He didn't often directly mention being ill at all, and Nica said he never talked about it again to her. If the doctors had told him he had brain damage from drugs, he didn't say so. Or if he knew and told her, his secret was safe with her.

A Steinway was set on the second floor in the studio where Monk and Nellie had always been welcome to stay. Nellie kept the family apartment in New York and visited Weehawken frequently, sometimes bringing food, particularly vegetable juices that she had squeezed herself. Nica was not much of a housekeeper or a cook, visitors observed, serving TV dinners. She was a pet lover, and had a house teeming with cats. Beginning with a few Siamese cats, which were fruitful and multiplied, she ended up with over 100 cats living on the ground floor and in the basement-boiler room, befouling those areas with their odor, and giving the house its nickname, the Cat House. One visitor, pianist Joel Forrester, recalled that she had a favorite cat named Pookie, which she claimed looked like Monk. Nica had her own quarters; Monk had his upstairs.

Harry Colomby, among many others, thought Nellie had always been grateful to the baroness for her help with Monk. Bob Jones had noticed how Nellie always made sure she bought perfume for Nica in Europe, though Jones was certain Nica could just as easily have bought it in America. But Nellie liked pleasing Nica with little mementos. Some people thought that Nica paid many of Monk's bills—his medical bills in particular. By this time, Monk wasn't working very much.

Monk trusted Nica to care for him. Toot said the family thought it was a good idea to get his father out of New York, away from everyone—although musicians, who used to visit him, rarely did anymore even when he lived in New York. Monk's sister Marion had the romantic idea that Monk and Nica had once had a romantic involvement and that Monk trusted Nica above all others with his welfare by the time he moved to Weehawken. That idea might be considered heresy by people who had marveled at the wonderful job Nellie had accomplished by her loving commitment and loyalty to Thelonious.[1] Everyone who knew them had witnessed their closeness earlier in their lives. But some people, who saw Monk with the baroness in public, actually mistook Nica for his wife. George Wein thought Monk and Nellie loved each other, and Monk was simply impressed by the baroness's title, money, and power to get things done for him.

Monk still rehearsed occasionally, said a few musicians, who played with him in the Weehawken studio. But Monk definitely showed no interest in moving back to New York City. He didn't even want to go there again. Jeffrey, Ridley, and Toot, who were among his visitors, didn't play a single gig with Monk in 1973 and 1974. Monk made two appearances in 1975. On March 28th, he performed at Carnegie Hall with his group, with the addition of Lonnie Hillyer on trumpet. John S. Wilson of the *New York Times* gave the concert a fine review, saying: "Mr. Monk, now looking like a biblical patriarch, as his beard has turned pepper and salt on his cheeks and gray below the chin, was in fine fettle as he reached into his huge bag of compositions for old familiar pieces . . . and for some seemingly new ones that showed the old familiar characteristics." Wilson mentioned in passing that he felt a sense of monotony in the long run, possibly because both Monk and Paul Jeffrey took long solos. Lonnie Hillyer, an excellent trumpeter, was rather colorless in this setting, according to Wilson; but Wilson was also unimpressed by Charlie Rouse during his days with Monk. Wilson said Jeffrey managed sudden bursts of physical energy, and Larry Ridley's improvisations were imaginative, while Toot played "unobtrusive but steady support on drums." Then Monk played solo at the Newport Jazz Festival in the summer of 1975—"one of the high points of that event," wrote Wilson.

After that, Monk didn't play in public again for another year. One day, when Paul Jeffrey was visiting him at the baroness's house, and they were watching television together, Monk said, "You didn't think I could stay in the bed this long." Jeffrey said that Monk knew exactly what he was doing; he liked to watch TV.

Whitney Balliett took a very dim view of Monk's performance at the Newport Jazz Festival in 1976, writing in *The New Yorker*. "His . . . appearance . . . was painful. His playing was mechanical and uncertain, and, astonishingly, his great Gothic style had fallen away."

In 1976, Thelonious went to Bradley's, a prominent piano jazz club thriving at the time in Greenwich Village, during a week when Barry Harris was playing the upright piano there. For one of the sets, Monk tapped him on the shoulder and said he wanted to play. Bradley Cunningham, the club's owner, was so excited by Monk's performance that he didn't sleep for three days afterward.

Around this time, Harris was also scheduled to play a concert at Carnegie Hall. He asked Monk, "Why don't you come by and play something?" Monk didn't reply. Harris told "the people downstairs," the baroness and her other houseguests, to bring Monk to the performance. When the time came, "in walked Monk to Carnegie Hall, and sat in and played the whole thing," Barry recalls. "I got paid and didn't have to play at all."

As far as anyone knew, Monk never touched a piano again.

NOTES

Personal interviews: George Wein, Dr. Everett Dulit, Ray Mosca, Michael James, Reverend John Gensel, Leroy Williams, Ron McClure, Joel Forrester, Harry Colomby, Bob Jones, Nellie Monk, T. S. Monk Jr., Larry Ridley, Paul Jeffrey, Barry Harris.

1. Oscar Pettiford had said that Alsbrook, born in Minneapolis, influenced his own playing.

2. Larry Ridley detected some tension between Monk's siblings and Nellie—Nellie who had known she was special, too, and had been proud of her own and her relatives' achievements. Some tension would be especially clear to Ridley after Monk died, though Ridley never understood what it was about. Yet Nellie and Marion Monk White maintained cordial relations.

Thomas W. Monk, Sr., Marion Monk White, and Thelonious, c. 1980. Courtesy of Marion Monk White and nephews

15 Last Glimpses

"There's such a thing as you be tired," said his brother Thomas, visiting Thelonious in Weehawken.

"That's right," Monk said, "I retired."

During his last years in Weehawken, neither Marion Monk White nor Thomas thought that Monk seemed ill. But he didn't want to play the piano anymore. Marion and Thomas, taking some walks with Thelonious, believed that their brother had withdrawn from his former interests.

He had not retired to enjoy life, as he had spiritedly told Pearl Gonzalez in Mexico that he had wanted to do. He did less and less, and his sojourn in Weehawken was tantamount to a hospitalization. Nellie said that Monk didn't see any point in going on stage to play when he didn't feel inspired to do it anymore. She claimed that after the 1976 concert, he had been offered $100,000 to perform ten concerts, and he turned them down, saying it was not enough money. The story may be apocryphal, but Nellie, who had cared for him so much, definitely wanted to emphasize how important and highly esteemed he remained even in his final years.

Whenever several musicians, among the most intuitive people in the world, have the same opinion about a sensitive situation, one is well advised to listen to them carefully. Although some simply couldn't understand what had happened to Monk, many accepted Randy Weston's opinion that Monk felt he had done a great deal and was finished. "That's for you," Randy said, summing up what he believed to be Monk's attitude about his music career and legacy. "He came, expressed beauty, and left," Weston said succinctly, expressing the profound sea change that occurred in Monk's life. This explanation satisfied those musicians who loved Monk's music and didn't dwell on his drug use.

Nellie maintained that Thelonious had simply taken too many drugs, and he had not suffered a creative burnout. "Thelonious did what he wanted to do when he wanted to do it," she said in 1996. That was the Thelonious she had known and loved, and that is who he remained.

Dr. Everett Dulit offered a more comprehensive analysis of Monk's behavior through his entire life. When he was in his 20s and 30s, Monk concentrated on creating his music. This gave many people the impression that he was withdrawn, but actually he had known what was going on around him, but simply had blocked out extraneous signals. He may or may not have been suffering at this point from an underlying mental illness, but he was able to exploit his sometimes strange behavior for his own ends. Dr. Dulit believes that "The theatrical element [in Monk's behavior] was very evident and reflected the intact, undamaged part of his mental functioning. That's always the case with people who are highly intelligent and highly creative and unique and want to be interesting. If they are a little bit crazy, they tend to dress it up into a form that can seem normal—purposeful eccentricity. And they can shape their behavior."

For example, if someone has an involuntarily twitching arm, he can purposely smooth down his hair when his arm twitches. Then it can seem as if the twitching is a normal movement. An eccentricity can be something that a person might *want* to do, if it pleases him and other people watching it.

"Monk's eccentricity was amusing to so many people and never really off-putting; he always seemed like a comical figure and loved to say mysterious things that people couldn't understand, as a mystic does," said Dr. Dulit. Monk wasn't willing to be perfectly clear. The guru isn't willing to be led by the acolyte; the guru's tradition of being mysterious gives him a sense of superiority over the mystified. "I think that's what was going on with Monk," Dulit explains.

If there was a real mental illness, with accompanying delusions and hallucinations, underlying Monk's eccentricity, he was able at least to control this illness as a young man. As a particularly gifted, intelligent man, he could tame the demon, even if he couldn't stop it, and could reshape it in a way that became more socially acceptable through his music. Dr. Dulit's hunch was that Monk's eccentricity "was not 100 percent self-created, but to say there was some input from some kind of mental illness isn't to take away from him the remarkable ability to shape it into an interesting form, his music." Other people simply called this ability Monk's "genius."

Monk traded on the pleasure of being unique. His behavior brought him attention, made him seem charming, astonishing, and unsettling, and gave him power over others, said Dr. Dulit.

"The late phenomena [of Monk's behavior by the 1970s] seem to me definitely to have to do with damage and deficit and malfunction of the central nervous system [because of drugs]. "That's a syndrome we recognize well," said Dr. Dulit. So Monk's early behavior may have had little or nothing to do with his final withdrawal, which in fact was caused by unrelated brain damage:

> Drug use caused his organic mental syndrome—doctors call it OMS—rather than a psychogenic mental syndrome from psychology or learned behavior. His withdrawal was the least of it. The point is: his brain wasn't working at that time very well. He was clearly an impaired, damaged person with a damaged central nervous system. His behavior wasn't voluntary. Nobody works like that, not talking for a year. From a physician's point of view, it is ridiculous to say that Monk

didn't speak because he had nothing to say, as some of Monk's friends believed.[1]

Still, Nica tried to rekindle Monk's interest in music. She brought a new friend, the young pianist Joel Forrester, to the house and asked him to play the piano outside the door of the room where Monk had established his presence. Nica hoped that the sound of the piano would inspire Monk to play again. Forrester noticed that sometimes Monk opened the door to hear the piano better, and sometimes he closed it. Small interchanges of that sort with Monk inspired Forrester enormously.

Forrester sometimes sat with Monk in Monk's small room for periods of time, with neither of them saying anything. Forrester was sure that Monk was still thinking of new music, and that his mind was restless. "His mind was active, and he hadn't stopped hearing music," Forrester theorized, though he didn't think Monk "heard" music being played on any particular instrument.

Nica also brought a masseur to the house in the hope that massages would stimulate Monk to walk around and prevent him from wanting to get back into bed. But nothing roused Monk for long. The masseur told Forrester that Monk had confided in him that he was sleeping a lot to make up for all the times he had gone for days without sleep.

Nica met Forrester in the West Boondocks Club, where Forrester occasionally had gigs, located on the West Side of Manhattan. She quickly befriended Forrester and his wife. For a two-year period, in 1979 and 1980, Nica welcomed Forrester to her house. Forrester recalled:

> Nica was attempting in a hundred different ways . . . to find out whether Thelonious Monk could be brought out of himself. During that time he spent most of his time dressed in a full suit of clothes [and hat, others recall], and lying on a day bed . . . with his piano just outside the room in that glorious, sunlit larger room that faced the Hudson River. And . . . in a sense I was in on the level of the witch doctors, massage artists, and others whom the baroness brought in a vain attept to figure out whether Monk might respond to some invitation to live in a fuller way.

Nica with Joel Forrester. Photo: Ariel Warner.

One day, Forrester, Barry Harris, and a very young pianist who was a friend of Harris's and was patently influenced by Art Tatum, took their turns playing the piano for a little while, "all with Monk in the next room," Forrester recalled. "Monk that day did what he would do with my [solo] sessions, which was this: if he liked what was being played, he would lean over and open the door to his day room, and if he didn't like it, he would close the door. And in the course of that day, he opened and closed the door quite a bit." Forrester had become used to the sound of Monk's door slamming and creaking open, and from those simple actions, Forrester took inspiration to play as well as he could and focus on his own compositions (which seemed to please Monk more).

An Egyptian-born jazz pianist, Samir Safwat—who studied with Barry Harris and was introduced to the baroness's household, where he became a friend of Nica's daughter, Berit, and a frequent visitor in 1981—noticed that Nellie, Nica, and everyone else in the house—Toot and other relatives and friends who visited—focused completely on Monk. "He isn't feeling well, they said to each other in various ways, and what can we do about it?" Safwat remembered. A musician, who had worked with Monk in one of his regular groups, recalled that Monk actually wasn't eating well, or even stopped eating for a while sometime during these years.

Occasionally Safwat, who didn't own a piano then, took the liberty of practicing in Nica's house. Once he brought Monk some food, and saw that his room was adequate, with its own bathroom, a television set, furniture, and a window with a decent view, though not the view of the Hudson River and the New York skyline that Monk could have seen from the big studio where his piano stood a few feet from his bedroom door. From where he lay alone in his bed, he couldn't see anything coming up the Hudson, none of that lively river traffic.

Steve Lacy visited once in 1981. "I called, and Nica said it would be good if I came out." Lacy spent a few hours talking to Monk—or more correctly, *at* Monk, "but he hardly said a word. He finally brightened up a little bit and said a couple of words, but it wasn't the same Monk that I knew," Lacy said. He didn't know what had happened to cause Monk's loss of appetite. "I call it appetite. Appetite is the most important word in this whole thing—an appetite for play, for life, for food, for work. All these appetities. If you lose your appetite, you're dead. And he lost his appetite. Just before he died, he had no appetite; he didn't talk, didn't eat, didn't play the piano. People would try to make him play, but no." Nothing worked.

Lacy believed that Monk's mental attitude was aggravated, if not actually caused, by all the substances he had dabbled with: "If you handle too many things, after a while, you can't handle them anymore. That's my version of it, really. There comes a point where you can no longer handle it. It starts to get to you. And you get diminishing returns." Lacy's visit saddened him.

Barry Harris, who spent a great deal of time in the Weehawken house when Monk lived there, and then lived there himself, would later comment about Monk's music in a documentary, "Thelonious Monk: American Composer." However, even though they coexisted in Nica's househould, they didn't have a great deal to do with each other,

Joel Forrester and others observed. Monk had little to do with anyone. Nica said he barely spoke to her or Nellie some days.

After interviewing Nica about Monk toward the end of 1981, and never having read any medical reports, Whitney Balliett wrote in *The New Yorker* that Nica said:

> "No doctor has ever put his finger on what is wrong with [Monk], and he has had every medical test under the sun. He's not unhappy, and his mind works very well. He knows what is going on in the world, and I don't know how, because he doesn't read the newspapers and he only watches a little telly. He's withdrawn, that's all." It's as though he had gone into retreat. He takes walks several times a week, and Nellie comes over from New York almost every day to cook for him. He began to withdraw in 1973, and he hasn't touched the piano since 1976. He has one twenty or thirty feet from his bed, so to speak, but he never goes near it. When Barry Harris visits, he practices on it, and he'll ask Monk what the correct changes to "Ruby, My Dear" are, and Monk will tell him. Charlie Rouse, his old tenor saxophonist, came to see him on his birthday the other day, but Monk isn't really interested in seeing anyone. The strange thing is he looks beautiful. He has never said that he won't play the piano again. He suddenly went into this, so maybe he'll suddenly come out.[2]

But Balliett thought that Monk knew he wouldn't re-enter a life of activity in music.

During the first week of February 1982, Monk became ill and was taken to Englewood Hospital, where he lay in a coma for about ten days. Nellie remembered that he talked to her there, but the Reverend John Gensel, who visited Monk three times during his final illness, said that Monk remained mute in a coma brought on by an aneurysm in the brain. On February 17, Monk died.

A cerebral aneurysm usually results from an inherited weakness of the wall of a blood vessel. One may be born with it or develop it; it's like a time bomb. One can even suffer from a seizure-disorder associated

Monk's funeral, St. Peter's Church, New York. Photo: Mitchell Seidel

with it. However, the odd spells or interludes of withdrawal Monk suffered were not caused by an aneurysm. An aneurysm is like a bubble on a tire. It can, in rare cases, be a slow leak—it can bleed, stop, bleed again, and stop, over a period of years. And then it can burst, and the person might die.

Monk's funeral, which lasted a long time—three hours and fifteen minutes—was held at St. Peter's Church, on 54th Street and Lexington Avenue, in New York. Reverend Gensel prepared the service with Nellie and the family, who wanted the casket open. Though the Lutheran church didn't usually permit it, Reverend Gensel made an exception for Monk. "The funeral was incredible," he recalled. "The place was jammed. Big bands and small groups played. Everyone wanted to be in it—to play music or to speak. It was a very emotional service. There were one hundred seats reserved for the family, and we had to put people behind the altar." One musician saw someone move Monk's hands in the coffin, when people filed by.

Eddie Bert (trombone), Ben Riley (drums), Paul Jeffrey (sax), and Larry Ridley (bass) playing at Monk's funeral. Photo: Mitchell Seidel

Monk was buried in Ferncliffe Cemetery in Hartsdale, New York, in a plot owned by Nellie Monk. Nellie continued to live in her apartment in New York City.

Monk's daughter Barbara "Boo Boo" Monk died of breast cancer in 1984 in San Diego, California, and was buried near her father in the family plot at Ferncliffe.

Nellie Monk, far left, backstage at the 1992 Thelonious Monk International Drum Competition. Photo: Mitchell Seidel

Nellie and Toot relinquished the apartment on West 63rd Street in 1985. "It represented too much pain," Toot said.

Nica, who had been born on December 10, 1913, died on November 30, 1988, and a crowd attended her memorial service at St. Peter's Lutheran Church. Thelonious S. Monk, Jr., delivered one of the eulogies, reminding everyone that, if it had not been for the baroness, the great Charlie Parker would probably have died in the street.

Toot, who now was known as Thelonious S. Monk, Jr., played the drums in recording studios and led his own groups in jazz clubs. With the support of his aunt, Marion Monk White, he was legally appointed by New York Surrogate Court to take charge of his father's estate.

Eventually he was contacted to head a project that became the Thelonious Monk Institute. As chatty and extroverted as his father was taciturn, Toot, slender like his mother, speaks very rapidly and proudly about his work with the institute.

Toot first visited the Monk family home in Rocky Mount, North Carolina, at the end of the 1980s. "It was enlightening to a northerner," Toot said:

> I had never seen a town with a railroad track that went through the middle of town, and all the whites lived on one side of the track and all the black folks lived on the other side. I said to myself: "This is the real thing here, they are still into it."
>
> But they love Thelonious Monk. The Thelonious Monk Institute of Jazz started as an effort by fairly peripheral family members in Rocky Mount who wanted to honor Thelonious. They called me. The next thing you knew, we had so much support that the town of Rocky Mount became involved, and then Durham, North Carolina, wanted to be involved. But the project outgrew Rocky Mount before ever getting off the ground there.
>
> The incubator was the Beethoven Society of America. Maria Fisher, a founder of that society, took it upon herself to help my relatives put together this project, to build a community center in Rocky Mount. She was based in Washington, D.C., and she and these peripheral family members reached a point where she realized there would have to be a direct involvement with my father's immediate family. She called me. The relatives had no rights, no control over the estate, and they didn't know me and had no contact with me. To function, the institute needed my involvement. That's when I got involved.
>
> I had already been chairing the Thelonious S. Monk Foundation, which had been started by my sister Boo Boo. It was really my sister's campaign that had West 63rd Street named for Thelonious. The family members who had never known Thelonious got their idea for an institute from her. Unfortunately, she died.

So I took it over and became chairman. We've been steam-rolling ever since.

"We're in nine different places," he said at the beginning of 1996:

We have classes at the New England Conservatory. We have an international competition well known in the world, and a program with the Los Angeles Lakers, called Los Angeles Jazz Sports, involving two high schools, one in south central Los Angeles and one in another magnet school in suburban Los Angeles. And a program starting in Washington, D.C., with the Washington Bullets, and a National Basketball Association program, and an exchange program with Italy, and we'll embark on a program with Universal Studios with their theme park in Florida, a twenty-six-million-dollar program. We just received the biggest donation in the history of jazz education, two million dollars from Nissan. We're also televising this year's competition. (The show turned out to be a tribute to the Thelonious Monk Institute, which aired on ABC on December 28, 1996.)

We have a program called *Jazz in the Classroom* involving master's teaching, broadcasting a clinic live to eleven million kids in classrooms. And I have just returned from Thailand for the U.S. Information Service. I've made a trip to South Africa before this, for the State Department. And we've had programs in public schools in New York and in North Carolina. And in Los Angeles a program will start with U.C.L.A. And we're getting into a jazz history program with Harvard University. We've gone from an operating budget two years ago of half a million dollars to this year's $3.5 million. So we're very busy—busier than anyone's ever been in jazz education. And all this was born out of an effort in Rocky Mount.

"This is an amazing, huge, wonderful thing that came out of nothing," he reflected, "out of a humble situation."

Billy Dee Williams, Toot, and David Williams at the 1992 Thelonious Monk
International Drum Competition, Lincoln Center, NY. Photo: Mitchell Seidel

NOTES

Personal interviews: Thomas Monk, Marion Monk White, Nellie Monk, Randy Weston,
Dr. Everett Dulit, Joel Forrester, Samir Safweat, Steve Lacy, the Rev. John Gensel, T. S.
Monk Jr.

1. Though he had discussed Thelonious Monk's case with the doctor who treated
Monk in 1971, Dr. Dulit believed he would have developed his theory even if he had not
had spoken with him. "And [my theory] is fully compatible with what [the Beth Israel
psychiatrist] said," Dr. Dulit said.
2. Balliett (1982).

Postscript

Question to pianist Tommy Flanagan, renowned as one of the best interpreters of Monk's music: "How do you approach Monk's music?"

Tommy Flanagan, waggling his fingers a little in front of his chest: "Carefully."

Compositions

Thelonious Sphere Monk registered the following 91 compositions with Broadcast Music Inc. (BMI)

A
Ask Me Now

B
Ba-lue Bolivar Ba-lues
Bemsha Swing (composed with
    Denzil Best)
Blue Five Spot (Five Spot Blues)
Blue Hawk
Blue Monk
Blue Sphere
Boo Boo's Birthday
Brake's Sake
Bright Mississippi
Brilliant Corners
Bye Ya

C
Children's Song
Coming on the Hudson
Crepuscule with Nellie
Criss Cross

E
Epistrophy (composed with Kenny
    Clarke)
Eronel (composed with Idrees
    Sulieman and Sadik Hakim)
Evidence

F
Fifty-Second Street Theme
Four in One
Friday the 13th

G
Gallop's Gallop
Get it Straight
Green Chimneys

H
Hackensack
Hornin' In
How I Wish
Humph

I
I Go To Work
I Mean You
In Walked Bud
Incident Ly
Introspection
It's Over Now, Well, You Needn't

J
Jackie-ing

L
Let's Call This

Sessionography

The following sessionography was based on my own research plus the previous work of:

1. *The Complete Riverside Recordings.*
2. *Thelonious Monk-Discography*, compiled by Dan Morgenstern, dated November 1, 1981.
3. *Seventy Years of Recorded Jazz, 1917–1987*, by Walter Bruyninckx, privately published by the author, Lange Nieuwstraat, 2800 Mechelen, Belgium, noting Monk's recordings as leader only.
4. *Monk on Records*, by Leen Bijl and Fred Cante, noting Monk as leader and sideman on recordings. Order Address: Fred Cante, Deurloostraat 27, 10078 HR, Amsterdam, Holland.
5. Howard Mansfield's discographies listed on the Thelonious Monk homepage: www.achilles.net/~howardm/tsmonk.html

The following listing contains the dates, places, personnel, and titles of the songs recorded, omitting details of original releases and reissues, as well as alternate takes. Monk himself recommended that people listen to his recordings in the order they were recorded. This is a very good idea, because you can trace his development from the freshness of his first recordings, which are invariably hypnotic, to the occasional veneer, or patina, of practiced, commercial success on some of his recordings on the Columbia label. This judgment should not subtract a scintilla of importance from the later recordings.

When possible, the "original" album and reissue information is given following session information, thanks to my editor Richard Carlin. The early recordings made for Blue Note and Prestige were originally on 78s, and have since been reissued in various ways; the original Riverside and Columbia LPs also have appeared and reappeared under various catalog numbers. And, no doubt, these recordings will continue to be reissued in various formats as new technologies are introduced.

Note: More recordings or tapings are included in some discographies, but they do not warrant inclusion here. For one thing, many would be virtually impossible to obtain. A good example is a taped peformance of the Thelonious Monk Sextet on the "Tonight Show" hosted by Steve Allen, which is cited in the book itself but not commercially available. In general, this book's discography omits any recordings not made for a recognized label and emphasizes recordings made by Monk for Blue Note, Prestige, Riverside, and Columbia.

I. EARLY AND UNOFFICIAL RECORDINGS

THELONIOUS MONK, *with*

1. CHARLIE CHRISTIAN, guitarist, generally regarded as the leader.
   Joe Guy and another (tp), Don Byas, Kermit Scott (ts), Christian (g), Nick
   Fenton (b), Kenny Clarke (d).
   New York City, Minton's Playhouse, possibly May, definitely 1941.
   Note: There are several versions, or opinions, about the personnel on this
   tape. Possibly Kermit Scott is not on this.

   Up On Teddy's Hill
   Down On Teddy's Hill
   Stompin' at the Savoy
   Charlie's Choice (Topsy), also called Swing to Bop

2. DON BYAS, tenor saxophonist, generally regarded as the leader.
   Joe Guy and another (tp), Don Byas and another (ts), probably Nick Fenton
   (b) and Kenny Clarke (d), Helen Humes (voc).
   New York City, Minton's Playhouse, 1941.

   I Can't Give You Anything But Love
   Indiana
   Stardust, with Humes
   Exactly Like You, with Humes
   (Some sources say Monk played on tapings at Minton's with Roy Eldridge
   and Joe Guy and Hot Lips Page as leaders in 1941. Those tapings are not
   included in this discography.)

3. COLEMAN HAWKINS, quartet leader.
   Hawkins (ts), Monk (p), Edward Robinson (b), Denzil Best (d).
   New York City, December 19, 1944.
   Flying Hawk
   Drifting on a Reed
   On the Bean
   Recollections

4. DIZZY GILLESPIE, orchestra leader.
   Gillespie, Elmon Wright, Dave Burns, John Lynch, Talib Dawud, possibly
   Kenny Dorham (tp), Alton Moore, Leon Comegys, Charles Greenlea (tb),
   Howard Johnson, possibly Sonny Stitt (as), Ray Abrams, Warren Luckey (ts),
   possibly Leo Parker (bs), Monk (p), Milt Jackson (vb), Ray Brown (b), Kenny
   Clarke (d).
   New York City, broadcast from Spotlite Club, May and June, 1946.
   Things to Come

One Bass Hit
Second Balcony Jump
Groovin' High
An Original Jump Tune, Title Unknown
Our Delight
The Man I Love
Ooo Bop Sh'bam
'Round Midnight (partial)
Ray's Idea
Cool Breeze

II. BLUE NOTE YEARS

Reissue note: All of Monk's Blue Note recordings, along with various outtakes, are collected on CD as Blue Note 781510/781511.

5. THELONIOUS MONK SEXTET
Idrees Sulieman (tp) Danny Quebec West (as), Billy Smith (ts), Monk (p), Gene Ramey (b), Art Blakey (d).
New York City or Hackensack, October 15, 1947, on the Blue Note label.
Humph
Evonce
Suburban Eyes
Thelonious

6. THELONIOUS MONK TRIO
Monk (p), Gene Ramey (b), Art Blakey (d).
New York City or Hackensack, October 24, 1947, on the Blue Note label.
Nice Work If You Can Get It
Ruby, My Dear
Well, You Needn't
April in Paris
Introspection
Off Minor

7. THELONIOUS MONK QUINTET
George "Flip" Taitt (tp), Sahib Shihab (as), Monk (p), Bob Paige (b), Art Blakey (d).
New York City, November 21, 1947, on the Blue Note label.
In Walked Bud
Monk's Mood
Who Knows?
'Round Midnight

8. THELONIOUS MONK QUARTET
   Milt Jackson (vb), Monk (p), John Simmons (b), Shadow Wilson (d), Kenny ("Pancho") Hagood.
   New York City, July 2, 1948, on the Blue Note label.

   All the Things You Are (Hagood in)
   I Should Care (Hagood in)
   Evidence
   Misterioso
   Epistrophy
   I Mean You

9. CHARLIE PARKER AND HIS ORCHESTRA
   Dizzy Gillespie (t), Charlie Parker (as), Monk (p), Curley Russell (b), Buddy Rich (d), on Mercury/Clef.
   New York City, June 6, 1950.
   Bloomdido
   An Oscar For Treadwell
   Mohawk
   My Melancholy Baby
   Leap Frog
   Relaxin' with Lee

10. THELONIOUS MONK QUINTET
    Sahib Shihab (as), Monk (p), Milt Jackson (vb), Al McKibbon (b) Art Blakey (d).
    New York City, July 23, 1951, on the Blue Note label.
    Four in One
    Criss Cross
    Eronel
    Straight. No Chaser
    Ask Me Now (Shihab and Jackson out)
    Willow. Weep For Me (Shihab out)

11. FRANKIE PASSIONS, vocalist, leader.
    Unknown tp, b, d; some sources say Charlie Rouse (ts); Monk (p)
    Probably New York City, 1950s, the Washington label
    Especially to You
    Nobody Knows. Nobody Cares

12. THELONIOUS MONK SEXTET
    Kenny Dorham (tp), Lou Donaldson (as), Lucky Thompson (ts), Monk (p), Nelson Boyd (b) Max Roach (d).
    New York City, May 30, 1952, on the Blue Note label.
    Skippy

Hornin' In
Carolina Moon
Let's Cool One

III. PRESTIGE RECORDINGS

13. THELONIOUS MONK TRIO
Monk (p), Gary Mapp (b), Art Blakey (d).
Hackensack, N.J., October 15, 1952, on the Prestige label
Little Rootie Tootie
Sweet and Lovely
Bye-Ya
Monk's Dream
Blakey Out, Max Roach (d) in, Oct. 18, 1952 (some sources give as December 18, 1952).
Trinkle, Tinkle
These Foolish Things
Bemsha Swing
Reflections
Reissue note: Material from the October 15 and December 18, 1952 sessions, along with two tracks recorded on September 22, 54, appeared on the LP *Monk's Moods* (Prestige 7159; on CD as Original Jazz Classics [OJC] 010).

14. THELONIOUS MONK QUINTET
Julius Watkins (frhn), Sonny Rollins (ts), Monk (p), Percy Heath (b), Willie Jones (d).
Hackensack, N.J., November 13, 1953, on the Prestige label.
Let's Call This
Think of One
Friday the Thirteenth

15. THELONIOUS MONK QUINTET
Ray Copeland (tp), Frank Foster (ts), Monk (p), Curley Russell (b), Art Blakey (d).
Hackensack, N.J., May 11, 1954, on the Prestige label.
We See
Smoke Gets in Your Eyes
Locomotive
Hackensack
Reissue note: Material from the November 13, 1953, and May 11, 1954 sessions was issued as *Quintets* (Prestige 7053), on CD as OJC 016.

16. THELONIOUS MONK SOLO
    Monk (p).
    Paris, June 7, 1954, on the Vogue label.

    Manganese (We See)
    Smoke Gets in Your Eyes
    Portrait of an Eremite (which is actually Reflections)
    Off Minor
    Eronel
    'Round Midnight
    Reflections (which is actually Evidence)
    Well, You Needn't
    Hackensack

17. THELONIOUS MONK TRIO
    Monk (p), Percy Heath (b), Art Blakey (d).
    Hackensack, N.J., September 22, 1954, on the Prestige label.
    Work
    Nutty
    Blue Monk
    Just a Gigolo (Monk solo)

18. SONNY ROLLINS QUARTET
    Rollins (ts), Monk (p), Tommy Potter (b), Art Taylor (d).
    Hackensack, N.J., October 25, 1954, on the Prestige label.
    I Want To Be Happy
    The Way You Look Tonight
    More Than You Know
    Reissue note: Material from the November 13, 1953, September 22, 1954, and
    October 25, 1954 sessions was collected on the LP, *Work!* (Prestige 7169), on
    CD as OJC 059; one track from the October 25, 1954 sessions was also
    included on Rollins's LP, *Movin' Out* (Prestige 7058).

19. MILES DAVIS ALL STARS
    DAVIS (TP), MILT JACKSON (VB), MONK (P), PERCY HEATH (B), KENNY
    CLARKE (D).
    HACKENSACK, N.J. DECEMBER 24, 1954, ON THE PRESTIGE LABEL.
    Bags Groove
    Bemsha Swing
    Swing Spring
    The Man I Love
    Reissue note: On CD as OJC 347.

IV. RIVERSIDE

Reissue note: The complete Riverside recordings made between 1955 and 1961, including outtakes, have been collected on a 15 CD set (Riverside RCD 022-2), a total of 153 tracks in chronological order.

20. THELONIOUS MONK TRIO
Monk (p), Oscar Pettiford (b), Kenny Clarke (d).
Hackensack, N.J., July 21 and 27, 1955, on the Riverside label
Mood Indigo
It Don't Mean a Thing
Sophisticated Lady
I Got It Bad
I Let a Song Go out of My Heart
Caravan
Black and Tan Fantasy
Solitude (Monk solo)
Reissue note: Originally on LP as *Plays Duke Ellington* (RLP 12-201); on CD as OJC 024.

21. GIGI GRYCE QUARTET
Gryce (as), Monk (p), Percy Heath (b), Art Blakey (d)
New York City, October 15, 1955, on the Savoy label.
Shuffle Boil
Brake's Sake
Gallop's Gallop
Nica's Tempo

22. THELONIOUS MONK TRIO
Monk (p), Oscar Pettiford (b), Art Blakey (d).
Hackensack, N.J., March 17, 1956, on the Riverside label.
Liza
Memories of You (Monk solo)
You Are Too Beautiful
Just You, Just Me
Hackensack, April 3, 1956, on the Riverside label.
Honeysuckle Rose
Darn That Dream
Tea for Two
Reissue note: Originally *The Unique* (RLP 12-209); on CD as OJC 064.

23. THELONIOUS MONK QUINTET
Ernie Henry (as), Sonny Rollins (ts), Monk (p; celeste on Pannonica only),
Oscar Pettiford (b), Max Roach (d).
New York City, October 9, 1956, on the Riverside label.

Pannonica
Ba-lue Bolivar Ba-lues
New York City, Oct. 15, 1956
Brilliant Corners
Clark Terry (tp), Sonny Rollins (ts), Monk (p), Paul Chambers (b), Max
Roach (d, tympani).
New York City, December 7, 1956.
Bemsha Swing
I Surrender, Dear (Monk solo)
Reissue note: Originally *Brilliant Corners* (RLP 12-226); now OJC 026.

24. THELONIOUS MONK SOLO
New York City, Apr. 5, 1957, on the Riverside label.
I Don't Stand a Ghost of a Chance With You.
I Should Care
'Round Midnight
New York City, April 12 and 16, 1957.
April in Paris
I'm Getting Sentimental over You
Monk's Mood (Add John Coltrane (ts) and Wilbur Ware (b), New York City, April 16, 1957.)
Functional
All Alone
Reissue note: Originally *Thelonious Himself* (RLP 12-235); on CD as OJC 254.

25. SONNY ROLLINS SEXTET
J. J. Johnson (tb), Rollins (ts), Monk (p), Horace Silver (p), Paul Chambers
(b), Art Blakey (d).
New York City, April 14, 1957, on the Blue Note label.
Misterioso
Reflections (Johnson and Silver out)

26. THELONIOUS MONK QUARTET
John Coltrane (ts), Monk (p), Wilbur Ware (b), Shadow Wilson (d), on the
Riverside label.
New York City, April 16, 1957.
Monk's Mood (Shadow Wilson out)
Note: For the next three tunes, Orrin Keepnews, the session's producer, put
the recording date as "probably July 25 in New York City." Morgenstern
chose April 16. "Monk on Records" chose July or August 1957. Bruyninckx
chooses July. In short, there are several possibilities.

Nutty
Ruby, My Dear
Trinkle Tinkle
Reissue note: On CD as OJC 039 along with tracks recorded on June 25 and 26, 1957.

27. THELONIOUS MONK WITH ART BLAKEY
AND THE JAZZ MESSENGERS
Bill Hardman (tp), Johnny Griffin (ts), Monk (p), Spanky De Brest (b), Blakey (d).
New York City, May 14 and 15, 1957, on the Atlantic label.
Rhythm-a-ning
Purple Shades
In Walked Bud
Evidence
Blue Monk
I Mean You
Reissue note: Originally Atlantic 1278; on CD as Atlantic 781332.

28. THELONIOUS MONK SEPTET
Ray Copeland (tp,) Gigi Gryce (as), Coleman Hawkins (ts), John Coltrane (ts), Monk (p), Wilbur Ware (b), Art Blakey (d).
New York City, June 25 and 26, 1957, on the Riverside label.
Epistrophy
Abide with Me
Crepuscule with Nellie
Well, You Needn't
Ruby, My Dear (Copeland, Gryce, Coltrane out)
Off Minor
Reissue note: Originally *Monk's Music* (RLP 12-242); on CD as OJC 084.

29. MULLIGAN AND MONK
Gerry Mulligan (bs), Monk (p), Wilbur Ware (b), Shadow Wilson (d).
New York City, August 12, 1957, on the Riverside label.
Straight, No Chaser
Rhythm-a-ning
I Mean You
Aug. 13, 1957,
'Round Midnight
Sweet and Lovely
Decidedly
Reissue note: Originally Riverside RLP 12-247; on CD as OJC 301.

30. CLARK TERRY
    Terry (flglhn), Monk (p), Sam Jones (b), Philly Joe Jones (d).
    New York City, Hackensack, May 7 and 12, 1958, on Riverside label.

    In Orbit
    Pea-Eye
    One Foot in the Gutter
    Trust in Me
    Let's Cool One
    Argentia
    Moonlight Fiesta
    Buck's Business
    Very Near Blue
    Flugelin' the Blues
    Reissue note: Originally Clark Terry's LP, *In Orbit* (RLP 12-271); on CD as
    OJC 302.

31. THELONIOUS MONK QUARTET
    Johnny Griffin (ts), Monk (p), Ahmed Abdul-Malik, (b), Roy Haynes (d).
    Five Spot Cafe, New York City, August 7, 1958, on the Riverside label.
    Light Blue
    Coming on the Hudson
    Rhythm-a-ning
    Epistrophy
    Blue Monk
    Evidence
    Misterioso
    Let's Cool One
    Just a Gigolo (Monk solo)
    Nutty
    In Walked Bud
    Five Spot Blues
    Reissue note: Some tracks originally issued on *Misterioso* (RLP 12-279); on
    CD as OJC 206; additional tracks issued on *Thelonious in Action* (RLP 12-
    262); on CD as OJC 103.

32. THELONIOUS MONK QUARTET AT THE FIVE SPOT
    John Coltrane (ts), Ahmed Abdul-Malik (b), Roy Haynes (d).
    Five Spot Cafe, New York City, September 11, 1958.
    Trinkle Tinkle
    In Walked Bud
    I Mean You
    Epistrophy
    Crepuscule with Nellie
    Reissue note: Issued for the first time in March 1993, as a CD entitled

Discovery (Blue Note 799786). This historic recording was done informally at the Five Spot by John Coltrane's first wife, Naima, on a portable, reel-to-reel tape recorder.

33. THELONIOUS MONK ORCHESTRA AT TOWN HALL
Donald Byrd (tp), Eddie Bert (tb), Robert Northern (frhn), Jay McAllister (tuba) Phil Woods (as), Charlie Rouse (ts), Pepper Adams (bs), Monk (p), Sam Jones (b), Art Taylor (d), Hall Overton arranger.
Town Hall, New York City, February 28, 1959.

Thelonious
Friday the Thirteenthth
Monk's Mood
Little Rootie Tootie
Off Minor
Crepuscule with Nellie
Reissue note: Originally Riverside RLP 12-300; on CD as OJC 135.

34. THELONIOUS MONK QUINTET
Thad Jones (cnt), Charlie Rouse (ts), Monk (p), Sam Jones (b), Art Taylor (d).
New York City, June 2, 1959, except where otherwise noted, on the Riverside label.
Jackie-ing (June 4)
Straight, No Chaser
Played Twice (June 1)
I Mean You
Ask Me Now
Reissue note: Originally 5 By Monk By 5 (RLP 12-305); on CD as OJC 362.

35. THELONIOUS MONK SOLO
Monk (p).
San Francisco, October 21 and 22, 1959, on the Riverside label.
Blue Monk
Remember
Ruby, My Dear
Round Lights
Everything Happens to Me
You Took the Words Right Out of My Heart
Bluehawk
Pannonica
There's Danger in Your Eyes, Cherie
Reflections
Reissue note: Originally *Thelonious Alone in San Francisco* (RLP 12-312).

36. THELONIOUS MONK QUARTET PLUS TWO
    Joe Gordon (tp), Charlie Rouse, Harold Land (ts), Monk (p), John Oré (b),
    Billy Higgins (d).
    The Blackhawk, San Francisco, April 29, 1960, on the Riverside label.

    Let's Call This
    Four in One
    I'm Getting Sentimental over You
    Worry Later (San Francisco Holiday)
    'Round Midnight
    Epistrophy
    Reissue note: Originally At the Blackhawk (RLP 12-323); on CD as OJC 305.

37. THELONIOUS MONK QUARTET
    Charlie Rouse (ts), Monk (p), John Oré (b), Franklie Dunlop (d).
    Olympia Theater, Paris, April 18, 1961, on Riverside label.
    Jackie-ing
    Rhythm-a-ning
    I Mean You
    I'm Getting Sentimental over You
    April in Paris (Monk solo)
    Epistrophy
    Off Minor
    Just a Gigolo (Monk solo)
    Well, You Needn't
    Hackensack
    Reissue note: Originally RLP 003/004; on CD as OJC 670.

38. Same personnel at Teatro Lirico, Milan, Italy, April 21, 1961, on the Riverside
    label.
    Jackie-ing
    Straight, No Chaser
    Bemsha Swing
    Crepuscule with Nellie
    San Francisco Holiday
    Rhythm-a-ning
    Body and Soul (Monk solo)
    Epistrophy
    Reissue note: Originally RLP 002; on CD as OJC 488.
    Note: Some sources mention live recordings by Monk with the Quartet in
    Bern, Switzerland; and Italy, in 1961.

V. COLUMBIA RECORDINGS

39. Same personnel, New York City, October 31, 1962, on the Columbia label.
Bye-Ya
Bolivar Blues (probably November 1, 1962)
New York City, November 1, 1962.
Bright Mississippi
Body and Soul (Monk solo)
November 2, 1962
Just a Gigolo (Monk solo)
Monk's Dream
New York City, November 6, 1962.
Five Spot Blues
Sweet and Lovely
Coming on the Hudson
Rhythm-a-ning
Hackensack
Reissue note: Originally *Monk's Dream* (Columbia 8765).

40. At Birdland, varied dates in February 1963, and according to Dan Morgenstern and Bruyninckx, on the Alto label.
Bright Mississippi
Epistrophy
Birdland
'Round Midnight
Birdland
Sweet and Lovely
Evidence

41. Same Personnel, New York City, February 26, 1963, on the Columbia label.
Tea for Two (Rouse out)
Criss Cross
New York City, February 27, 1963.
Eronel
Don't Blame Me (Monk solo; liner notes for the Columbia reissue say this song was recorded on March 29, 1963.)
New York City, February 28, 1963.
Think of One
New York City, March 29, 1963.
Crepuscule with Nellie
Pannonica (Butch Warren replaces John Ore)
Reissue note: February 26 to March 29, 1963 sessions originally *Criss Cross* (Columbia 2038); on CD as 4469184 ("Pannonica" was added to CD).

42. THELONIOUS MONK QUARTET
Sankei Hall, Tokyo, May 21, 1963, on Columbia.

Straight, No Chaser
Pannonica
Just a Gigolo (%ONK SOLO)
Evidence
Jackie-ing
Bemsha Swing
Epistrophy
I'm Getting Sentimental over You
Hackensack
Blue Monk
Epistrophy (theme)
Evidence
Reissue note: On CD as Sony 466552.

43. THELONIOUS MONK QUARTET AND
PEE WEE RUSSELL AT NEWPORT
Charlie Rouse (ts), Monk (p), Butch Warren (b), Frankie Dunlop (d).
Newport, R.I., July 4, 1963, on the Columbia label.
Light Blue
Criss Cross
Add: Pee Wee Russell (cl)
Nutty
Blue Monk
Reissue note: Originally *Live at Newport*; reissued as the first CD as Columbia
C2K 53585 (2-CD set also includes Miles Davis's 1958 live performances).

44. THELONIOUS MONK BIG BAND
Thad Jones (cnt), Nick Travis (tp), Eddie Bert (tb), Steve Lacy (ss), Phil
Woods (as, cl), Charlie Rouse (ts), Gene Allen (bs, cl, b-cl), Monk (p), Butch
Warren (b), Frankie Dunlop (d), Hall Overton, arranger.
Philharmonic Hall, Lincoln Center, New York City, December 30, 1963, on
the Columbia label.
I Mean You
Evidence
Oska T
Four in One
Epistrophy
When It's Darkness on the Delta (Monk solo)
Bye-Ya
Light Blue
Also, at the same concert, THELONIOUS MONK QUARTET
Charlie Rouse (ts), Monk (p), Butch Warren (b), Frankie Dunlop (d).

Played Twice
Misterioso
Dunlop out; Ben Riley (d) joins group.
Reissue note: Originally an edited version appeared on LP as Columbia 2164;
the full concert is on CD as 57636.

45. THELONIOUS MONK QUARTET
Rouse, Monk, Warren, Riley.
New York City, January 29, 1964, on the Columbia label.
Shuffle Boil
Nice Work If You Can Get It (Monk solo)
New York City, January 30, 1964.
Stuffy Turkey
Shuffle Boil
Epistrophy
February 10, 1964, on the Columbia label.
Lulu's Back in Town
Brake's Sake
Reissue note: January 29–February 10 sessions originally issued on *It's Monk's
Time*; on CD as Columbia 468405.
March 9, 1964, on the Columbia label.
Memories of You (Monk solo)
Tea
Butch Warren out; Larry Gales (b) joins group.
New York City, October 6, 1964, on the Columbia label.
Liza
I Love You (Monk solo)
October 7, 1964, on the Columbia label.
Children's Song
October 8, 1964, on the Columbia label.
Pannonica
Just You, Just Me
April in Paris
Reissue note: March 9–October 8, 1964 sessions Originally issued as *Monk*
(Columnbia 2291).

46. THELONIOUS MONK SOLO
Monk (p).
Los Angeles, October 31, 1964.
I Surrender, Dear
Sweet and Lovely
Everything Happens to Me
I Should Care
North of the Sunset

47. THELONIOUS MONK QUARTET
   Personnel same as on October 8.
   Jazz Workshop, San Francisco, October 31 or November 2, 1964.

   All the Things You Are

48. THELONIOUS MONK SOLO
   Monk (p).
   Los Angeles, November 2, 1964.
   These Foolish Things
   I Hadn't Anyone 'Til You
   Dinah
   I'm Confessing
   Monk's Point

49. THELONIOUS MONK QUARTET
   Personnel same as on October 31 or November 2.
   Jazz Workshop, San Francisco, November 3 or 4, 1964.
   Honeysuckle Rose
   I'm Getting Sentimental over You
   Bemsha Swing
   Reissue note: Material recorded at the November concerts is available on CD
   as *At the Jazz Workshop* (Columbia 469183).

50. THELONIOUS MONK SOLO
   Monk (p).
   New York City, February 23, 1965.
   Ask Me Now

51. THELONIOUS MONK QUARTET
   Same personnel as on November 3 or 4, 1964.
   Brandeis University, Waltham, Mass., February 27, 1965.
   Well, You Needn't
   Same personnel.
   Village Gate, New York City, March 2, 1965.
   Ruby, My Dear (Monk solo)
   Honeysuckle Rose (quartet)
   Introspection (Monk solo)
   Darn That Dream (Monk solo)
   Reissue note: The album *Solo Monk* (Columbia 2349) was culled from various
   solo tracks made between October 31, 1964, and March 2, 1965; various
   other tracks recorded between May 21, 1963, and May 2, 1965, made up the
   quartet album *Misterioso* (Columbia 2416).

52. THELONIOUS MONK QUARTET

Same personnel, probably at Palais de la Mutualité, Paris, March 18, and Maison de l'O.R.T.F., Paris, March 20, 1966, on the Japanese Byg label, taken from French broadcasts. (In some sources, not all the following titles are given.)

I Love You
Lulu's Back in Town
Just a Gigolo (Monk solo)
I'm Getting Sentimental over You
Sweet and Lovely
Off Minor
Crepuscule with Nellie
Epistrophy
Monk's Mood
Ruby, My Dear
Blue Monk
Hackensack
Evidence
Straight, No Chaser
'Round Midnight

53. THELONIOUS MONK QUARTET

New York City, November 14, 1966, on the Columbia label.
I Didn't Know about You
This Is My Story, This Is My Song (Monk solo)
November 15, 1966.
Locomotive
January 10, 1967.
Straight, No Chaser
Japanese Folk Song
Between the Devil and the Deep Blue Sea (Monk solo)
We See

Reissue note: The original, edited album was issued as *Straight, No Chaser* (Columbia 9451); the full tracks were restored on CD as 64886.

Note: Some discographies list a recording made for the Columbia label by Monk with Dave Brubeck, with an unknown bassist and drummer, at the Pueblas Artes Festival in Mexico; another version states that this recording included Monk, Gales, Riley, Rouse, and Brubeck, and was made in May, 1967. However, the recording appears never to have been released by Columbia.

54. THELONIOUS MONK QUARTET AND
OCTET ON EUROPEAN TOUR

Details of personnel on each recorded song are not clear in the discographies. Probably *Quartet*: Charlie Rouse (ts), Monk (p), Larry Gales, Ben

Riley; and *Octet*: Clark Terry (flglhn) Ray Copeland (tp), Jimmy Cleveland (tb), Phil Woods (as), Johnny Griffin (ts).
Various European locations, October and/or November, 1967, on the Unique Jazz label.

Blue Monk (with Clark Terry)
Hackensack (Ray Copeland out)
Ruby, My Dear (Ray Copeland out)
We See
Probable live performance recording in Paris, November 14, 1967, Thelonious Monk Quartet only.
I Love You (Monk solo)
Lulu's Back in Town
Just a Gigolo (Monk solo)
I'm Getting Sentimental over You
Sweet and Lovely
Off Minor
Crepuscule with Nellie
Epistrophy

55. THELONIOUS MONK QUARTET
New York City, December 14 or 19, 1967, on the Columbia label.
Ugly Beauty
Green Chimneys
December 21, 1967, on the Columbia label.
Boo Boo's Birthday
New York City, February 14 or 24, 1968, on the Columbia label.
(Rouse out.)
Thelonious
Raise Four
Easy Street
(Add Jon Henddricks, voc.)
In Walked Bud
Reissue note: December 1967–February 1968 sessions originally issued on *Underground* (Columbia 9632); on CD as 460066.

56. THELONIOUS MONK BIG BAND
Bobby Bryant, Freddie Hill, Conte Candoli (tp), Mike Wimberly, Lou Blackburn and/or Bob Bralinger, Billy Byers (tb), Ernie Watts (as), Ernie Small (bars), Homer Scott, Buddy Collette and/or Gene Cipriano (reeds), plus Charlie Rouse for solos (ts), Monk (p), Howard Roberts (g), Larry Gales (b), Ben Riley, John Guerin (d), Oliver Nelson arranger and conductor. (Morgenstern omits Roberts [g].)
Los Angeles, November 19, 1968, on the Columbia label.
Let's Cool One

Reflections
Little Rootie Tootie
Monk's Point
Straight, No Chaser
November 20, 1968.
Just a Glance at Love (composed by Teo Macero)
Brilliant Corners
Consecutive Seconds (composed by Teo Macero)
Trinkle Tinkle
Reissue note: Originally *Monk's Blues* (Columbia 9806).

VI. FINAL RECORDINGS

57. THELONIOUS MONK QUARTET WITH A JAPANESE BIG BAND
Paul Jeffrey (ts), Monk (p), Larry Ridley (b), Lenny McBrowne (d).
Tokyo, Koseinenkin Hall, live recording, October 4, 1970. Probably on the
Far East label and never released on Columbia, according to Paul Jeffrey.
Straight, No Chaser
Don't Blame Me
Evidence
'Round Midnight
Blue Monk

58. THE GIANTS OF JAZZ
Dizzy Gillespie (tp and p); Kai Winding (tb), Sonny Stitt (as, ts), Monk (p),
Al McKibbon (b), Art Blakey (d).
Paris, fall, 1971, on the Lotus label.
'Round Midnight
Tour de Force
I Mean You
Tin Tin Deo (Monk or Dizzy at p)
Same personnel, Victoria Theater, London, November 14, 1971 (two
concerts), on the Atlantic label.
Tin Tin Deo (Dizzy on tp and p)
'Round Midnight
A Night in Tunisia
Everything Happens to Me
Blue Monk
Tour de Force
Woody'n You
Allen's Alley
Blue 'N' Boogie

59. THELONIOUS MONK TRIO/SOLO
Monk, Al McKibbon (b), Art Blakey (d).
London, November 15, 1971, on the Black Lion label.

Blue Sphere (solo Monk)
Hackensack
Nice Work If You Can Get It (Monk solo)
Criss Cross
Something in Blue (Monk solo)
Evidence
Jackie-ing (Monk solo)
Nutty
I Mean You
The Man I Love (Monk solo)
Ruby, My Dear
Little Rootie Tootie (Monk solo)
Misterioso
Trinkle, Tinkle (Monk solo)
Crepuscule with Nellie (Monk both solo and with quartet)
Darn That Dream (Monk solo)
My Melancholy Baby (Monk solo)
Reissue note: The complete Black Lion sessions are available either as a 3-CD set (7601-2) or individually as 760101; 7660116; and 30083.

60. GIANTS OF JAZZ
Dizzy Gillespie (tp), Kai Winding (tb), Sonny Stitt (as/ts), Monk (p), Al McKibbon (b), Art Blakey (d).
Switzerland, November 12, 1972, on the Philips label.
Straight, No Chaser
Thelonious
Epistrophy
Don't Blame Me
I'll Wait for You
Sweet and Lovely

Videography

Straight, No Chaser, Warner Brothers, Inc., produced by Charlotte Zwerin and Bruce Ricker, executive producer Clint Eastwood.
Thelonious Monk, American Composer, 1991 East Stinson, Inc., Tony Byron/Multiprises.
Jazz on a Summer's Day, videotape, Raven Films, 1959, 1987.

The above three films are available as home videos.

Other videos of Monk have been made and may also be available, though they are generally more difficult to find than the most popular ones listed above.

The best of these is *Monk in Oslo*, The Thelonious Monk Quartet, April 15, 1966, Rhapsody Films, Inc., which portrays Monk as a charismatic, commanding leader and demonstrates his piano technique, particularly his use of the two-handed, Harlem stride style.

Also of great interest are:
Thelonious Monk: Japan-Europe, 1961/63, containing performances by Monk solo and with his quartet in Japan, 1963; Europe, 1964; and Paris, 1970; VidJazz 2, and *Thelonious Monk Quartet: Monk in Europe*, containing performances by Monk solo in Berlin, 1969, and with his quartet in London, 1965, Vidjazz 18.

Thelonious Monk also makes brief appearances on documentaries not focused on him, such as *Piano Legends*, hosted by Chick Corea, Video Artists International; and *Celebrating Bird: The Triumph of Charlie Parker*, 1987 Toby Byron/Multiprises, Sony video.

Bibliography

BOOKS

Alkyer, Frank, ed. 199[?]. *Down Beat: Sixty Years of Jazz*. Milwaukee: Hal Leonard.
Balliett, Whitney. 1991. *Goodbyes and Other Messages*. New York: Oxford University Press.
Buin, Yves. 1988. *Thelonious Monk*. Paris: Pol.
Chilton, John. 1990. *The Song of the Hawk*. Ann Arbor: University of Michigan Press.
Davis, Miles, with Quincy Troupe. 1989. *Miles*. New York: Simon & Schuster.
Deffaa, Chip. 1996. *Jazz Veterans: A Portrait Gallery*. Fort Bragg, Calif.: Cypress House Press.
de Wilde, Laurent. 1996. *Monk*. Paris: Editions Gallimard.
Fitterling, Thomas. 1987. *Thelonious Monk: Sein Leben, Seine Musik, Seine Schallplatten*. Germany: OREOS Verlag; rev. ed. (in English), Berkeley Hill Books, forthcoming 1997.
Giddins, Gary. 1985. *Rhythm-a-ning*. New York: Oxford University Press.
Gillespie, Dizzy, with Al Frasier. 1979. *To Be or Not to Bop*. New York: Doubleday.
Gitler, Ira. 1966. *Jazz Masters of the Forties*. New York: Macmillan.
Goldberg, Joe. 1965. *Jazz Masters of the fifties*. New York: Macmillan.
Gordon, Max. 1980. *Live at the Village Vanguard*. New York: St. Martin's Press.
Hentoff, Nat. 1961, reprt. 1975. *The Jazz Life*. New York: Da Capo.
Keepnews, Orrin. 1986. *Thelonious Monk: The Complete Riverside Recordings*. Liner notes.
Kernfeld, Barry, ed. 1988. *The New Grove Dictionary of Jazz*. New York: Grove Dictionaries of Music.
Lyons, Len. 1980. *The 101 Best Jazz Albums*. New York: William Morrow.
Ponzio, Jacques, and François Postif. 1995. *Blue Monk*. France: Actes Sud.
Schuller, Gunther. 1989. *The Swing Era*. New York: Oxford University Press.
Spellman, A. B. 1985. *Four Lives in the Bebop Business*. New York: Limelight Editions.
Stewart, Rex. 1973. *Jazz Masters of the Thirtiess*. New York: Macmillan.
Wakefield, Dan. 1995. *New York in the Fifties*. New York: Grove, Weidenfeld.
Williams, Martin. 1992. *Jazz Changes*. New York: Oxford University Press.
———. 1989. *Jazz in Its Time*. New York: Oxford University Press.
———. 1973; rev. 1987. *The Smithsonian Collection of Classic Jazz*. Washington, D.C.: Smithsonian Institution Press.
———. 1970. *Jazz Masters in Transition, 1957–1969*. New York: Macmillan.

————. 1970. *The Jazz Tradition*. New York: Oxford University Press.

Wilmer, Valerie. 1977. *Jazz People*. London: Allison and Busby.

ARTICLES

Andrews, Colman. 1972. "Two Evenings in the Manne-hole." *The Staff*, Mar. 10.

Balliett, Whitney. 1959. "Jazz Concert: A Celebration for Monk." *The New Yorker*, Mar. 7.

————. 1982. "Notes and Comments," *The New Yorker*, Mar. 1.

Baraka, Amiri. 1980. "Bang Bang/Outishly." A poem.

Batten, Jack. 1966. "Let's Rejoice: Monk's Back in Town." *New York Daily Star*, Nov. 1.

Buin, Yves. 1971. "Caught in the Act." *Down Beat*, March 4.

Brown, Frank London. 1958. "Thelonious Monk." *Down Beat*, Oct. 30.

Coltrane, John, in collaboration with Don DeMichael. 1960. "Coltrane on Coltrane." *Down Beat*, Sept. 29.

Crouch, Stanley. 1979. "Thelonious Monk: Playing Possum with Genius." *Village Voice*, Aug. 13.

————. 1982. "Monk's Dancing Shoes," *Village Voice*, Aug, 31.

Dance, Stanley. 1963 (?). "Three Score: A Quiz for Jazz Musicians." *Metronome*, undated clipping.

Dufty, Maely Daniele. 1960. "The Prophet's Exile to the Tombs—Return." *New York Citizen Call*, Jul. 2.

Ellison, Bob. 1966. "Pianist Nutty Enough To Be a Comedian." *Toronto Daily Star*, Feb. 18.

"Encounter: An Interview with Thelonious Monk and Dolores Wilson." *The Telegram*, Toronto, Nov. 12, 1966.

Farrell, Barry. 1964. "Jazz: The Loneliest Monk." *Time*, Feb. 28.

Favoino, Gabriel. 1961. "The Jazz Beat: T. Monk, Architect." *Chicago Sun Times*, Mar. 18.

Feather, Leonard. 1966. "Thelonious Monk: Blindfold Test." *Down Beat*, Apr. 21.

Gerard, Warren. 1966. "The Monk: 'Everybody's Different, Man!" *Toronto Globe & Mail*, Nov. 5.

Gerein, Warren. 1966. "The Monk-Like Mr. Monk." *Toronto Daily Star*, Nov. 5.

Giddins, Gary. 1976. "Rabbi Monk Reasserts His Master." *Village Voice*, Apr. 12.

Gonzalez, Pearl. 1971. "Monk Talk! An Uncommon Interview." *Down Beat*, Oct. 28.

Gottlieb, Bill. 1947. "Thelonious Monk—Genius." *Down Beat*, Sept. 24.

Grove, Gene. 1960. "The New World of Jazz." *New York Post*, Nov. 14.

Hentoff, Nat. 1956. "Just Call Him Thelonious." *Down Beat*, July 25.

————. 1959. "Jazz," *Esquire*, Oct.

————. 1960. "The Private World of Thelonious Monk." *Esquire*, April.

————. 1960. "The Jazz Baroness." *Esquire*, October.

Holley, Eugene, Jr. 1994. "The Education of Bud Powell." *Village Voice*, June 28.

Kanzler, George. 1982. "Monk carried 'genuis' one step beyond." *Sunday [Newark] Star Ledger*, Feb. 21.

Keepnews, Orrin. 1948. "Thelonious." *Record Changer*, April.

Keepnews, Peter. 1982. "Monk's Music: Wrong Is Right." *Down Beat*, December.

"Kennedy's Death Causes Tour and Concert Cancellations," *Down Beat*, Jan. 2, 1964.

Kosner, Edward. 1960. "Thelonious Monk Gets a Key to the City," *New York Post*, June 18.

Kotlowitz, Robert. 1961. "Monk Talk." *Harper's*, Sept.

Lapham, Lewis. 1964. "Monk: High Priest of Jazz." *The Saturday Evening Post*, April 11.

"The Magnificent Monk of Music." *Ebony*, May 1959.

McDonald, Jo. 1964. "Mongo, Flip, and Monk." *Village Voice*, Aug. 6.

McLellan, John. 1960. "Le Jazz Hot Is Often Cool." *Boston Traveler*, Jan. 21.

————. 1961. "Thelonious Monk Quartet Exciting." *Boston Traveler*, Apr. 13.

McNamara, Helen. 1959. "This Jazz Hero Can Do No Wrong." *Toronto Telegram*, May 8.

————. 1964. "Thelonious Monk . . . Joker or Genius." *Toronto Telegram*, Apr. 25.

————. 1964. "Monk Show Flies Low." *Toronto Telegram*, Apr. 27.

————. 1967. "Noncomformist of Accomplishment." *Toronto Telegram*, Aug. 11.

————. 1968. "Just Too Much at One Time." *Toronto Telegram*, June 10.

Mitchell, Sammy. 1971. "Caught in the Act." *Down Beat*, Mar. 4.

Nelson, Don. 1961. "Monk's Tune a Great One." *Sunday News*, Nov. 19.

Nichols, Herbie. 1944. "Jazz Milieu." *Music Dial*, 1944.

"The Night that Monk Forgot the Music." *New York Amsterdam News*, Aug. 13, 1960.

Norris, John. 1966. "Late—But Great." *Toronto Telegram*, Nov. 1.

————. 1967. "Monk Puts His Mark on Everything." *Toronto Globe & Mail*, Aug. 22.

————. 1968. "Monk Brings Real Jazz to the Jazz Festival." *Toronto Daily Star*, June 8.

Peck, Ira. 1948. "The Piano Man Who Dug Be-Bop." *P.M.*, February 22.

Piazza, Tom. 1995. "How Two Pianists Remade (and Upheld) A Tradition." *The New York Times*, Jan. 1.

Rouse, Charlie. 1987. "Interview," trans. by A. David Franklin. *Cadence*, June.

————. "Same Old Unusual Story." *Down Beat*, May 12, 1960.

Scott, Patrick. 1964. "Monk's Piano Chases the Gathering Chaos." *Toronto Globe & Mail*, Apr. 27.

————. 1966. "Thelonious, Musak or Pumpkins." *Toronto Globe & Mail*, Nov. 1.

Simon, George T. 1948. "Bop's Dixie to Monk." *Metronome*, Feb.

Smith, Charles Edward. 1958. "Madness Turned Out To Be Musicianship." *Nugget*, Oct.

Stokes, W. Royal. 1975. "Jazzing Up the Curriculum." *The Washington Post*, Mar. 13.

Thomas, Ralph. 1964. "Fans Too Much Jazz for Monk." *Toronto Daily Star*, Apr. 27.

Williams, Martin. 1961. "Thelonious Monk." *Down Beat*, Dec. 21.

———. 1963. "Arrival without Departure." *Saturday Review*, April 13.

———. 1966. "Yesterday's Monk—Again" *Saturday Review*, Jan. 29.

Wilmer, Valerie. 1965. "Interview with Thelonious Monk." *Down Beat*, June 13.

Wilson, John S. 1959. "Thelonious Monk Plays His Own Works" *New York Times*, Mar.

———. 1960. "Concert Is Offered by Thelonious Monk." *New York Times*, Feb. 9.

———. 1963. "Thelonious Monk, Unworldly from Way Back." *New York Times*, Dec. 29.

———. 1964. "Monk's Jazz Group Heard at Carnegie." *New York Times*, June 8.

———. 1966. "Monk and Gillespie Share Bill at Carnegie." *New York Times*, Jul. 2.

———. 1970. "Jazzmen of 1950's Play in Holmdel." *New York Times*, Sept. 7.

———. 1976. "Thelonious Monk Is in Fine Fettle with a Quintet." *New York Times*, Mar. 28.

———. 1982. "Friends Pay Tribute to Monk with His Music." *New York Times*, Feb. 23.

———. 1982. "Monk Tribute at Town Hall Tonight with Barry Harris." *New York Times*, Apr. 23.

Wilson, Russ. 1970. "Thelonious Monk Opens at S.F." *Oakland Tribune*, Oct. 16.

Wyatt, Hugh. 1982. "Thelonious Monk, Bop Pioneer, Dies." *Daily News*, Feb. 18.

Many brief recording and performance reviews, and brief news items, have also been used as references.

Disclaimer

The author has made every effort to identify the sources of original publication of copyright material cited in this work and make full acknowledgment of its use. If any error or omission has occurred, it will be corrected in future editions, provided the appropriate notification is submitted in writing to the publisher or author.